Nathaniel Hawthorne

A MODEST MAN

Nathaniel Hawthorne

Nathaniel Hawthorne

A Modest Man

EDWARD MATHER Jackson

GREENWOOD PRESS, PUBLISHERS
WESTPORT, CONNECTICUT

Copyright 1940 by Thomas Y. Crowell Company

Originally published in 1940
by Thomas Y. Crowell Company, New York

Reprinted with the permission
of Christy & Moore, Ltd., London

Reprinted from an original copy in the collections
of the University of Illinois Library

First Greenwood Reprinting 1970

Library of Congress Catalogue Card Number 77-110834

SBN 8371-2594-4

Printed in the United States of America

I forewarn you, dearest, that I am a most unmalleable man; you are not to suppose because my spirit answers to every touch of yours that therefore every breeze, or even every whirlwind, can upturn me from my depths.

—FROM A LOVE LETTER WRITTEN BY
HAWTHORNE TO HIS FUTURE WIFE

Author's Note

BETWEEN 1864, when Hawthorne died, and the present time, a number of books have been written about him. They have been of two kinds. Henry James, writing as only Henry James could, but with inadequate material at his disposal, traced Hawthorne's literary development, and so wrote a book which was a biography but which was at the same time literary criticism and a chapter of literary history. In recent times Newton Arvin with much more material at his disposal has given a somewhat fuller and different treatment. The other kind has been written by the descendants of the author. They are a mine of information but they are eulogistic memorials in which no adverse criticism of motive or behavior is permissible. In these Nathaniel Hawthorne and his wife Sophia appear as examples of almost inhuman perfection. This approach to Nathaniel was suggested by the action of his widow, who had no hesitation in expurgating and, worse still, in altering the manuscripts of his private papers in order that after his death the author of *The Scarlet Letter* should be shown to the world as a paragon of virtue. In honoring their father and mother the descendants inevitably emasculated their personalities.

Apart from works of which Nathaniel Hawthorne is the eponymous interest, his name appears in all critical and historical reviews of the development of letters in New England.

In the journals, biographies and autobiographies of his famous contemporaries, his name appears time without number. In these he appears either as a small part actor or as one among a number of American writers.

In these pages I have treated the biography of Hawthorne as that of a man rather than that of an author, as that of a man with a peculiar personal history, a history which constitutes a study in human behavior. As an Englishman I have been particularly interested in his years of residence in England and in his violent opinions concerning the English.

My thanks are due to the Marquis of Crewe, K.G., P.C., who has not only opened up for me the Muniment room of Madeley Manor, but has supplied me with other information. He is the son of the Mr. Monkton Milnes, later to be known as Lord Houghton, who is so frequently mentioned in these pages. Another son of one of Hawthorne's friends has also helped me, but for some reason I do not understand but will respect, he does not wish to be quoted as having contributed anything to the new material.

Though at the end of this volume I have given a short list of the many works I have consulted, there is a name to which all who write of Hawthorne in our times must make acknowledgment. To Professor Randall Stewart of Yale University we all owe a great debt of gratitude for his editing of the text of *The American Notebooks*, the property of the Trustees of the Pierpont Morgan Library, and particularly for his notes which appear at the end of that volume, published by the Yale University Press.

E. M.

Contents

Illustrations

Nathaniel Hawthorne

A MODEST MAN

Prologue

ALL of Nathaniel Hawthorne's contemporaries have testified to his strangeness. He puzzled them; but though he resisted all influences, rejected all advice, and discouraged even those whom he really liked from approaching too close, he attracted them, too. It was easy enough to gain a general impression of the man, to make a sketch of his character. But once a more detailed drawing was attempted the design of the whole went awry. Recognizing this, they asked themselves, "Why?" and searched around for an answer. It was easy enough to see that because of his early environment he had grown up a young man given to long periods of seclusion. And in that seclusion his reading, extensive though it was, was nothing more than an unregulated browsing. To men like Emerson, Longfellow, James Russell Lowell and Oliver Wendell Holmes, men disciplined to serious study, such indiscriminate consumption of literature must have but one result—a vagueness of opinion. But were his opinions ever vague? They had to confess that they were not—only queerly orientated. That is to say, not theirs.

The evidence concerning him was conflicting. He shunned society, which was unfortunate; for the intelligentsia of New England was socially minded to an exaggerated degree. They talked so much that it is remarkable that they found time for work. It was odd that, shunning society as he did, Hawthorne

almost always accepted their invitations. It is clear enough
that socially he was difficult. When he came to a party, the
guests forever turned their eyes toward him because of his
great good looks. But he sat in a corner as mum as could be.
He was not in a daze or dream; he was listening. He had no
conversation. But once the party was over, once he was outside in the dark, his tongue could become loosened and he
would fling himself into the fun and entertainment of conversation rather in the same way he used to fling himself across the
ice on his skates while Mr. Emerson was quietly and cleverly
circling round and round, doing figures-of-eight and concen-
tric circles.

Then it was said that he was an unhappy man, a very unhappy man; and that someone should try to make him happy.
He must be unhappy to be so preoccupied with problems of
conscience. Yet he was as happily married as a man could be
and adored his wife and delighted in his children. He was certainly harassed by many matters—some of them minor. But he
could laugh, as Longfellow knew, heartily. He was simple and
honest enough not to feign appreciation of the intellectual
jokes of the intellectual society in which, because of the Misses
Peabody, he lived. His sense of humor was there but he kept
it up his sleeve. When Lowell made one of his puns, he expected it to be recorded. It would appear in his "Works" any-
way. They were right when they said Hawthorne was the sort
of man who could never coöperate. That was true. But they
might have rewarded him with some marks for trying. He
worked like a Trojan at Brook Farm, that idealistic community
which was Ripley's contribution to the science of living. His
attempts at collaboration with Longfellow failed because Long-

fellow failed him. What is strange is that they made no complaint against him, so far as we know, where they had just cause of complaint: namely in his attacks, now thinly veiled, now openly expressed, upon the opinions his clever companions held and upon their behavior. The explanation may be that in those hypercritical circles of Boston, Cambridge and Concord, there was too much open criticism already of the endeavors of each and all, for anyone to dare to complain. Because his books still sell in considerable quantities after so many decades, and because his place is assured in any history of English literature, it must not be supposed that all his friends thought highly of him as a writer. Lowell, of course, thought him a genius. But Ellery Channing and Emerson were not flattering. Longfellow's praise was considerable, but Longfellow was apt to praise. It was the man that they thought great, not his work as a writer of fiction. Difficult, unresponsive and unsocial as he was, or as they found him, they could not leave him alone. For thirty years Emerson tried to win his confidence. Yet he failed —he who with that one exception never failed, he who had the world and his wife at his feet. And when Hawthorne died in '64, Emerson sadly records in his journal that he would regret for all time that he had not tried harder! Which is an impressive epitaph.

1

Antecedents

HE WAS a strange link to find at the end of that particular ancestral chain. It was always a matter of wonder to him that he should be there. Not that more than two links of that chain had ever resembled each other in the least. The American chain of the Hathorne family (for it was Nathaniel, the novelist, who changed the spelling of the name) began with two heavy links—with William, the Speaker and Captain of Militia, and his son, Judge John. Here were men who seemed to have started a line of descent which would remain of the "governing classes," would be prosperous. They would be merchants, magistrates and militiamen; sit on the Bench, and occupy a seat in the Assembly. But that was not to be. For the third link was hardly a link at all—a mere ring—a small farmer with a name and nothing else.

Then, of all improbable changes, the chain became a sea-chain, roughly forged but very strong. . . . There was Bold Daniel, a captain in the merchant service and a privateer; he was followed by another sailor, Nathaniel, who went away to sea and never came back. And then came the strangest link of all, Nathaniel Hawthorne, the introspective and retrospective novelist, hanging there and wondering how he had got there, at the end of the Hathorne chain.

To suggest, as has been suggested, that Nathaniel Hawthorne was some kind of a *revenant,* come out of the seventeenth century to dwell in the nineteenth, is to deprive him of his chief characteristic. He had not come out of the past to dwell in the present. The desired movement was in the opposite direction. Because of the peculiarity of his early environment there was a time in his youth when the past seemed very much more real to him than the present, knowing as he did much more about the past than he did of his own times. And then later, as he emerged from his seclusion into the midday glare of a contemporary light, his desire was to get back into the shade of the past. At times, one must concede, he seems to have succeeded. That he remained uncertain of the historic sequence of events in other sections of his own country is one of the most surprising traits in his character. In his work as in his life, his New England antecedents are of paramount importance.

The reason which prompted William Hathorne to leave the soft climate of southern England to face the rigors of life on the edge of the American wilderness as one of the Massachusetts Bay colonists, we do not know.

We must suppose, therefore, that William Hathorne came to New England for the same reasons as did the vast majority of other emigrants. Because of bad times they came to "better themselves." They came because the broad Church of England which was being whittled down to a narrower church, was being whittled from the edge they liked most. They came believing that in the wilderness they would be able to have the kind of Bible-class authority under which they wished to live. Whether by malice aforethought or by the deliberate design of a few or by mere accident (it seems impossible to decide by which or by a combination of which now), the authority set up was very different from that which the emigrants had anticipated. Government was conducted by the smallest of oligarchies, by a local committee of Bay Company's shareholders, at most by about a score. By taking with them the physical thing, the charter, the few shareholders who sailed from England in the *Arabella* had done something extraordinary. The Bay Company became domiciled in America.

The advantages thus gained, not by the promoters but by the local agents of the Bay Company, were promptly taken and made use of to the fullest extent. It is a common accusation against English chartered companies that the officers of the company usurp the function of officers of the Crown. It is an easy accusation to make and has often been an easy one to sustain. Organization and discipline in an undeveloped territory, even if that territory was originally the property of the Crown, must in effect if not in theory, be government. But here in Massachusetts is a special case. The local representatives of the Bay Company, knowing perfectly well what they were doing, imposed upon the emigrants a form of government which was not a local variant of the Home Government but theoretically and ideologically an entirely different political system. By good management or by chance, we are not sure which, a few men with no political experience whatsoever got control. To give a name to that system of government is to invite criticism. It was certainly an oligarchy and the members of it were certainly Calvinists. The difficulty arises only when the admission is made that they were Puritans; for Puritans in England were at that moment "the Opposition." They opposed but were not in revolt against King or Established Church, much as they disliked both.

Two principal men stand out head and shoulders above all others: Endicott and Winthrop. In the year 1628 a certain Captain Endicott, a Dorset man, left England in charge of an advance party of the Bay Company. Of his English past we know nothing. He has a permanent place in the history of the United States.

In an intolerant age—for if Archbishop Laud was intolerant, so were the Puritans—Endicott stands out as an example of an intolerant and aggressive Englishman. The job entrusted to him was a difficult one, and no doubt his exaggeratedly clear perception of his duties to the Company and to God were a great asset in the colonization of Massachusetts. He had to prepare the way in his territory (in which already lived a number of Englishmen and the native Indians) for the Bay Company's emigrants, who were to arrive within the next year or two, and to make this new country "safe" for his Genevan political and religious convictions. And he did. Endicott was not a great man, but he was a strong man, as a leading Nazi or Fascist is "strong." As an executive officer he was without any doubt efficient.

And then in 1630 came Winthrop—Governor Winthrop— in the *Arabella* with the first colonists, with men who were land-hungry, with men who wanted to better themselves and who believed that in America, though they were risking all in the venture, life might after a time, an arduous time, be lived as they believed it should be. With this first migration of colonists came William Hathorne, the ancestor of Nathaniel.

Winthrop, a Suffolk squire and a small office-holder under

the government, had done most of the spade work in the promotion of the Company, and there had been much to do. The original conception of it and the money for it came from a group of neighboring country gentlemen living in that part of Lincoln which is known as Holland, in Norfolk and in Suffolk. At forty-four years of age Winthrop found himself governor of the Company and nominal leader at least of the little oligarchy in Massachusetts. The magnitude of the task he had undertaken must have been very apparent upon his arrival. The Massachusetts wilderness was not a land flowing with milk and honey. He arrived to find that eighty of Endicott's men settled at Salem had died during the winter; that food was scarce; and that disease might be expected, as it did, to take heavy toll of their numbers. It was under these depressing circumstances that Winthrop had to organize his men and set them immediately to the work of building sufficient houses on the sites selected for the future townships, so that all might have some sort of protection before the winter set in. They must harbor their resources. They must work as they had never worked before.

The Bay Company's colonists just managed to survive that winter, which was exceptionally severe, though their sufferings from cold and inadequate nourishment gave some reason to think that an immediate removal of the whole colony to the warmer climes of Providence was advisable if not necessary. Winthrop was not of that opinion. Yet it is not unreasonable to suppose that the difficulties he and his colleagues experienced in that first year did much to put him in a frame of mind to acquiesce in the despotic theories of government advised by the extremists. He was no lover of liberty, either of conscience or action, and he had no faith in democracy. But he was a noble character and a kindly man, keen only on making a success of the work which had been entrusted to him. It is with some surprise that we find him in later years at the head of an authoritarian state, persecuting those who did not conform to the state religion, selling Indians as slaves and driving out from the borders of the Bay Company's territory those who did not agree with the party's program.

Within four years of Winthrop's landing trouble came; for the English colonists, finding themselves disenfranchised, began in their informal town meetings to complain of the despotic control which the Company's magnates exercised. Not for this had they left the England of Charles I and Archbishop Laud. As this unrest coincided with the difficulties which the governing body were having in obtaining a quorum for their meetings, and as the number of emigrants was increasing, the time was opportune for a change. For the change could still be made without upsetting the authority of the Company. Extend the vote to *members* of the Congregational Church (a select few of those who *attended* church), and make magistrates of a selected few of these. Then it would become clearly the duty of the clergy, as it would be the delight of the new magistrates, to keep the oligarchs in power. It must have seemed a most satisfactory solution, if an obviously illegal one. But like many other very clever solutions, particularly those which can be described as tricky, it had strange results. For Winthrop and the Rev. John Cotton were placed in the hands of the extremists; the one believing that the English connection was essential to the life of the colony, had done his best to cut that connection; and John Cotton, who professed that he was still a member of the Church of England, became a leader in the congregation of Genevan Calvinists. Theocracy, none the less, was established. And though Dudley and Endicott, knowing that the clergy were to a man reactionaries, must at times have smiled, Winthrop and Cotton were happy; for God was guiding them.

William Hathorne, as we have seen, arrived in the *Arabella* with Winthrop in 1630, being then only twenty-two years of age. He settled in Dorchester, but in 1636 he was persuaded to move to Salem where he was given grants of land. He had already been admitted to the select circle of freemen in 1634. He was clearly a very promising young man; it was clear, too, that having been chosen by Salem he must have been even then as stout a Calvinist as anyone could want. Before he was forty years of age he was "Mr. Speaker."

There are certain inherent difficulties in theocracy as a form of government. Herr Hitler and the leaders of the Nazi Party can change their minds. Signor Mussolini and his Fascists can reverse a policy. They can think again. But the executive in a theocracy, though not necessarily controlled by a priesthood, having accepted one particular formula of faith, can only "think again," if the priesthood or ministry agree that a mistake has been made. There could, for example, have been no mistake made when it was decreed that only *members* of the Church could have the vote. It was therefore obvious that anyone who had an entirely different faith, Christian though he might mistakenly think it, must live outside the orthodox formula's dominions. There was no room in Massachusetts, for example, for antinomians—people who refused to accept a label.

There is another inherent difficulty in authoritarianism. Outsiders always want to get in, whereas those who have been expelled, once outside, seem to prefer to remain outside. The desire to run a danger, even though the motives for running it are of the highest order, is a constant factor in practical politics. Massachusetts was no place for the Quakers, who were democrats, if not anarchists, and who, because they believed in the inner light of self-revelation, had no great faith in the Bible as a source of inspiration. And yet they came. Endicott was Governor at that time, and in William Hathorne he found a most zealous lieutenant. They stripped them, they exposed them, they beat them and they hanged them. The people were against the theocrats; but the reactionary clergy and the reactionary junta were all-powerful. This is how the descendant of William Hathorne was to describe one of the scenes two hundred years later:

Joshua Buffum is standing in the pillory. Cassandra Southwick is led to prison. And there a woman—it is Ann Coleman—naked from the waist upward, and bound to the tail of a cart, is dragged through the Main-street at the pace of a brisk walk, while the constable follows with a whip of knotted cords. A strong-armed fellow is that constable; and each time that he flourishes his lash in the air, you see a frown wrinkling and twisting his brow, and, at the same instant, a smile upon his lips. He loves his business, faithful officer that he is, and puts his soul into every stroke, zealous to fulfil the injunction of Major Hawthorne's warrant, in the spirit and to the letter. There came down a stroke which has drawn blood. Ten such stripes are to be given in Salem, ten in Boston and ten in Dedham; and, with those thirty stripes of blood upon her, she is to be driven into the forest. The crimson trail goes wa-

vering along the Main-street; but Heaven grant that, as the rain of
so many years has wept upon it, time after time, and washed it all
away, so there may have been a dew of mercy, to cleanse this
cruel blood-stain out of the record of the persecutor's life!

So much violence is difficult to account for. Though Massachusetts was beyond doubt the most successful colony in New
England, men worked just as hard in Rhode Island and in
Connecticut. A stern attitude towards life was of course the
order of the day in those parts. Not only did the Puritan mind
reject the sociological view that a certain amount of amusement was necessary if amusement was to be kept innocent, but
the conditions of existence in Massachusetts seemed to require
all the hours of daylight for a man and his family to win the reward of survival. So much ferocious zeal in the seats of government, while the immigrants were "cutting out the wood" and
cleaning the new fields, has the appearance more of fear than of
sound policy.

There was no immediate cause for fear, but there was a cause
for nervousness on the part of the theocrats. Owing to conditions in England the number of immigrants who were true
colonists exceeded all expectations. As the numbers increased
the distance between the base of the administration on the seacoast and the "frontier" increased too. Men on a frontier, faced
with an enemy, form those sorts of ties with one another which
produce democracy in its purest form. Could the governing
clique on the seaboard maintain its control?

The parsons, of course, could be trusted implicitly. For them
theocracy was a very pleasant form of government; for without them it could not exist. So it was that though most of them
arrived in America as Low Churchmen protesting against the

hierarchy of the High Churchmen at home, they soon learned that the more they retreated towards Genevan Calvinism, the greater was their power in a theocracy.

So many good men and true have been born and have died in the faith which is named after the Frenchman Jean Calvin that care must be taken not to give unnecessary offence by speaking ill of it. His primary theological discovery—which was a re-discovery—may today look singularly tame; but it was one which gave a strong instrument of mental torture to those who were in authority. It was that all were not worthy of be-coming members of the church. The unworthy must be ex-cluded. Who then were the unworthy? *One must inquire.* The private lives of all became the concern of each. In Calvinism there was no room for mercy; and there is no room for mercy in an authoritarian state. The Englishman Froude, writing an *apologia* of Calvinism, wrote this long and very dreadful sen-tence: "To represent men as sent into the world under a curse, as inevitably wicked—wicked by the constitution of his flesh, and wicked by eternal decree—as Doomed, unless exempted by special grace which he cannot merit, or by any effort of his own obtain, to live in sin while he remained on earth and to be eternally miserable when he leaves it—to represent him as born unable to keep the commandments, yet as justly liable to ever-lasting punishment for breaking them, is alike repugnant to reason and to conscience, and turns existence into a hideous nightmare." For the sanity of New England it was fortunate that there were by now thousands of strong Englishmen who must have been far too busy digging, ploughing and cutting down trees to give their attention to the problem of whether they were among the eternally damned or not. That the Hawthornes and the Cottons and the rest of the theocrats believed that they were "exempted by special grace" goes without saying.

William Hathorne was a deputy, Speaker of the House, a merchant and a magistrate. He was the father of eight children. He was also a major in the Militia during the Indian Wars. In the year 1666 King Charles II in a circular to the colonies in America expressed his satisfaction with all of them except Massachusetts, whose attempts at independence caused him grave concern. By royal command he ordered the colony to send over to London four or five of their agents that they might answer a number of charges. Specifically named were Bellingham and William Hathorne. All refused to go. It is a proof, however, that in London at least William Hathorne was considered to be one of the principal men in these things.

The story of John, the son of William, lingered long in the memory of the Hawthorne family, as it probably lingers still; for he was connected with one of the strangest events which ever befell the colony.

No sadder day could be imagined by the people of Massachusetts than the day when Charles II revoked their charter. Their theocracy and with it their independence was gone. In their hour of adversity there seemed to be but one man to whom the Congregationalists could turn, and that was to the Rev. Increase Mather of Harvard, who had married the famous old John Cotton's daughter, and who was the most awe-inspiring preacher of his day. And no one was more convinced of his predestined call to leadership than was the Rev. Increase

Mather. For the Mathers excelled in vanity as well as in in-
defatigability.

Charles died. James came to the throne. And with the Declaration of Indulgence the people of Massachusetts, seemingly
quite ignorant of the true purport of that declaration, breathed
again. Dramatically—the Mathers did everything dramatically
—Increase Mather slipped away across the Atlantic to congratulate the new King and to see whether, after suitable congratu-
lation, His Majesty would grant him another charter. He
landed in England in May 1688, which was an unfortunate
year in which to arrive; for William of Orange arrived, too, in
November; and James fled from London in December.

Increase Mather was now a diplomat and an astute one. For
four years he remained in England and at the end of that time
he returned to America, not having got all that he wanted but
eminently pleased with himself. King William had been adamant on two points. The franchise must be extended to free-
holders. And the King himself must appoint the Governor and
other officials. So theocracy was ended after all. In theory, yes:
in practice (with any luck), no. That was, as Increase Mather
congratulated himself, where he and his ability came in; for the
new election packed the Assembly with his theocrats, and the
Governor appointed by the King was the man of his own
choice. But he had not accounted for the doings of his own son
during his absence.

Young Cotton Mather has had his apologists, of whom he
himself was the most energetic. His diaries alone would seem
to condemn him, and in the eyes of his people he eventually became utterly discredited. Vanity was no doubt his besetting
sin. It was the kind of vanity which goads a man to set up futile

records—records in fasting, records in prayer, in hours of preaching, in hours of reading and in the number of works written and published. In quantity he excelled, in quality he lamentably failed. His father away, Cotton Mather, being the *locum tenens* of his father's church, must make his mark and cause his sensation. He would create an atmosphere of superstitious terror in Boston and the neighborhood. He would search for witches. He was to succeed better than he ever could have expected.

Judge John Hathorne of the Salem witchcraft trials made the family name known to every child who after his time attended the village school. Nathaniel Hawthorne was never allowed to forget that he had had a great-great-grandfather who had added a brief chapter to American history.

In the year 1692 there lived in Salem village a Congregational Minister called the Rev. Mr. Parris, who had formerly lived in the West Indies as a trader. With him from the Indies came three native servants. The Rev. Mr. Parris concerned himself overmuch with psychic phenomena, witchcraft and palmistry. He seems to have been a man of no consequence and less esteem in his suburb. Mr. Parris's tricks and his talk went first to his head, then to those of his West Indian servants and finally to those of three small girls who were in and out of the house all day—his daughter aged nine, his niece aged eleven, and their playmate aged twelve, the daughter of the parish clerk. Children's minds in those days carried a full and sufficient store of horrifying matter—the more gruesome stories from the constantly studied Old Testament, as well as frightening tales told by the older generation of the Indian Wars. To add to these some alarmist reports of the presence of witches among them, was sufficient to unbalance the minds of such children as by nature happened to be hypersensitive and as such were mentally weak. So it happened that the Parris children, going unreproved, began by producing the strange phenomena which they imagined would be the effect of bewitchment and so continued until their hysteria was uncontrollable. They "threw fits," cataleptic and epileptic; they bit the dust; they saw yellow birds and red cats and other things which no one else could see; they were bitten by imaginary snakes and were pricked by pins. They became a center of interest. Jealousy and the contagion of hysteria soon produced similar results in other children, some of whom were almost certainly genuine schizophrenics and epileptics. They began to lie, to make accusations. Witchcraft was a capital offence.

Mr. Parris and another parson were convinced that the children were bewitched. It was all turning out as the Rev. Cotton Mather in his wonderful sermons in Boston said it would. Unless God-fearing men went out and searched diligently for the Devil's agents, the witches, Lucifer would yet regain the territories which he had lost to the theocrats. This was a case for the courts, said Mr. Parris; and to the courts they went. John Hathorne was one of the two examining magistrates.

It would be wrong to place all responsibility for the Salem atrocities upon the shoulders of John Hathorne. He was not alone as was Judge Jeffreys on the Bloody Assize. The law recognized the possible existence of witches, and the crime of practising witchcraft was considered sufficiently heinous for the fitting punishment to be death. But there are black marks against him. He must have known that the special courts set up were illegal. Even though he may have believed the "evidence" of the afflicted children, may have believed too that witches really did fly on broomsticks through the night, there is no excuse whatsoever for him to have presumed as he did that every man and woman (the vast majority of whom had led blameless lives) brought before him was "guilty" before ever they opened their lips. He and he alone could have stopped the persecution at the outset. He did not do so.

For six months superstitious terror reigned in Salem. Men testified against their relations. No one trusted his neighbor. Some nineteen men and women were hanged, one man was tortured by crushing until life was extinct and some two hundred were imprisoned as witches.

The picture of John Hathorne sending up prisoners to a higher court, an illegal one too, knowing that after his cross-examination only a miracle could save them from the death-sentence, may be unattractive; but the behavior of the Mathers is not particularly attractive either by our standards. Hathorne, though discredited, was promoted. He became a judge of the Supreme Court. But he died a poor man. It was the hour of sunset in the fortunes of the Hathorne family.

It was an old wives' tale no doubt—but it survived—that John Hathorne and his family had been cursed by two of his victims. They all of them knew of the curse of Rebecka Nourse; but it was not until 1838 that Nathaniel Hawthorne was told the story of Philip English. The daughter of Philip English was supposed to have married one of John Hathorne's sons. If this were true, then the blood of curser and accursed had mingled in the second generation. It was a story which the novelist was not to forget. We meet it again in the *House of the Seven Gables*.

2

Beginnings

CURSE or no curse, the fortunes of the Hathorne family declined gradually during the eighty-seven years which separated the death of Judge John and the birth of him who was to change his name to "Hawthorne" and become America's first great novelist. Did Nathaniel Hawthorne believe in the curse? On occasions he came near to believing it. In his gloomiest moments there were times when he wished there had been no such story. It was unforgettable. But that the decline was due to the curse, he comforted himself, was a totally unnecessary postulate. The inevitability of the decline and fall of family fortunes—to which one must admit there are some notable exceptions!—became part of his philosophy of life. It was with evident delight that he records yet another family disappearing or another megalomaniac building a mansion, which, according to him, could never possibly be occupied even by the grandchildren. His anti-aristocratic principles were in part at least due to the events recorded in his own family history.

Members of well-known families in "reduced circumstances" have a habit of exaggerating the affluence of their ancestors. Judge John of the Salem trials left a will which like all wills tells nothing of net personality. He certainly left some debts; for he had never repaid Mr. Higginson, the London banker, the sum of fifty-three pounds for hospital and funeral expenses incurred for his son John, nor had he repaid his son Ebenezer the improbably large sum of four hundred pounds borrowed, nor yet the twenty-five pounds he had from Joseph. It seems possible that he left very little else than the family property in Salem.

The son who succeeded and who was to carry on the line was Joseph, who may have started life as a sailor but who is known as the farmer. Just at a time when decades of affluence were to be enjoyed by the towns on the seaboard, Joseph left the town for the fields. If this was unfortunate it was unfortunate too that living as he did until '62, he missed making a fortune, as many made theirs, out of the high prices obtainable for agricultural products due to the Seven Years' War. His son Daniel went to sea at a time when going to sea had its rewards. He was of the right age to be in charge of a privateer during the War of Independence. Though his bravery is recorded in the word "bold," and his encounters with the English were the talk of the day, the rich prizes which formed the nucleus of great fortunes for other privateersmen did not fall to him. He died leaving a widow, a large family, a little house in Union Street, and some property in Salem which he had exchanged for the old Hathorne houses in the town.

The family was getting poorer and poorer; but there was yet a fine chance for the revival of the family fortunes. Nathaniel, Daniel's sixth child and eldest surviving son, who was born in 1775, was put by his father into the mercantile service. He was to be a sailor too. As one daughter was to marry John Crowninshield and another was to marry Simon Forrester, the sons of merchant princes, and as great fortunes were to be made in the next three decades in shipping, it is possible that

Daniel died thinking the prospects of young Nathaniel were good. The great change in the management and finance of shipping fleets which has occurred between those times and our own makes it only too easy for a snobbish mistake to be made. Our merchants and bankers of today may send their sons into the Navy, but they do not send them into the mercantile marine with a view to their becoming a captain in a fleet of vessels owned by a company of which they are directors. However, they did so in the times with which we are concerned, and in much later times too. Banking, insurance and shipping were still new fields of endeavor as joint enterprises. On both sides of the Atlantic there lived many families of considerable fortune who were as pleased to see their sons on the poop as in the counting house. Where the ships plied regularly between ports from which the crew might be expected to suffer a high mortality from tropical or Eastern diseases, one of the sons might be put to the study of medicine so that the commodore of the fleet, his brother, might have expert advice at his disposal. So Sarah Crowninshield and Rachel Forrester, the sisters of Captain Nathaniel, might with a stretch of imagination, be considered as realizable assets in the prospects of the Hathorne family. Those dreams of commercial prosperity were never to materialize. Young Captain Nathaniel Hathorne, who had married the daughter of his next-door neighbor, Miss Elizabeth Clarke Manning, by whom he had two daughters and a son, sailed one day for Surinam, Dutch Guiana. That was in 1808. He never came back. His ship, with flag at half mast, returned to Salem without him. He had died in Surinam of yellow fever.

Because Nathaniel Hawthorne's father died at the age of thirty-three and the family was poor, the widow and her three children returned to the maternal home across the garden, which separated the Manning house from the little old house in Union Street in which the children had been born. From that time until Hawthorne rather late in life was able to fend for himself, the Hathorne children were the charges of the Manning family. Mrs. Hathorne returned to the fold she liked so well, her own family. Dearly as she loved her husband, she had disliked all Hathornes save him. From the children's point of view this might have been, and perhaps was, short-sighted policy. The money was, obviously, in the pockets of Aunt Hathorne Crowninshield and Aunt Hathorne Forrester. Elizabeth Clarke Manning had fallen in love with a young sea captain of honorable family and of remarkable good looks—which his son inherited. She had certainly not fallen in love with or married the rest of the Hathornes. They were hard, stern and bad-mannered. The Mannings were cultured people. Mrs. Hathorne herself was without doubt a cultured woman. When her boy flatly refused to accept a tip of five dollars from Uncle Forrester the influence of the mother was clearly discernible.

There is all the difference in the world between being unsociable, as were the Hathornes, and "reserved" as were the Mannings, or so the Mannings thought. The young bride, Miss Manning, had left the many-windowed, gray mansion on Herbert Street and become the wife of the young captain who lived with his mother in the house on Union Street—a large cottage—which was only across the backyard. The young widow and her three small children traipsed back to the Manning house on Herbert Street. She returned with her children and a morbid psychological trouble from which she was never to be free until her dying day. To her this return no doubt seemed satisfactory. It was not charity she was accepting—and charity it would have been if she had accepted the protection of Crowninshields and Forresters; she was returning to her "ain folk." But for this Nathaniel, her son, might have become a banker.

The house which Hawthorne's grandfather had bought was as simple, architecturally, as a child's drawing. A clap-boarded face to the cobbled street was pierced by three cottage windows on the second floor, by two and the front door on the ground floor. The deep roof, with its one formidable-looking chimney sticking out of the middle, provided space for attic bedrooms. There were thousands of just such modest dwellings in America, all built to the simplest design. That house and some other town property were all that Captain Hathorne could leave to his widow.

The family of Mrs. Hathorne's generation of Mannings had once consisted of nine brothers and sisters, but was reduced in size at this time. There were enough of them, however, to make Mrs. Hathorne's share of the father's estate small indeed. The father died leaving one of those enormous land concessions in Maine which at a slightly later date were to be the object of reckless and therefore disastrous speculation for so many New Englanders. Old Manning had obtained his many thousand acres around Raymond and Casco at the end of the eighteenth century when the going was good. On his death there was no separation of these assets, and Robert Manning was appointed administrator or managing trustee; his business was to sell by lots of about a hundred acres until, if ever, the whole property was disposed of. Robert was consequently not the owner of the Raymond estate, as has sometimes been stated.

The brother who took up permanent residence on the estate as a trader was Richard and the management of the land development eventually passed to him. Richard's place was at Raymond. Robert, though in control, only visited the property upon which they were building a mansion. Robert's real place was in Salem, where with his brother William he ran an Eastern stagecoach business with offices in the Herbert Street house.

The place is Salem, the year is 1808. The deportment expected of a young widow during the period of her mourning was fixed by certain recognized rules. Whether her grief was genuine or not, and the genuineness of the grief of Madame Hathorne (as she was to be known thereafter) needed no demonstration, a widow was expected to keep herself to herself behind a purdah, seeing even her most intimate relations but seldom. With three healthy children romping round, in a house in which lived or came to stay so many brothers and sisters and sisters-in-law, Madame Hathorne in her great sorrow was only too rigorous in her acceptance of the deportment expected of her: she went behind the curtain; and she remained there for the rest of her life. On one occasion and one occasion only, she is reported to have taken a meal with her children—to their infinite surprise. Her morbidity was to have a profound effect upon two of her children. She was a sane woman, even an intelligent one, and took great interest in the welfare of her children. She saw them at an approved hour, probably every day, as she saw her brothers, the Mannings. Her food was left on a tray outside her bedroom door.

In a bustling household the peculiar behavior of the mother was accepted by the children as the way "mother" behaved. It

was only very many years later, when Hawthorne saw what
the perpetual hibernation of his mother had done to himself
and to his sister Elizabeth, that he wrote critically of her. The
house was full of aunts, uncles and cats; and such, they imagined, was life. The sponsorship of Uncle Robert does not seem
ever to have been the result of spontaneous affection. Some
member of the family must look after Nathaniel. Robert paid
for his education, it is true; but Richard was helpful occasionally, and William put him for a time to a desk in the offices of
the Manning stagecoach business, which in William's mind
was the very best thing for the boy.

Of the infancy of Nathaniel, the son of Captain Hathorne,
the fosterchild of the Mannings, we know little. A curly-headed
boy with broad shoulders and exceptional good looks; a boy
at times reserved, at times rather violent; a boy who was so sensitive of criticism that when his suffering became acute, when
chaff had gone beyond a joke, he could black an eye without
any feeling of remorse; but a boy who, though he liked cats,
could still just once sling a cat by its tail over the fence and not
be sorry, appears healthy, normal and even ordinary. Such,
however, has been the adoration of his descendants and rela-
tives that in their biographical writings much of the small
amount which is known of that period bears the obvious mark
of the pleasant afterthought. A very ordinary little boy, who
disliked his lessons, when nine years old he had an accident. He
was playing bat and ball and probably his ball hit him on the
foot with some violence. At least the ball hit his foot with such
force that the damage was sufficiently serious for a number of

doctors, one after the other, to be called in. Allopathy was tried (by trying to prove that it was not his foot which hurt him), homeopathy was tried (by giving him a regulated diet of pills) and some crude form of osteopathy, which reads more like an experiment in weights and measures. Even Dr. Peabody, his future father-in-law, was called in. As he is known as a bibliophile dentist who became a chemist, the child perhaps deserves our pity. Nathaniel wrote a despondent letter to his Uncle Robert. Two doctors have failed him, he complains, "Maybe he will do me some good, for Dr. B. has not and I dont know as Dr. K. will." He was then nine years old. He had not been to school for four weeks, "and I dont know but that it will be four weeks longer." It was going to be nearly four years longer.

To lie on the floor brought him most relief. He surrounded himself with heavy volumes from the shelves of the Manning house wherein he was secluded. He read the books—classics of literature such as one would expect to find in the Manning house, little else—and when tired of reading, he could lie there and make the cats jump back and forth over "jumps" made out of the tomes of the family library. The first period of loneliness and of seclusion had been forced upon him by a childish accident. His companions were not boys but cats and books—Shakespeare, Milton, Pope and Thomson; Froissart, Spenser, Bunyan and Rousseau.

At times he could hobble about on crutches; at times he could attend school; but there was always Dr. Worcester (the Dr. Worcester of the dictionary) who would come in—an act of professional, though not perhaps gratuitous, duty—and give this boy of such strange charm some homework. And nothing is more endearing in Nathaniel Hawthorne than his confession in later life that he used the foot to avoid school. To make such a confession the pain and the loneliness had to be forgotten. As an old man he remembered only the "dodge."

3

Maine

"I LIVED in Maine like a bird of the air," Nathaniel Hawthorne said, "so perfect was the freedom I enjoyed."

The war of 1812–1814 was over. The danger of a Canadian invasion of the State of Maine was consequently removed. Land sales had begun again which called Robert Manning to Raymond constantly. Richard had settled in Raymond permanently. His trade too was looking up. It was a period of great activity. The big house, so much bigger than the other houses that it was known locally as "Manning's Folly"—though it did not look like a folly to those who came from the coast, but just a plain, comfortable building—was nearing completion. Richard married Susan Dingley, the daughter of Captain Dingley, the miller—a name perpetuated in Dingley's Brook—and so the interests of the family or of part of the family became more and more centered in the principal township on the estate. In the next twenty-six years the Mannings disposed of no less than twelve thousand acres in small lots.

The reason for Madame Hathorne's departure from the family house in Salem is not known. It is not improbable that, seeing the unhealthy life which she was leading there—her exaggerated mourning seemed to have no end—the family persuaded her to move. But perhaps they had not intended her to move so soon; for when she arrived, the house her brothers were building for her was only just begun, and the big house was not finished, so that she and her children had to lodge with one of the tenants.

The town-bred boy, the son of a sailor, arrived in Maine, and Maine in those days, or all of it but a stretch along the coast, was a real frontier state. Civilization existed in only one or two valleys and along the seaboard. The rest was wilderness, as much of a wilderness as Massachusetts when the first Hathorne arrived in America from England. Nathaniel was a strong boy, and from the time when he recovered from that accident to his foot—a recovery not due to the science of his doctors—he was never to be ill—in body—until that mysterious decline, fifty years later, from which he never recovered. As a boy and as a man he was to be envied that body, those strong hands, strong legs and broad shoulders.

Yet it was here in the place he loved best perhaps of any place in which he lived, that a change came over him. Or so he affirmed, though with his family history known it is difficult to believe that the cause and effect were such as he surmised in after life. He believed that those happy days in Maine encouraged in him his accursed "habits of solitude." That the removal from town life to a life in the depths of the country redirected the currents which were running through the excellent conductor of his imagination, is no surprise. The boy who had startled visitors to the house in Herbert Street by the recitation of a strange and inappropriate Shakespearian sentence now suddenly came face to face with the strangeness of woods, streams, forests and lakes. Though there were other boys to bathe with and skate with; though he learned how to bring down partridges with his fowling piece and to catch trout from the streams, there was something even better than that—to get away, to get lost, to identify himself with the mysterious in nature. His vivid imagination which had made him dramatize every situation in the playground and town garden, now was only satisfied with following a stream to its source as if the search were of the utmost importance, or peering down into a pool, seeing his own face and seeing through it and beyond it another face, the face of a girl, a face more beautiful of course than that which any other girl had ever been blessed with. Tracker, Indian and frontiersman were the rôles he played. They were games which had to be played alone. Beyond him to the north and to the northwest lay the vast territories of that state which Longfellow described as a wild and grander example of the English Lake District—a wonderful playground. ". . . here I ran quite wild, and would I doubt not, have willingly run wild till this time [forty years later] fishing all day long, or shooting with an old fowling piece; but reading a good deal too, on the rainy days, especially in Shakespeare and *The Pilgrim's Progress* and any poetry or light books within my reach."

Back in Herbert Street he felt, not unnaturally, very lonely and depressed. His sisters, upon whom he relied for his only companionship, were in Maine; he was in Massachusetts. "I do not know what to do with myself here," he wrote to Elizabeth. "I now go to a five-dollar school—I that have been to a ten-dollar one. 'O Lucifer, son of the morning, how art thou fallen!' I wish I was but in Raymond, and I should be happy."

All men, perhaps without exception, have shown in their youth a revolt against growing up. However roseate tomorrow's dawn may seem, the twilight of the present day is very attractive. There is a "sadness" remembered when many another real sadness is forgotten, in "putting on trousers." To his Uncle Robert Manning he wrote a diplomatic letter. Referring to the school, with real schoolboy adroitness he says, "It's not dear enough [We must remember that Hawthorne always smiled at the Mannings as superior people.] and not near enough, for it is up by the Baptist Meeting House." Uncle Robert would have known all this. "There is a pot of excellent guaver jelly now in the house and one of preserved limes and I am afraid they will mould if you do not come soon, for it's esteemed sacrilege by Grandmother to eat any of them now because she is keeping them against somebody is sick and I suppose she would be very disappointed if everybody was to continue well and they were to spoil." To his sister Louisa he writes, "Wish I could again savagize with you." To his mother he writes hoping that his gun is safe in the closet, "Oh how I wish I was again with you, with nothing to do but to go a gunning. But the happiest days of my life are gone." His sister Louisa joined him in Salem in the summer of 1820, for, poor thing, little knowing how useless this would be to her, she was taking dancing lessons, and Elizabeth followed in 1821 when Uncle William gave her an enormous Leghorn bonnet, which entirely enveloped her head and which cost Uncle William fifteen dollars.

From the uncles' point of view, he was no easy boy to place. He continued to write bad poetry. "I am full of scraps of poetry; can't keep it out of my brain. Tell Ebe [Elizabeth] she's not the only one of the family whose works have appeared in papers." He had been tried in the stagecoach office—a part-

time job at a dollar a week and the promise of a suit of clothes—
but showed not the slightest interest in the work. He had expressed a wish to go to sea. This desire was rightly suspect. He
had only to express it for Madame Hathorne to become crazy
with apprehension; for though her husband had not been
drowned but had died of yellow fever in a South American
port, she blamed the sea for her bereavement. To give them
their due, the uncles never seemed to have taken this proposition seriously.

As early as March 1820 Robert Manning had made up his
mind to send Nathaniel to college. "I have left school," he
writes to his mother, "and have begun to fit for college under
Benjamin L. Olivier, Lawyer."

"I dreamed the other night that I was walking by the Sebago;
and when I awoke was so angry at finding it all a delusion, that
I gave Uncle Robert (who sleeps with me) a most horrible
kick. I don't read so much now as I did, because I am more taken
up in studying. I am quite reconciled to going to college, since
I am to spend the vacations with you. Yet four years of the best
part of my life is a great deal to throw away. I have not yet
concluded what profession I shall have. The being a minister is
of course out of the question. I should not think that even you
could desire me to choose so dull a way of life."

It is a statement of opinion as little flattering to the ministry
as to his mother.

"Oh no, mother, I was not born to vegetate forever in one
place, and to live and die as calm and tranquil as—a puddle of
water. As to lawyers, there are so many of them already that
one half of them (upon a moderate calculation) are in a state of
actual starvation. A physician, then, seems to be 'Hobson's

choice'; but yet I should not like to live by disease and in-
firmities of my fellow creatures. And it would weigh very heavily on my conscience, in the course of my practice, if I should
chance to send any unlucky patient *ad infernum* which being
interpreted is, 'to the realms below.' Oh that I was rich enough
to live without a profession! What do you think of my becoming an author, and relying for support upon my pen? Indeed I
think the illegibility of my hand writing is very author-like.
How proud you would feel to see my works praised by the re-
viewers, as equal to the proudest productions of the scribbling
sons of John Bull." And so on.

The contemptuous phrase, "the scribbling sons of John
Bull," is reminiscent of a much older Hawthorne, an American
author suffering from the lack of an international agreement
on copyright. As a phrase written by a schoolboy it is a re-
minder of the anti-British feeling consequent upon the war of
1812. The letter as a whole brings to mind a much shorter letter written by Henry Wadsworth Longfellow when he would
have been about the same age as his future friend Hawthorne.
Longfellow too at a very early period in his life had seen his
literary efforts in print. "Somehow and yet I hardly know
why, I am unwilling to study any profession. I cannot make a
lawyer of any eminence, because I have not a talent for argument; I am not good enough to be a minister—and as to Physic,
I utterly and absolutely detest it."

Uncle Robert's choice of a college was Bowdoin. For this
choice there were two very good reasons: Bowdoin was cheap
—board about $2 a week, college expenses $14.49 a term—and
Bowdoin was within thirty miles of Raymond. It was an obscure college which had been in existence only some twenty-

five years, and at the date of Hawthorne's arrival had just been taken over by the State of Maine. Few people outside Maine would ever have heard of it. Nothing much would have been expected to come out of Bowdoin, a little country college of the plainest description, situated near the pleasant village of Brunswick. Of the one hundred and eight undergraduates there during Hawthorne's time, quite a number made a name for themselves in after-life, though none of them seem ever to have attributed even a modicum of their success to Bowdoin. The instruction given was no doubt sufficient unto the requirements of positions which the graduates were expected to take up. The discipline was good: the general tenor old-fashioned and Calvinistic. (One student was fined for taking too long walks on the Sabbath!) What seems to have appealed most to the undergraduates was its topographical position; it was a hideously ugly college set in surroundings of great beauty and charm.

In September 1821 Nathaniel Hawthorne mounted the Boston-Portland stagecoach and went bowling toward the New Hampshire border. He had never been to a boarding school or to a public school; at the age of seventeen he was leaving home and the protection of his family for the first time. During its progress along the short seaboard of New Hampshire three other young men bound for Bowdoin joined the stage—Franklin Pierce, future President of the United States; Cilley, the brilliant Cilley, who was to die so young in a duel; and Mason, who was to become Hawthorne's roommate. All were freshmen except Pierce, who had already been up at Bowdoin for one year. What Emerson was many years later to call the "disastrous friendship" of Hawthorne and Pierce had begun, a friendship which only ended forty-three years later when the ex-President tip-toed into Hawthorne's bedroom and found him dead.

Arrived at Bowdoin, Nathaniel Hawthorne, a remarkably good-looking youth, but because of his painful shyness abrupt in manner, found himself one of thirty-eight freshmen, of whom he already knew two. He and Mason, though they seemed to have little in common, stuck together. Among the freshmen he met for the first time after his arrival were three who, like Pierce, were to remain his lifelong friends—Horatio Bridge from Augusta, Maine, and the two Longfellows, Stephen—the delightful Stephen, who never made much of a name for himself—and little Henry Wadsworth, a boy as precocious as he was pretty, who was entering Bowdoin at the early age of fourteen years.

The man who might have given us so many more interesting details of Nathaniel Hawthorne at Bowdoin was his friend Horatio Bridge who knew him intimately then and remained his occasional companion until 1864. But Bridge when he wrote his little book was a very old man and he was writing a memorial of this one friend who had become famous. Not only had his excellent memory lost something of its finer edge—if it ever had one—but he had joined the band of the faithful. He had become one of the panegyrists, defending the memory of a man who needed little defense and writing obscurely when clarity would have served his ultimate purpose far better. Yet even in Horatio Bridge the idiosyncracies of the young Hawthorne of Bowdoin are apparent. It is the destruction of the letters written after Nathaniel left Bowdoin which is the real loss.

From the first Nathaniel Hawthorne seems to have decided that there were things he could not and would not do. There were things that he would and could do very well. He could stand up and with his head on one side make excellent translations from the Latin. He could write good Latin prose too. Astoundingly good was his English. But then, having already considered in his own mind the possibility of devoting his life to literature, his English was something too personal and too important for him to be pleased with the praise he got for it. What he could not do was anything which concerned mathematics and metaphysics. What he refused to have anything to do with was public oratory, recitations and organized games. He had tried "declaiming," as it was called, before ever arriving in Brunswick. Once was enough. Let them fine him: nothing would induce him to stand up on a platform.

What he dearly loved about Bowdoin was everything which reminded him of Raymond. In the dedication of the *Snow Image* to Bridge (1850) he recalls their times at Bowdoin together, "at a country college, gathering blueberries in study hours under those tall, academic pines, or watching the great logs as they tumbled along the current of the Androscoggin, or shooting pigeons or grey squirrels in the woods, or bat-fowling in the summer twilight, or catching trout in that shadowy little stream which, I suppose, is still wandering riverward through the forest, though you and I will never cast a line in it again; two idle lads, in short (as we need not fear to acknowledge now) doing a hundred things that the Faculty never heard of, or else it would have been the worse for us. . . ." He enjoyed Ward's tavern too, an inn conveniently placed on the campus; for he liked drinking wine (he had a very strong head) and he liked playing cards. In the Navy Club, which seems to have been a supper club, meeting at Ward's, he was made commander, and he was also a member of the Androscoggin, which existed for the purpose of playing five-card loo. His keenness for cards, which he soon lost, came near to being his undoing. For the members of the club were caught in a raid by the college authorities. "All the card-players in college have been found out—my unfortunate self among the number. One has been dismissed from college, two suspended, and the rest, with myself, fined fifty cents each." President Allen officially informed Madame Hathorne of the disgrace of her son. The stakes must indeed have been low and the wine cheap for Nathaniel Hawthorne, even in his very mild and retiring way, to have taken part in them. For during his college years he was always short of cash and always short of presentable or suitable clothes. His impecuniousness and the deficiencies in his wardrobe caused him constant trouble and untold worry.

The little college of Bowdoin was divided by two such societies: the one conservative and superior, the other, the Athenean, liberal and progressive. Hawthorne's democratic mentality as well as his inheritance made him an obvious candidate for the Athenean, just as young Henry Longfellow was destined by his inheritance and by his views—comfortable and well-upholstered views on everything—to belong to the rival society. The societies were nominally literary clubs and indeed did have their own libraries.

How very admirably the compulsion to join one society or the other suited Hawthorne's social inferiority complex can easily be imagined. He liked Mason for no other reason than that he had met him on the coach and was his roommate. They are described as friends with nothing in common but a room. Horatio Bridge attracted him, too, though they had nothing in common except rather silent walks. But the Athenean Society provided him with leaders—with heroes. The one was Franklin Pierce and the other was Jonathan Cilley. Had Emerson been the sort of man to understand lifelong loyalties, he would have realized that for Hawthorne to give up Pierce because his presidential campaign was anathema to the intellectuals would have been as improbable and unnatural as for Bronson Alcott to make a fortune.

Frank Pierce and poor Jonathan Cilley were all that Hawthorne was not. Pierce, after a period of revolt against the authorities, became a plodder, a hard worker, an organizer and eventually chairman of the committee of the Athenean Society. A slender boy of medium height, he was popular, warmhearted, courteous and affable to his fellow undergraduates. Hawthorne was warm-hearted too; but the warmth was poked away inside him and seldom warmed others. Cilley, though nothing of a scholar, had a great influence at Bowdoin. He was a man without guile, who liked his fellow men and was anxious to talk with them. As a future politician he practised the arts of oratory and debate, knowing "the tongue to be his peculiar instrument." His unpretentiousness and kindness are very evident, and Hawthorne loved him. His early death in a duel when the prospects of his political career seemed brilliant made Hawthorne utterly miserable. Cilley never professed to understand Hawthorne, nor could he account for Hawthorne's admiration of him. For Hawthorne's moments of expansiveness were as surprising as they were few; he expressed his sympathy and understanding more often with a smile than with a word. Not that he was meek or feeble: physically he was strong; he was courageous; he was a dangerous youth to enrage. But he seemed always at bay, like a magnificent animal who refused to come out of the thicket, or one which was there because it was wounded. As for Horatio Bridge—he just liked him. Bridge was practical and accommodating. Both Bridge and Pierce, in fact, though they were to outlive Hawthorne, were not to outlive their love of him.

In the year 1825 Nathaniel Hawthorne returned to his mother and sisters in Salem—returned with as little idea what he was going to do with his life as when he had written to his mother in 1821.

4

I Shall Soon Go Back

IF we were to believe Hawthorne explicitly, there would be very little to put into a chapter concerning the next eleven years of his life, from 1825 to the first months of 1837. And if we were to respect his wishes we would make no attempt to pry into it. For to him the idea that anyone could get to know him and his behavior through his writings or learn from them his inward troubles, was repugnant. When anyone suggested that it could be done, he went to his notebook and wrote a violent protest.

In his biographical notes prepared for his friend Stoddard in 1853, he writes:

It was my fortune or misfortune, just as you please, to have some slender means of supporting myself; and so, on leaving college, in 1825, instead of immediately studying a profession, I sat myself down to consider what pursuit in life I was best fit for. My mother had now returned, and taken up her abode in her deceased father's house, a tall, ugly, old, grayish building (it is now the residence of half-a-dozen families), in which I had a room. And year after year I kept on considering what I was fit for, and time and my destiny decided that I was to be the writer I am. I had always a natural tendency (it appears to have been on the paternal side) toward seclusion; and this I now indulged in to the utmost, so, that, for months together, I scarcely held human intercourse outside of my own family; seldom going out except at twilight, or only to take the nearest way to the most convenient solitude, which was oftenest the seashore,—the rocks and beaches in that vicinity being as fine as any in New England. Once a year, or thereabouts, I used to make an excursion of a few weeks, in which I enjoyed as much of life as other people do in the whole year's round. Having spent so much of my boyhood and youth away from my native place, I have very few acquaintances in Salem, and during the nine or ten years that I spent there, in this solitary way, I doubt whether so much as twenty people in that town were aware of my existence.

Meanwhile, strange as it may seem, I had lived a very tolerable life, always seemed cheerful, and enjoyed the very best bodily health. I had read endlessly all sorts of good and good-for-nothing books, and, in the dearth of other employment, had early begun to scribble sketches and stories, most of which I burned. Some, however, got into the magazines and annuals; but, being anonymous or under different signatures, they did not soon have the effect of concentrating any attention upon the author. Still, they did bring me into contact with certain individuals. Mr. S. G. Goodrich (a gentleman of many excellent qualities although a publisher) took a very kindly interest in me, and employed my pen for the *Token*, an annual. . . . From the press of Munroe & Co., Boston in the year 1837, appeared *Twice-Told Tales*. Though not widely successful in their day and generation, they had the effect of making me known in my own immediate vicinity; insomuch that, however reluctantly, I was compelled to come out of my owl's nest and lionize in a small way. Thus I was gradually drawn somewhat into the world, and became very much like other people. My long seclusion had not made me melancholy or misanthropic, nor wholly unfitted me for the bustle of life; and perhaps it was the kind of discipline which my idiosyncrasy demanded, and chance and my own instincts, operating together, had caused me to do what was fittest.

A man of forty-nine years of age, with his most important literary work done, looks back on his life as a young man and finds that after all it was not so unpleasant. The anodyne of domestic felicity and public recognition has worked. Just as by some merciful providence the human mind does not record in memory or at least cannot recall from memory the experience of physical pain but only its associated thoughts and happenings, so with the passage of time mental anguish fades and only the behavior consequent upon it remains vivid. Hawthorne's story as told to Stoddard conveys an inaccurate impression.

Returned to Salem from Bowdoin, he found that his mother was keeping to her room for longer hours than ever; that his intelligent sister Elizabeth was keeping to her room too; and that even young Louisa, who had so valiantly fought the family battles for him, was keeping herself more and more to herself. He came back to the Manning house in Herbert Street and found Mannings going about their business as usual, but he found his mother and two sisters living the life of recluses. And there never seems to have been a moment's doubt by which mode of life he would be attracted. He, too, would have food left on a tray outside the door of his upper room. He, too, would agree that though he might meet his mother and sisters once a day, further intercourse was unnecessary. They would mind their own business, keep their own hours. When it was dark Nathaniel would go for his walk. Elizabeth would go for a walk too, also in the dark, but of course alone. How could he believe in 1853 that the natural tendency towards seclusion came from the paternal side?

It is no doubt true that when he took possession of that upper room, he had no idea he was to spend eleven years of his life there in loneliness and seclusion. He did not then recognize his inherited propensity to keep out of other people's way. There may have been an intention to choose in his own good time what part he was fitted to take in the active life of the community in which he lived. But it was a choice which would only have to be taken in the event of his proving to his own satisfaction that he was unfitted to follow the profession of letters. For a young man with no literary connections whatsoever and for one who had cut himself off from all intercourse with the few friends he had made at Bowdoin (with one exception, Horatio Bridge, who lived in another state) this was going to be something very difficult to prove. It was going to take a long time. There must be tentative efforts at composition, after which the constant submission of manuscripts to editors and publishers would test the interest of his work. Since he masked his identity with a variety of pen names and used the Salem post office as an address, it was improbable that editors would take very much interest in him until he had had so many articles published that by the style of his writing they could easily recognize his work. It was possible that several years would have to pass by before he got his proof. As long as the Mannings were prepared to keep him under their roof, his own small stock of money would last a long time. His living expenses were indeed low. He could afford to wait for his proof. Meanwhile time and his youth were passing.

To the Mannings their nephew must have seemed as unsatisfactory as a nephew could be. They had paid for his education and had received, from a cousin sent to Bowdoin to find out how he was getting on, a most excellent report. Perhaps they received their first intimation that their nephew might

prove "difficult" in the future when Nathaniel violently objected to this eulogistic report's ever having been given. He
wished it to be clearly understood that he himself saw no reason why he should be expected to make a success of any profession or career. Though Madame Hathorne, disliking all
others who were Hathornes or bore the name, had made it improbable that Nathaniel's rich aunts would persuade their hus-
bands to take him into their businesses, the Mannings themselves were quite capable of placing him well either in Salem
or Boston. They soon discovered that all helpful suggestions
were considered as unwarrantable interference with his freedom of mind and action; and discovered too that he was going
the way of his mother and his sister Elizabeth into seclusion.

It is perhaps improbable that had they known that their
nephew was not entirely idle in that upper room but that he
was assiduously practising the craft of fiction, they would have
been pleased. An author was not what was wanted in that
family but a young man who would go into the stagecoach business, into real estate, or become a produce merchant. But Hawthorne had sworn his two sisters to secrecy—an oath which
Elizabeth in later life regretted—and to his Manning uncles he
appeared a useless and deplorable member of the family. As far
as they could see, he did nothing whatsoever. His only occupation was to read old books and play with the cats. He remained
indoors all day, only going out at night. He had no friends
with the exception of a carpenter's son and one or two village
louts. Yet he was a man of intelligence, good looks and remarkably good health. They seemed to have wasted their
money. When they made one final effort, all they succeeded in
doing was to drive him temporarily from the house. "Some con-

duct of the friends among whom he resided in his native village was constructed by him into oppression." [1] A lonely spirit in revolt, he traveled to Niagara, covering most of the distance on foot. He was soon back. That upper room had an irresistible attraction for him, and like a carrier pigeon he knew his loft. Thenceforth he ignored the existence of Mannings.

No man can ever have begun his career as a writer of fiction with less material to work with than did Nathaniel Hawthorne. His experiences in childhood and in adolescence had been singularly featureless. At Bowdoin he had been so much more the spectator of life than a participator in it that he could not expert to find much to use there. In contemporary events he took little or no interest. His reading had been mostly in the classics of a former period or of another age. There had been no apprenticeship to a trade or profession. There had been no years on an office stool or in a lawyer's chambers. The prospects of one so lacking in experience would not have seemed encouraging even though the lucid prose style, from the first something more than competent and soon to be perfected as a medium of expression, was a rare and invaluable gift. No one could have foreseen that what is most individual in the mature Hawthorne's writings—the immateriality of his inventions and the semblance of reality standing for reality itself—would have its origins in the poverty of the stuff from which he must make his first stories. Necessity forced him to imagine what he did not know. Failures disciplined his mind so that at last his imagination, working on the thinnest material, produced fiction which, though always inclined towards the fantastic, described

[1] *Journal of a Solitary Man.*

a credible world. It was ever an Hawthornian world—but a world none the less, not discovered but created. What he described as the "disciplining of my idiosyncrasies" was a painful process.

It was only natural, perhaps inevitable, that he should have turned to historical subjects for his first essays in the craft of fiction. This we know he did though we have none of those stories in its original form and only one—*Alice Doane's Appeal*—as he rewrote it years afterwards for the *Token*. Setting aside these historical pieces for a time, he began the longer and more difficult task of writing a novel. Though the story was his own invention, for the background of the action he used his experiences at Bowdoin. Though it must be confessed that *Fanshawe*, the product of these labors, has no interest at all as literature, it has some biographical importance. Hawthorne thought well of it when he had finished it. He had written it secretly; he was to publish it anonymously; and he was to pay for its printing out of his own small moneys. But though the style was good and a number of copies did get into circulation, there was little in the book to attract attention, and in fact it attracted hardly any. Ashamed of its failure, he became ashamed of the work itself. He called in all copies unsold and destroyed them. This was easily done. What was not easy was to discover all copies sold to retailers in order to buy them back and destroy them too. He must have succeeded remarkably well, for copies of *Fanshawe* are a rarity.

The failure of his first book only confirmed his belief in the value and importance of secrecy—which from now on becomes a strongly drawn trait in his character. Horatio Bridge recalled that before leaving Bowdoin Hawthorne had suggested that they should correspond with each other when, living in different states, they could no longer meet except on rare occasions. Even for this private correspondence Hawthorne urged the importance of using pen names as an aid to freer expression and without a thought chose the name "Oberon." Bridge, the most unoriginal of all men, after a moment's thought, chose "Arthur." To conceal himself in the shadows of anonymity even while he revealed himself in his own works pseudonymously, to act and live secretly, to be unidentifiable by his fellow men —these were Hawthorne's wishes, and they were all variations of the same trait. It was with something akin to pride that a handful of people—not more than twenty—in his own home town knew of his existence. Of those twenty perhaps five at the most, and they sworn to secrecy, knew what he was doing. With the withdrawal and destruction of the copies of *Fanshawe*, secrecy became more precious to him than ever.

Living more than ever in the shadows beneath the roof of the Herbert Street house, Nathaniel turned again to the subjects first thought of for his stories and began to study seriously the early history of New England. It was a congenial and interesting task, but for a youth so introspective it was one which was to pose grim problems of conscience and to encourage depressing views of human behavior. So much of the early history of New England and of the history of his own family was one and the same that he was able to feel something akin to personal responsibility for the deeds of his ancestors, or at least a responsibility to find justification for their more questionable acts. From earliest youth Nathaniel would seem to have been a fierce patriot, it being understood that New England and not the United States was the object of his veneration. In that

William Hathorne had been one of the founders of the Commonwealth of Massachusetts and his son John had been among those who without question helped to consolidate the colony. They were ancestors to be proud of. But as undemocratic theocrats willing to persecute their fellow men for the establishment of religious doctrines, the most important of which were repellent to Nathaniel, they were men whose lives must be regretted. The problem has the appearance of a very old one: whether the end can ever justify the means. Hawthorne was unwilling to answer the question finally. To know all might be to understand, in which case forgiveness would be unnecessary. He delved deep into the melancholy literature of the times. Anyone who has made a prolonged study of the works of Increase and Cotton Mather knows that after a time it is not the sanity of those authors which is questioned but the reader's own. The *apologias* of hysterical Calvinists have the same effect on some as the case books of psychoanalysts. It becomes uncertain in which mind the neurosis exists. Hawthorne's daily life was too somber for such studies, not undertaken as historical research but as material for fiction in which problems of conscience must be faced, to have anything else than a morbid effect on his mind. It was not quite the time either, after the failure of *Fanshawe*, to study his family history—a history which was one of gradual but steady decline over some two hundred years. Every child in the village school knew something of William and John Hathorne. Would a later generation of school children ever know of him? Perhaps the Mannings were right in thinking that in him the Hathorne stock had touched rock bottom? To comfort himself he evolved his theory of the inevitability of the decline of famous families—a recurrent theme in his work—and took an almost vicious interest in discovering other cases similar to his own.

He was to use the material resulting from these inquiries over many years and with great success. But the first use to which he put it was to result in a failure far more damaging to his equanimity than had been the failure of *Fanshawe*. Of the *Seven Tales of my Native Land* we know nothing, for the very good reason that he burnt them. They met, as he describes it, a "brighter destiny" than publication. "They fed the flames; thoughts meant to delight the world and to endure for ages, had perished in a moment, and stirred not a single heart but mine." He did not burn his *Seven Tales* because they were so often found returned to the Salem post office. He burnt them because on rereading them he was profoundly shocked by the morbidity of the imagery they contained. He was horrified by what he had written and therefore destroyed the manuscripts in order that others might not discover the gruesomeness of his fantasy-thinking. It was a deed of incendiarism which must have cost him more in mental distress than any other literary sacrifice he was ever to make. And if one judges from the stories—some of them gruesome enough—which he published shortly after this, one must suppose that those he destroyed were macabre indeed.

The work upon which he was engaged, its subject matter and the circumstances under which it was performed had combined to foster the growth of all that was unhealthy in his imagination. He became obsessed by fantasies of resurrection, his ancestors rising from their tombs in filthy shrouds or in the everyday garments which they happened to be wearing when buried. He pictured himself walking down Broadway in a shroud, to the horror of those who passed him on the sidewalk. He cultivated the most unamiable pleasures, which, though he was soon to renounce them, remained as recurrent themes throughout his literary career. He became part Paul Pry, part Peeping Tom. From behind the curtains of his window in the upper room of the Herbert Street house, he spied on the goings and comings of the people of Salem in the street below. When darkness came he prowled round the town and peeped through the chinks left between carelessly drawn curtains. He could see. He could never be seen. He believed that by this unabashed spying on the lives of others he could understand the pattern of their lives far better than they could ever get to understand it. "The most desirable mode of existence might be that of a spiritualized Paul Pry, hovering invisible round man and woman, witnessing their deeds, searching into their hearts, borrowing brightness from their felicity and shade from their sorrow, and *retaining no emotion peculiar to himself*." Those words, put here into italics, express in themselves the reason why at a later period he came to the conclusion that this mode of life was a false one. Throughout his entire writing career, however, he frequently reverts to the attraction of seeing without being seen and allows his characters to climb up trees, to peep from behind curtains and unabashed to spy down from towers and upper rooms.

"M. du Miroir," one of his autobiographical pseudonyms, was the lonely, frightened counterpart of Paul Pry. He turned from the window from behind the curtains of which he had been peeping and sat himself down before the looking-glass. He communed with himself. He examined himself in the glass. It was something of a comfort in his loneliness to find himself not quite alone, for though M. du Miroir seemed to do every-thing that he did, it was done looking-glass-wise, in reverse order; and it was a subject of play for his over-stimulated imag-ination to suppose that the man in the glass might be thinking other thoughts than those that Hawthorne was thinking and might even get bored with mimicry and behave independently. Of schizophrenia he knew nothing. He most certainly was not a sufferer from duality of personality, yet he cleft himself in twain partly for company's sake and partly as a device for the invention of fictional material. The looking-glass in the upper room is of serious importance in the biography of the man. From it he evolved his one and only philosophic theory (for he was anything but a philosopher), namely that what appeared to us as Reality was not even simply a looking-glass reflection of it but probably a reflection of a reflection, each mirror being slightly distorting, so that we might have to be born again many times before it was granted unto us that we should com-prehend Reality.

This habit of looking at himself in the glass had another more immediate and more disturbing effect. After the burning of the *Seven Tales* he continued to write stories on the same themes, stories which established his position in that *genre* of fiction, and the themes of many of those stories concerned death, decomposition and physical resurrection. His imagina-tion was necrogenic to a marked degree. He suffered, one sup-poses, from necrophobia, and he was soon to become a necro-phile. The transition is explicable. Of death he had no fear. Though in his fantasy-thinking he might be haunted by the idea of semi-decomposed bodies rising from their graves, he could not be seriously disturbed by imagining such an unpleas-

The Study in the Tower

Hawthorne's Inkstand

ant eventuality occurring to his own body. The idea which tormented him was the idea of watching in the glass for the first signs of that slow but certain deterioration of the body, which he considered became marked before a man was thirty years of age and which would end in death. It was the contemplation of corruption in life, not the corruption of the corpse, which terrified him. He was remarkably good-looking; yet there was no vanity in him. He was a man, too, who, in spite of the apparent unhealthiness of his mode of life, was never to suffer so much as a stomach ache until he was fifty years old. He was enamored of death because of a morbid horror of physical deterioration which he believed became noticeable in all men from an early age. Therefore he must die young. Being unwilling to witness his own decline, he must make great haste to establish what would no doubt be a posthumous place in the literature of his time and country. A few years would suffice; and then before anyone had a chance to notice that old age was creeping over his body he must die. He was a young man in his twenties.

Once every year sunlight and fresh air were let into his life. He left the upper room with its curtained windows and went upon an excursion. He walked and rode all over New England. His dreams of world-wide travel were not realized, but he got to know his own and the neighboring states almost as well as the drover, the drummer and the itinerant showman who were his companions. Away from his room and its pens and papers, out in the open air or standing by the bar of a roadside tavern listening to others talking, Hawthorne was as happy as a man could be. From his fiction we know that he traveled as far westward as Niagara—perhaps as far as Detroit. Southward he may have got as far as New York and northward as far as the Canadian border. In 1830 he traveled through Connecticut. In 1831 he was in New Hampshire visiting the Shaker community. In 1832 he went up by the Portland route to the high pass of the White Mountains, the old trade route for Canada-New England commerce, and, going over the top, returned by way of Lake Champlain and Burlington, a journey which produced material for two of the best stories of that period, *The Ambitious Guest* and *The Great Carbuncle*. From Brunswick to Martha's Vineyard, from Boston Bay to the Taconic Range, he knew his New England well and gained an observer's knowledge of life in the country districts of his region. In a month or two of every year he observed enough and collected enough material for ten months' work in the upper room, which in itself was no mean achievement.

Though the *American Notebooks* do not begin until the year 1837, it would seem probable that for the years between 1825 and 1837 he must have kept some journal, now lost, in which there would have been even fewer accounts of personal emotion and personal opinions than in those we have. In no place is his passion for secrecy more plainly displayed than in his working notebooks. Henry James, who admittedly knew the *American Notebooks* only in their bowdlerized edition, could see nothing of interest in them except that they showed quite clearly Hawthorne's preference for "plain people." And by plain people he meant the lower or lower middle classes, of whom James had no opinion or knowledge at all. Hawthorne had to live for fifty years before he discovered that there really were such things as class distinctions; and he had to cross the Atlantic and live in England to discover them.

Amusement, material for work, exercise and health—these things Nathaniel derived from his excursions. But there were displeasures too. There were times when he was made to feel uncomfortable; if those occasions came in quick succession he was made to feel guilty and the sense of guilt increased in intensity after he returned to his upper room. It is not difficult to see how his troubles arose.

No one on the road cared who he was. If he did not want any of the men whom he met to know his name, they were not interested in it. There was a rule of civility, a rule of the Open Road, which entitled a fellow traveler to receive an answer to the question, "What's your line of business?" or "What brings you here?" Was he tinker, tailor, soldier, sailor, apothecary or drummer? They were all of them earning their living in some creditable way. How was he earning his? "Every honest man should have his livelihood," the manager of a traveling theater reminded him. "You, sir, as I take it, are a mere strolling gentleman." Nothing of course would persuade Hawthorne to admit that he was an author and though he was not as yet perhaps earning a livelihood, his work—and it was some of his best—was being published. Another point, too, which was brought to his notice was that to *join with* someone in doing a job was a moral satisfaction. To be able to work beside a mate, work with him and work as well as he, must, however lowly the job, be a proof that one had a creditable capacity for earning wages or doing piece work. In his craft no one shared responsibilities and coöperated with fellow workers. The publishers and the booksellers dealt in finished goods so far as the author was concerned. As a craftsman he had no apprentices. He was a single-handed man who when at work never even had the chance to pass the time of day with an employer or with an acquaintance.

It is understandable that he should have magnified the errors of his mode of life into a vice, a vice of which he was secretly proud, but a vice against which he would in his writings warn all others who might adopt the profession of letters. Never for one moment did Nathaniel Hawthorne doubt that he had in him the stuff of which authors of fiction are made. But of what they are made he wisely did not pretend to know. His life frightened him, yet he deliberately chose to continue it as it had happened to be planned. His interest in death had to be transmogrified. Though he did not fear death he was afraid that it might come to him before he had written enough to establish even a posthumous reputation. Hawthorne was his own *Ambitious Guest*, who "could have borne to live an undistinguishable life, but not to be forgotten in the grave. Yearning desire had been transformed to hope: and hope, long cherished, had become like a certainty, that, obscurely as he had journeyed now, a glory was to beam on all his pathway—though not, perhaps, whilst he was treading it. But, when posterity should gaze back into the gloom of what was now present, they would trace the brightness of his footsteps, brightening as meaner glories faded, and confess that a gifted one had passed from his cradle to his tomb, with none to recognize him. 'As yet,' cried the stranger . . . 'as yet, I have done nothing. Were I to vanish from the earth tomorrow, none would know so much of me as you; that a nameless youth came up, at nightfall, from the valley of the Saco, and opened his heart to you in the evening, and passed through the Notch, by sunrise, and was seen no more. Not a soul would ask— "Who was he? Whither did the wanderer go?" But I cannot die till I have achieved my destiny. Then let Death come! I shall have built my monument!' " Faith in his own powers could hardly have been more forcibly expressed.

Difficult though the future inevitably seemed it was a glance back over his shoulder that gave him the shudders. In *Wakefield* he wrote, ". . . considered in regard to his fellow-creatures and the business of life, he could not be said to possess his right mind. He had contrived, or rather he had happened to dissever himself from the world—to vanish—to give up his place and privileges with living men, without being admitted among the dead. The life of a hermit is nowise parallel to his. He was in the bustle of the city as of old; but the crowd swept by and saw him not. . . . Yet changed as he was, he would seldom be conscious of it, but deem himself the same man as ever; glimpses of the truth, indeed would come, but only for a moment; and still he would keep saying, 'I shall soon be back,' nor reflect that he had been saying so for twenty years. Amid the seeming confusion of our mysterious world, individuals are so nicely adjusted to a system, and systems to one another, and to the whole, that by stepping aside for a moment a man exposes himself to a fearful risk of losing his place for ever."

5

Horatio Bridge Opens the Door

THERE was no knowing of course that the door to the world was ever going to open. And so it happened that, since he was no clairvoyant, his depression became deeper and deeper as the hour of his rescue came closer and closer. By the first months of 1836 he had written and published in periodicals and magazines the greater part of the work as a short-story writer which was to give him a permanent place among the eminent nineteenth-century writers in that genre. More, many more, were to follow. He was thirty-two years of age. He had been working for eleven years. But of the many editors to whom he submitted his work not more than two probably knew what he looked like. Of the many readers who admired his work, as he wrote anonymously, only Bridge, his mother and sisters, perhaps Pierce, and some of the editors knew the real name of the author.

Nothing is more difficult to assess than the contribution of S. G. Goodrich to Hawthorne's happiness and unhappiness. From reading the correspondence one gets the impression that Goodrich, as publisher and editor, thought that in Hawthorne he had found a writer who if kept anonymous or pseudonymous would bring him in larger profits than those which would be obtained by giving him personal publicity. By 1836 Hawthorne had already been for some six years in Goodrich's hands, though under no contract to him. And it was Hawthorne who was keeping alive Goodrich's *Token*. "I have made liberal use of the privilege you gave me," Goodrich writes, "as to the insertion of your prices in the *Token*. I have already inserted four of them; namely, *The Wives of the Dead, Roger Malvin's Burial, Major Molineaux*, and *The Gentle Boy*. As they are anonymous, no objection arises from having so many pages by one author, particularly as they are good, if not better than anything else I can get." Had Hawthorne insisted that his work was to appear under his own name, as he should have done, Goodrich, it is true, might not have been able to take so much for any particular issue; but Hawthorne would have become known to his New England public very much sooner. That Goodrich understood how to use Hawthorne's shyness, impecuniousness and ambitions to his own advantage and to the disadvantage of the author seems as apparent to us as it did to his friend Horatio Bridge. Quite properly Bridge advised against any break with Goodrich, but persisted in his recommendation that he should appear before the public as "Nathaniel Hawthorne" and be done for ever with hiding his talents behind varying noms de plume.

Difficult as it was to bear writing continuously for such small monetary reward or doing hack work for Goodrich, such as compiling articles for *Peter Parley's Universal History*, a popular magazine of potted information, a much more galling experience was in store for him. Early in 1836 Goodrich gave him the appointment of editor to his *American Magazine*, which was published in Boston. Hawthorne was pleased. His three friends, Bridge, Pierce and Cilley, were delighted. "It is no small point gained," wrote Bridge, "to get you out of Salem

. . . there is a peculiar dullness about Salem—a heavy atmosphere which no literary man can breathe." Now at last Hawthorne had a job which would provide him with the opportunity of getting into contact with men who were leading normal, hard-working lives. Away to Boston he went. "I congratulate you sincerely," wrote Pierce, ". . . enter my name as a subscriber to the magazine. Where do you board, and where is your office? If you do not write me soon, Hath, I will never write a puff for the *American Magazine* or say a clever thing of its editor."

For some months Hawthorne occupied the editorial chair. Though Bridge was afraid that he would soon tire of it, Hawthorne was determined to stick to his job and to make improvements in what it was his job to edit. He worked away.

But where was his salary? In June he wrote to Curtis and demanded what was owed him. The very same day Curtis replied: "In answer to your wish that the Company would pay you some money soon, I would say it is impossible to do so just now, as the Company have made an assignment of their property to Mr. Samuel Blake, Esq., for the benefit of their creditors. They were compelled to this course by the tightness of the money market and losses which they had sustained. We would like to have you, when in the city, sign the assignment. We shall continue the magazine to the end of the volume. Your bills from the 27th May will be settled by the assignee promptly."

B. Bewick & Co. was either on the rocks or nearly so. And Hawthorne went no more to Boston. It would have been an unfortunate experience for anyone: for Hawthorne it was about the worst thing that could have happened.

There was no break with Goodrich. By September he was owed money by the *Token*, too—$108. Goodrich is now using the broken-spirited Hawthorne to his advantage and is rude to him about his contributions to that wretched *Universal History*.

The *Token* was out by the middle of September, and Horatio Bridge writes again to Hawthorne expostulating with him for writing anonymously [1] but congratulating him upon his work. Hawthorne had continued to edit the *American Magazine* (from Salem presumably) until its last number, hoping evidently that the new owners would reappoint him as editor. That was not to be; for the new owner wished to edit his own magazine. But there was already in the air the prospect of publishing a book by "Hawthorne" (or rather for several years past there had been in the air a project which was being revived); and the book was to contain a collection of his tales, very much after the lines of *Twice-Told Tales*, as it was eventually to be called. This plan too going awry, Hawthorne's spirit wilted rapidly. It was all more than he could bear. And for the last quarter of the year 1836 he was in a suicidal mood.

It is impossible to assess at their true value Hawthorne's threats to do away with himself. Horatio Bridge, in Maine, became seriously alarmed. "I have just received your last and do not like its tone at all," Bridge wrote from Augusta, October 22, 1836. "There is a kind of desperate coolness about it that seems dangerous. I fear that you are too good a subject for suicide and that some day you will end your mortal woes on your own responsibility. However I wish you to refrain till

---

[1] It has to be remembered that anonymity was rather the rule than the exception in magazines and periodicals of that day in America.

next Thursday, when I shall be in Boston, *deo volente.* . . .
Be sure you come and meet me in Boston."

Bridge had already, in fact, as we know, taken steps to assure his friend's peace of mind by approaching the man he did
not know, the man whom by hearsay he disliked, Hawthorne's
editor-publisher S. G. Goodrich, in order that at long last a
book by his college friend might be published. Was there,
Bridge asked Goodrich, any pecuniary obstacle in the way of
publication? Goodrich replied, "I received your letter in regard to our friend Hawthorne. It will cost about $450 to print
1000 volumes in good style. I have seen a publisher, and he
agrees to publish it if he can be guaranteed $250 as an ulti-
mate resort against loss. If you will find that guaranty, the thing
shall be immediately put in hand." Bridge gave the guaranty at
once, stipulating only that the affair should be concealed from
Hawthorne. As an immediate result of this secret negotiation,
both Bridge and Goodrich were committed to telling Hawthorne a rare number of "white" lies. Goodrich begins by writing to Hawthorne that *he* has found a man, Mr. Howes, who
knows a man who will edit and provide the money for the publication of the book. Hawthorne must have written to Bridge,
and a blushing Bridge must have passed on the news to Cilley;
for by November 17 Cilley writes to Hawthorne asking, "What
sort of a book have you written, Hath? . . . I have no doubt
it will be good, but I assure you I'll find fault with it if I can!"
Cilley and Hawthorne had not seen each other since Bowdoin,
but their affection for each other had survived the years of
separation.

Meanwhile the lie was picking up trouble. Hawthorne, having distrusted Goodrich for years, now trusts him completely

and wishes to dedicate his first book to him. This is too much for Bridge. So Bridge writes an earnest, helpful but—poor man —a thoroughly dishonest letter. He begins, "Have you obtained the magazine again?" It is true that Hawthorne did hanker after an editorship. But as a first sentence in a letter it is deliberately misleading. "How does the book come on? I am anxious to see the effect it will produce, though nothing doubting of its success. I fear you will hurt yourself by puffing Goodrich *undeservedly*,—for there is no doubt in my mind of his selfishness in regard to your work and yourself. I am perfectly aware that he has taken a good deal of interest in you, but when did he ever do anything for you without a *quid pro quo?* The magazine was given to you for $100 less than it should have been. The *Token* was saved by your writing. . . . And now he proposes to publish your book because he thinks it will be honorable and lucrative to be your publisher now and hereafter, and perhaps because he dares not lose your aid in the *Token*. Unless you are already committed, do not mar the prospects of your *first* book by hoisting Goodrich into favour."

The letter is an unfortunate one, though the motives for writing it were beyond reproach. It was proper that Mr. Goodrich should not receive the thanks of Hawthorne for something he had not done. The thanks were due to Bridge (who having so severely criticized his friend for his love of anonymity, had become the anonymous benefactor) and in later years Hawthorne in a preface was publicly to bestow them where they were due. But Bridge, knowing Hawthorne as he did, should never have written that letter, one addressed to a young man with, as he thought, suicidal tendencies. What Hawthorne wanted far more than the acclamation of the crowd was the confidence of a publisher—a man in the trade. At long last Goodrich, whom he had long suspected wrongly of being a scoundrel, came forward (with Bridge's secret guaranty) as his champion. Bridge tells him to give no thanks to Goodrich because he does not deserve it. Hawthorne, his pleasure poisoned by the bitter pull which Bridge has given him, appears to lose interest in his book. He has lost his editorship; he has lost his job. We have as a consequence the situation of young Hawthorne, who should be anxiously and delightedly awaiting the publication of his first book (*Fanshawe* being forgotten), plaguing the very friends who had faith in his literary work to find him an editorship or some other permanent occupation.

After a slight delay—the fault of the printers—the "slim and elegant little volume" of *Twice-Told Tales* by Nathaniel Hawthorne was issued for sale on March 8, 1837.

It was indeed a slim little volume, just half the size and with only half the stories of the modern edition as we know it.[2] It was not likely to make much of a stir in the literary world of the day. And it did not. But it achieved what no one would have believed possible: it continued to have a steady sale for a hundred years. And in small quantities it is still selling. If it has not become a classic of English literature, its sales indicate that it is remarkably like one—a minor one admittedly. So Goodrich was right—Goodrich who had helped so many young poets and other literary lame ducks, but who seemed to have behaved so badly to Hawthorne—when he wrote to Bridge that in his opinion no call would be made on his guaranty. The little book got its notices. The little book sold satisfactorily but

[2] The second series appeared in 1842 and is now always added to the first.

no more than that. It had been published at a period when the historical pieces in it would be particularly attractive to many. Bancroft had about two years previously begun to publish his great American history in parts. Ticknor's advice to take an interest in the history of America would not reach the reading public; but Bancroft's work did. And since for so many it is more pleasant to read short stories than to read historical works, the attraction of the book (all merit ignored) was larger than might be supposed. Had it had less merit as literature the appeal would doubtless have been far greater.

Hawthorne now seemed on the threshold of success. He had waited long, perhaps too long, for public recognition—had waited behind the door which Bridge had thrust open. Would he come out and show himself? For now was the time. We have to remember that "Hawthorne" was still to the majority of people a pseudonym. His real name was Hathorne and his friends knew him as "Hath." Would he do something to make himself known?

There was one thing he was determined to do. Bridge had communicated with almost all of his old Bowdoin friends. But there was one with whom he must communicate himself. There was one free copy of the book which he must tie up and post himself, and the parcel must be addressed to Henry Wadsworth Longfellow, a young man, a younger man than he was, whom he had never once set eyes on since leaving Bowdoin College. And on the reception of that book and the accompanying letter he set great store. Would Longfellow, his very successful junior, remember "Nat Hathorne" or "Hath"? Yes, almost certainly; though without the letter there was the danger that Longfellow might not connect the author of *Twice-Told Tales* with his brother's friend at Bowdoin.

How two existences, both occupied with literature, could differ more than those of Longfellow and Hawthorne after they left Bowdoin it is difficult to imagine. Short as it then was, Longfellow's career had been amazingly successful. Though still under thirty he had achieved distinction in academic life. He had been one of those few, those happy few, who while still at their university are chosen as men to be pushed up the ladder of success. His own little college of Bowdoin gave him his first shove. He had no sooner given his farewell address than he was bidden to return. The Faculty of Bowdoin, small though that college was, had determined that they must have a chair of modern languages. Though Longfellow was no linguist he was a starred graduate. He was also the son of one of the principal lawyers in the state. Would he agree to be eventually installed in that chair—on conditions? The conditions were attractive. He must agree to go to Europe, expenses paid, to make himself proficient before taking up his duties. Longfellow accepted. He sailed for Europe, armed with letters of introduction. He was good at getting such things. The year 1826 was spent in France, 1827 in Spain. In 1829 he was in Germany and in that same year he was installed in his chair. He was just about to come of age. Though some of his pupils must have been older than he was, young Longfellow, for all his curls, his blue eyes, and his elegant clothes, was no boy. He was always quite sure of himself. He was a man of the world now, with the grand educational tour behind him and a creditable amount of serious study on record. Longfellow could always work.

How long so polished an American would have been prepared to remain as a professor in so rough a college as Bowdoin, even though it had been his own college, in his own State of Maine, near his own home in Portland is doubtful. If he had ideas of moving on he could hardly have expected that so brilliant a move would be open to him so soon. He was twenty-six years old when he received a letter from Josiah Quincy, the President of Harvard, telling him that Professor Ticknor had intimated to the authorities a desire to be relieved of his academic responsibilities. Ticknor, the professor-prince, was prepared to cast his cloak and would be happy if the cloak were to fall upon the shoulders of young Longfellow. Once more there were conditions. His German was weak. He must visit Europe once again. Even after a hundred years one can appreciate to some extent the excitement, the pride, and the visions of a brilliant future which the reading of that communication must have conveyed to the fortunate recipient.

In the year 1837 in which Queen Victoria came to the throne, in which Longfellow took up his duties at Harvard and in which Prescott published his *Ferdinand and Isabella*, Hawthorne sent his little book to Longfellow and the friendship between them began. It was to be a lifelong friendship. And for a time, for a decade or more, "friendship" justly describes their relationship. But as years passed they saw less and less of each other, and the neglect seems to have been Longfellow's fault. Yet glancing with one eye at Longfellow's progress through life and glancing with the other at Hawthorne's, one sees how increasingly difficult it must have been for them to fashion the bond of friendship from anything more concrete than memories or overlapping friendships.

As Henry Wadsworth Longfellow reappears, though with diminishing frequency, in these pages his position in relation to all the others who came into Hawthorne's life now the door is open, is worth establishing.

During the second and third decades of the nineteenth century Boston was as pleasant a place to live in for a man with money and intelligence as any place in the English-speaking world. The wealth of Boston, threatened first by the blockade and then by the new trade routes across the American continent, had miraculously recovered. Whereas formerly Boston, as the banking center of New England, had been dependent on shipping and the *entrepôt* trade, now her principal interests were in milling cotton and wool and in the manufacture of small goods. She was strangely lucky too that though she financially controlled these industries, none of them came to spoil her amenities. Old Boston at the mouth of the Charles River was preserved with all its charm. The distinguished traveler arriving by the Cunard liner from Liverpool and going no farther was surprised by the culture and the comforts of the well-to-do of New England. The Bostonians were renowned for their hospitality.

Up and across the Charles River the rural character of the famous village of Cambridge had not been touched. The professors of Harvard University after the day's work was done could read a book in a chair on the spacious lawns of their homes or could ride or drive into Boston to dine with friends or go to the play.

It was only natural that the merchant princes of Boston should be benefactors of their university of which they were so proud. What was strange was that the fathers should have encouraged the sons to stay over the river, to devote their lives and their fortunes to scholarship: stranger still that the zest for hard work which, combined with business astuteness, had built up those fortunes, should have been inherited in so large a proportion along with the wealth. The *jeunesse dorée* took up serious study with the same naturalness that the same small class today takes up polo. That they did not produce a genius was their misfortune, not their fault. If some of them lived in a style which it is unusual to connect with hard labor, the result of their industry is a record of their seriousness. Ticknor resigned his professorship because he was too busy, not because he wanted to relax. There were a number of these professor-princes. And there were author-princes too, men like Prescott who, struggling on with his great work, struggling heroically against blindness, and spending fortunes in Europe for archives to be opened and copies of manuscripts to be sent to Boston, worked for years in secret, and allowed busy Boston to consider him a slacker. Another author-prince was Motley, a serious historian if there ever was one, who allowed himself to be seduced in the end by the offer to play a part in history as a diplomat, and playing no part in history, never quite got back to his old style.

The elegant Mr. Longfellow, young as he was, was a clever choice as successor to Professor Ticknor. Scholastic social circles being what they were, are and presumably always will be, the new man was of course "not a patch" on the old. That was inevitable. Discarding his elegant continental fopperies and assuming his professorial black, thereby avoiding a repetition of the scandal of Bancroft who, returning from abroad, greeted a distinguished professor with a kiss (which was the end of Bancroft as far as Harvard was concerned), Professor Longfellow chose new methods to attract the confidence of undergraduates. Gathering his men around him, playing host at the end of the mahogany table, he talked delightfully of his meeting with Goethe and other European celebrities, praised the bouquet of old Provençal song and then, without his pupils' noticing it, got down to modern languages and modern literature in Europe. Longfellow "did his stuff," as we would say today, which was to "charm." He was well aware of the danger of his position as the substitute for the authoritarian Ticknor. And for a time he was unhappy. But his charm worked. And ever afterwards the man to put at the head of a mahogany table was Longfellow, the perfect host, the perfect chairman.

And then, just at the time when he must have been feeling strange and homesick (he had just written to his father telling him he might chuck everything), along came a book and a letter from Nathaniel Hawthorne, that peculiar but impressive youth he had known at Bowdoin.

"We were not," wrote Hawthorne, "it is true, so well acquainted with each other that I can plead an absolute right to inflict my twice-told tediousness upon you, but I have often regretted that we were not better known to each other."

Longfellow's response was immediate, and his pleasure, we must believe, whole-hearted. He wrote to Hawthorne and asked him where had been the secret nest of this New England lark. To which Hawthorne replied, "If you had pictured me as dwelling in an owl's nest, you would have been nearer the truth, for mine is about as dismal; and like the owl, I seldom venture abroad until after dark. . . . Since we last met—which I remember was in Sawtelle's room, when you read a farewell poem to the class—ever since that time, I have secluded myself from society. And yet I never meant such a thing, nor dreamed what sort of a life I was going to lead.

"I have indeed, turned over a good number of books; but in so desultory a way that it cannot be called study, nor has it left me with the fruits of study.

"There has been no warmth of approbation, so that I have always written with benumbed fingers.

"I have seen so little of the world that I have nothing but thin air to concoct my stories of; and it is not easy to give a life-like semblance to such shadowy stuff.

"To be sure, you could not well help flattering me a little; but I value praise too highly not to have faith in its sincerity."

Hawthorne's faith in Longfellow is very touching. It made him believe more than ever in the friends of his youth. Longfellow certainly did the very best thing which it was in his power to do. He sat down and wrote a complimentary notice of *Twice-Told Tales* for the *North American Review*, still at the height of its powers, still the authoritarian periodical of criticism. Boston was proud of her *North American*. It kept Boston on equal literary terms with Edinburgh and London. All the best men wanted to write for the review; and all did. The question of pay hardly, if ever, came into the contract. The time was approaching when the author-princes, so closely allied with the merchant princes, were to conduct the political opinion of this periodical into channels so far to the right of the

Whig group that young men were soon to tire of it. But at the time when Longfellow wrote his notice of *Twice-Told Tales* he could have done no greater service to Hawthorne.

Hawthorne, reading Longfellow's flowery eulogy, was delighted. He well might have been; for the young professor had been rash in his prophecies and extravagant in his praise. That Hawthorne should have been anxious to leave Herbert Street and go to Cambridge to see him and talk with him is proof of what good it had done.

And from then on until Hawthorne's death, they did see each other; and often. But either Hawthorne was too difficult or, far more probably, the social stratum of the one was so different from the social stratum of the other, that the political party to which Hawthorne with dogged faith always belonged, the ostracized Democratic party, made difficulties for the affable, charming and affectionate Professor Longfellow which prevented the two men from becoming intimate. Harvard had given Longfellow much—the cloak of Ticknor, a place in the Boston-Cambridge hierarchy, and the society of rich and intelligent men. It was not unnatural that the society should demand from Longfellow something in return—a willingness to become ripe, mellow and glossy before his time.

To show the loyalty of Hawthorne to Longfellow it is only necessary to remember that Hawthorne really came to admire Longfellow's poetry—he whose ears were deaf to the music of all poetry written after Elizabethan times. And that might have been put on Longfellow's tomb as a testimony of the admiration which he was able to attract. But there was a radical difference between them. They had chosen different clubs at Bowdoin and their choice then was a pointer to the road which each would choose in later life. The road which Henry Wadsworth Longfellow would always have taken would have been to the right, that which led to a full and rich life, "rich" in both senses of the word. The road which Nathaniel Hawthorne would have taken would always have been to the left, the road which led to artisans' dwellings, puppet shows and humble men. When Longfellow married *en seconde noce* the daughter of one of Boston's merchant princes, with the famous Craigie House thrown in as a wedding present, and Hawthorne married into the Concord circle, their social encounters were limited to the club dinners and the lecture hall.

In the first week in July 1837 Hawthorne left home to spend his annual holiday in the country with Horatio Bridge in his paternal mansion at Augusta, Maine.

Hawthorne was in holiday mood. He was merry, energetic, insatiably inquisitive and at times argumentative. He liked Bridge's large and only partly furnished house. He even liked the French tutor whom Bridge at that time was befriending, the silly little Alsatian, a M. Schaeffer, whom Hawthorne persisted in insulting by calling him a German, he calling himself French. His was not much of a job, going on foot from house to house giving lessons in French to the sons and daughters of Augustan townsfolk. Schaeffer was a sorry figure and owed much at that time to Bridge, who gave him bed and breakfast free so as to have someone to talk with in that empty house. For Bridge kept no regular domestic servants; he relied on a family he let live in the back quarters for cleaning such rooms as he used, for making the beds and for cooking the shoulders of lamb which he and Hawthorne ate cold for supper.

M. Schaeffer had no supper. He went empty to bed. He is reported, however, to have always done himself very well for breakfast. The midday meal they took at the hotel, which pleased Hawthorne immensely, for there was nothing that he liked better than the bar or the common room of a hotel. There a man could listen to everyone else's conversation and seldom be called upon to say a word. No plan of living could possibly have suited Hawthorne, an awkward guest, better: no fuss, no servants, no regular meals. If he did not want to join Bridge at the hotel, there was always a supply of bread, cheese and eggs —his favorite food—in the house.

But there was more than this to delight Hawthorne. A magnificent and refreshing river flowed past the house, a river (and he loved them all) up which he could travel by canoe, a river with tributaries each one of which was a separate exploration, a river with shingle banks upon which, having stripped off his clothes, he could lie naked beneath the July sun and let the water run over his body.

For Bridge, however, the river was something more than a vision of beauty. It was water power: it was, he believed, his fortune. He had not meant at the first, it is true, to put his entire realizable assets, amounting to some fifty thousand dollars, into the scheme—only perhaps half that sum and his territorial rights. The project was to build a dam across the Kennebec River just below his house, so as to provide more power for existing factories and provide power for the factories which would be built. All was going well when Hawthorne arrived there, except that the dam was costing about twice as much as the original estimate, and Bridge had had to put every dollar he possessed into the venture. Bridge was nervous; for if the dam broke or was left uncompleted, he was ruined. Hawthorne's amateur opinion of the look of the dam did not add, one imagines, to the confidence of the principal shareholder. He said it looked even in construction like a dam which had been already wrecked. True Hawthorne was no judge, and he was known to be ardent in supporting the cause of the preservation of rivers in their pristine glory and opposed to all industrialization.

Though all was still well with the dam during the time Hawthorne was staying at Augusta, disaster came; and came soon. A flood—of course, as Bridge writes, a bigger flood than had ever been known in the Kennebec valley—came down; it piled up against Bridge's dam and being discomforted by it, chose another route. And the route that the river chose was plumb through the middle of the promoter's paternal mansion. All was swept away—the investment, the house, everything. Within a year (which proves that Bridge did not brood over his woes) he was a purser in the American Navy. In that service he spent the rest of his working life and ended up as Paymaster of the Navy in Washington.

The big event of the visit was not the dam or the fishing expeditions, delightful as all these had been in one way or another: it was his meeting with Cilley, the youth who had fascinated him at Bowdoin, now a representative in Congress—Cilley the successful politician. He had not seen Cilley since Bowdoin days, though there had been correspondence between them, principally because Cilley had lost his bet that Hawthorne would marry before he did. The wager was a barrel of the best sherry-wine and Bridge, even in those far-off days, had been appointed as adjudicator. Cilley, having lost the bet, not unnaturally imagined that the payment of the debt would be made an occasion for drinking most if not all of the barrel of sherry. Bridge maintained with an unimaginative sense of justice that Hawthorne was owed a barrel of sherry. He must be paid, in sherry; there was no need for a party; and if Hawthorne wanted to drink the sherry, all of it and alone, he certainly could. So Cilley did not get his sherry party; Hawthorne got his barrel and Bridge was left with the reputation of being quite unnecessarily fussy.

The meeting of Hawthorne and Cilley after all those years, a meeting arranged by Bridge, is of importance because of what happened afterwards. Many must know the apprehensiveness with which a man receives the news that he is to meet the hero of his adolescence after years of separation. The hero himself, being quite unaware of the anxiety which the reunion is causing in the manly breast of an adult, approaches the meeting as his natural self and with pleasure perhaps—certainly with no sense at all of embarrassment. But the hero-worshiper of a past decade approaches the hero with apprehension, with embarrassment and consequently, being quite unnecessarily on his guard, even with hostility. It is not surprising, as some have thought, to find the former eulogies of Cilley suddenly, in the account of their meeting in Hawthorne's journal, replaced by a scathing criticism, in its turn to be replaced by that last and final eulogy which Hawthorne wrote only a twelve-month later on receiving the news that Cilley had been killed.

Approaching that meeting, Hawthorne evidently turned over in his mind the question: What was it in my youth that so fascinated me in Cilley? And another question: What is it

now in Cilley, a Democrat in Whig territory, a Democrat in
disagreement even with his own caucus, which so fascinates
the electors that he is returned by them as a Congressman?
There must be something, there must always have been something very meretricious about Cilley. Such is his answer. They
meet. Cilley as usual charms, as usual opens his heart and talks
as only Cilley could talk. His life is an open book and he likes
to read out of it.

There is no mistaking Hawthorne's carefully written sketch
of Cilley (Friday, July 28th) as anything but very uncomplimentary; and it becomes more uncomplimentary as it goes on.
They met like old friends, he says, and talked together almost
as freely as in college days. Cilley spoke touchingly and with
tears in his eyes of the death of his little daughter. Nevertheless . . . "he is a really crafty man, concealing, like a murder-
secret, anything that it is not good for him to have known.
There is such a quantity of truth, and kindness, and warm affections, that a man's heart opens to him in spite of himself; he
deceives by truth. And not only is he crafty, but when occasion
demands, bold and fierce as a tiger, determined and even
straightforward and undisguised in his manner—a daring fellow
as well as a sly one." [3] With Cilley's appearance he was as little
pleased. ". . . a thin face, sharp features, sallow, a projecting
brow, not very high, deep-set eyes; insinuating smile and look
when he meets you, or is about to address you. I should think
he would do away with this particular expression; for it lets
out more of himself than can be detected in any other way, in
personal intercourse with him." It is sharp criticism. The old
spell is evidently broken. Yet in the very next sentence Haw-

[3] R. S. edition of *American Notebook*, p. 20.

thorne announces his intention to go to Thomaston to see him.

To Thomaston he went on August 7th, and because Cilley was not able to put him up (he was not at all well off and had a wife and family), Hawthorne stayed in a comfortable boarding-house. Though he wrote four and a half pages in his journal about Thomaston, Cilley's name is only mentioned once. Yet he witnessed something there in Thomaston which corrected the bias of his opinion, an opinion at this moment clearly in Cilley's disfavor, an opinion founded partly on the natural mistrust of a grown man for his youthful enthusiasms, partly on his conviction (though Pierce was exempted) that a politician could not be an honest fellow from head to foot. And the conversion had to do with a cow. "Mr. Cilley's domestic habits were simple and primitive to a degree unusual, in most parts of our country, amongst men of so eminent a station as he had attained. It made me smile, though with anything but scorn, in contrast to the aristocratic stateliness which I have witnessed elsewhere, to see him driving home his own cow after a long search for her through the village. That trait alone would have marked him as a man whose greatness lay within himself." The cow, in fact, put everything right. By the end of the month Cilley and Hawthorne were in Boston together, drinking champagne on board an American man-of-war.

Did this renewal of a friendship, brief as it was to be, have any effect at all on the behavior of Cilley, who was so soon to meet his death? Did Cilley die because he believed that in fighting a duel he was only doing what Hawthorne had shown readiness to do? Did Hawthorne write his memorial address because he had been told that he was morally and by example

responsible for Cilley's exaggerated, out-of-date, and undemocratic rashness in accepting the challenge? The answer has always been a categorical "No." There are many who even go so
far as to attempt to prove that Hawthorne never issued a challenge at all. Hawthorne could never have written what he did
about Cilley's duel if he had been guilty of a like offence against
American standards of behavior. Hawthorne was not the man
—he who would never hurt a flea if he could avoid it—to risk
killing a man even if he at the same time ran the risk of being
killed himself. We must remember, however, that Hawthorne,
who had lived for years in an owl's nest and behaved rather
like an owl, was perhaps at that time—and very temporarily—
finding the light of the noon sun rather strong for him. Six
months before he had threatened to destroy himself. In his
youth he had been stubborn and had had flashes of violent and
dangerous temper.

The story is this, for what it is worth. Hawthorne having
ventured forth, got into some trouble with a girl. She was a
hoyden and having, so it appears, failed to make the impression
she wished on the handsome Hawthorne, she determined to
arouse his interest in her by confiding to him some dreadful
story of the way in which "his great friend" had treated her.
She succeeded in working him up to such an extent that though
the man was his best friend, he challenged him to a duel. "Hawthorne . . . who had never considered the possibility of a lady
being a deliberate and gratuitous liar . . . allowed her to de-
coy him into assuming towards her the attitude of a protecting
friend and champion. . . ." So wrote Julian Hawthorne in the
much disputed but long and carefully written passage in the life
of his father and mother which refers to "Louis" and "May,"

the fictitious names used to describe the incident without revealing the identity of the two protagonists. "She summoned Hawthorne to a private and mysterious interview, at which, after much artful preface and well-contrived hesitation and reluctance, she at length presented him with the startling information that his friend Louis, presuming on her innocence and guilelessness, had been guilty of an attempt to practise the basest treachery upon her; and she passionately adjured Hawthorne, as her only confidential and trusted friend and protector, to champion her cause . . . without pausing to make proper investigation, he forthwith sent Louis a challenge." Louis refused the challenge, made a full and adequate defense to the charge Hawthorne had made against him. "Hawthorne immediately called upon him, overwhelmed both by the revelation of the woman's falsehood and by his own conduct in so nearly bringing destruction upon a man he loved." He forthwith called on Mary too and "crushed" her, whatever exactly that may have meant.

Was it probable that Julian, Hawthorne's son, his father's stout defender, would have ever written this story at such length, if it was all made up, his own fancy or gossip? It seems highly improbable. And the story is deliberately told in order to bring forward its tragic consequence. The incident was known to a few friends who were no doubt startled when the recluse of Salem appeared as a challenger and a duelist. While the news was still fresh in their minds, Cilley received his challenge from Graves. A man called Watson Webb had changed the political opinion of his newspaper for a sum of fifty-two thousand dollars, a deal upon which Cilley commented truly in Congress. Webb sent a challenge by Graves which Cilley refused. Graves then challenged Cilley either to withdraw his statements or to plead parliamentary privileges. When Cilley refused, Graves, with whom he said he had no quarrel at all, challenged him to a duel. Why did Cilley accept the second challenge? Because, says his son, someone said, "If Hawthorne was so ready to fight a duel without stopping to ask questions, you certainly need not hesitate." Cilley accepted. Cilley was killed. "When Hawthorne was told of this, he felt as if he were as much responsible for his friend's death as was the man who shot him."

All this Julian is supposed to have invented. Horatio Bridge denies that Cilley was in any way influenced by Hawthorne's example, informs us that Hawthorne never in his hearing assumed any responsibility for Cilley's death. Remorse and responsibility are two totally different things. "Responsibility" in this instance would be a ridiculously severe self-accusation, but it may be that as the years passed, a momentary prick of conscience became remorse. Bridge does not, it is to be noticed, deny that Julian's account of Hawthorne's challenge and its refusal was invention, only that Cilley acted on Hawthorne's example. This is fortunate; for a recently discovered letter written by Hawthorne on February 8 in 1838, published by Mr. Randall Stewart and belonging to Miss Marian Bridge Maurice, seems to prove that Bridge knew very much more about the affair than he admits in his book. Hawthorne had appealed to him to come to help him, and at once. Advice would probably be useless, he was warned. It was all about a woman and he was leaving for Washington. Bridge might regret it, Hawthorne warned him, if he did not come at once. "Be mum!"

Hawthorne lived. But poor Cilley died on the other side of a barricade, "murdered," so the Democratic Party were prepared to think, as a too ambitious opponent to the power of the Whigs; killed by a man, as he had protested, with whom he had no quarrel at all.

Though knowing nothing of party politics Hawthorne became a Democrat after this tragic event. And this we must remember. Bridge, Cilley and Pierce were and always had been Democrats. Hawthorne had until then been democratic but not a Democrat, and the difference is by no means inconsiderable.

6

Enter Miss Elizabeth Peabody

THE warmth of public recognition, feeble though it had been, had brought him out as a rising thermometer brings out an hibernating animal from its winter retreat. Since no one could find him a job—though Bridge, Pierce and Cilley were doing their best—his was to be a brief summer. He was soon ready and even anxious to get back to his winter quarters, to the house in Herbert Street where his mother lived in the seclusion of her bedroom and his sister Elizabeth only became conscious that she was alive after the sun had set. It was the life he knew. He returned to it willingly.

And then who should come to disturb the peace of the house but Miss Elizabeth Peabody, a woman in her early thirties, whom they knew only by name as the daughter of that Dr. Peabody who had failed so lamentably to cure Nathaniel's foot when he was a boy. That was a very parochial description of that eager young woman. Elizabeth Peabody was a remarkable though not a particularly pleasing character. She would even at that time have shuddered at being described as Dr. Peabody's daughter not only because the matriarchal system prevailed in her family, the father and the four dead or dying sons being of no interest, but because she herself was so well known and so important in the intellectual world of Boston and Concord that she could well be expected to stand on her own feet, as it were.

And she did stand on them for no less than ninety years.

The assault on the stronghold of the recluses of Herbert Street was perhaps the most important event in Nathaniel Hawthorne's social life, regrettable though it seems to have to admit it. It was one of Miss Peabody's battle honors. It was a victory when the surprised and shocked defenders capitulated after a creditably sustained siege; and one must suppose that never in her long life did that indomitable lady find herself in greater need of a victory. She had just been guilty of a serious offense—for the great campaigner that she was, the most serious of all offenses—desertion in the face of the enemy. She had just ratted on poor Bronson Alcott and left him to the Boston mob, she who only a few months before had written a book which went into second edition proving that her friend Alcott was one of the greatest educationalists the world had ever seen. Badly bruised in that affray not by Bronson Alcott's enemies—she did not wait to face them—but by the pricks of her own conscience, she was determined to restore her reputation with the intelligentsia of New England by bringing before them an American of genius, a writer of tales and short stories whom she had eventually, after overcoming the greatest of difficulties, found barricaded, as it were, in a house in Herbert Street, Salem.

She was late in the day with her discovery. There was no secret whatsoever concerning the identity of the author. What she must be credited with is a successful assault on the house in Herbert Street, into which none but the oldest cronies of the family were ever allowed to set foot. She is to be credited with overcoming the females of that household and leading their only and treasured male away. It was she who lionized him and brought him to the attention of her eminent friends. To her Hawthorne was deeply indebted for his introduction to Sophia. After their marriage and even before it, Hawthorne found himself, often to his discomfort and because of his love for Sophia, in the company of men and women, brilliantly clever many of them, whose philosophy of life he openly distrusted. An obstinate wagoner, he refused to hitch his wagon load of talent to their stars. He chose to ride his own "dark horse of the night" as Emerson called it, and rode it well.

There are two accounts of Miss Elizabeth's assault on the Hathorne household. The one which she wrote herself (and as a biographer she was notoriously inaccurate, as Hawthorne twenty years later told her in the plainest terms possible) describes her search for the anonymous author. According to her from 1830 she had been interested in certain stories. They arrested her attention. They were written, she thought, by an *old* man; and to this unknown author she had addressed, but had not posted, a letter asking him how he knew that "sensitive natures are especially apt to be malicious"! "It was not until 1837 that I discovered these were the work of Madame Hawthorne's son.[1] It was a difficult matter to establish visiting relations with so eccentric a household; and another year passed away before Mr. Hawthorne and his sisters called on us. I was alone in the drawing room. As soon as I could, I ran upstairs . . . and said, 'O Sophia, you must get up and dress and come down! The Hawthornes are here and you never saw anything so splendid as he is—he is handsomer than Lord Byron!' " In her version there was no assault. Nathaniel and his sisters "came to call."

---

[1] Hawthorne's mother was never known except by the Peabodys other than as Madame *Hathorne*.

That at a later period, after the assault and capitulation, Nathaniel called upon the Peabodys frequently there is no denying. And the younger generation during her lifetime never let her down—they never exposed her as she so richly deserved to be exposed.

The other account, given by Mrs. Annie Fields, is as amusing as it is almost certainly authentic. Elizabeth Peabody had not been looking for a man at all, she had been looking for a female. Hearing that N.H. was a Hathorne of Herbert Street she jumped to the conclusion that the author was an authoress, the girl she remembered at her first school when both families were living in Union Street, the girl of whose talents she had been so very jealous—Elizabeth Hathorne. ". . . she concluded it must be Miss Hawthorne, as she did not remember having seen a brother.[2] On the strength of this information she called at the house, and asked to see Miss Hawthorne; but when only Miss Louisa presented herself, Miss Peabody devoted the powers of her eloquence to telling her what a genius her sister possessed. 'My brother, you mean!' was the response. 'It is your brother, then!' said Miss Peabody. 'If your brother can write like that, *he has no right to be idle.*' 'My brother never is idle,' answered Miss Louisa quietly."

Could anything be more typical of Miss Peabody, the school marm who has been caught out, than that rebuke, "He has no right to be idle"!

She was not at that time, we must remember, or for many years to come, either the famous old "Grandmother of Boston," which she became; or the "Mother of the American Kinder-

---

[2] *Nathaniel Hawthorne* by Annie Fields. Kegan Paul, Trench & Co. and Small, Maynard & Co., Boston, 1899.

garten," another sobriquet; or even Henry James's famous "Miss Birdseye." Nor had anyone at that time even thought of calling her "the most dissolute woman in Boston," which was young William James's nonsensically witty criticism of an old and revered lady. She was Miss Elizabeth Peabody, an energetic and interfering female in her early thirties.

That branch of the Peabody clan had to work for their living. There was no fund of bonds or income from real estate behind them; and, as the males were feeble, Mrs. Peabody and Miss Elizabeth had to fend for themselves. At the age of sixteen, consequently, Elizabeth Peabody opened her own school in her own home, her two sisters, Mary and Sophia, being among her first pupils.

Then fortune smiled on her. She became what was then called "amanuensis" or, as we would say now, "literary secretary" to Dr. Channing. To have worked in such intimacy with so fine a character was a privilege of which she should have been and was proud; for Channing was intellectually head and shoulders above his contemporaries. An unfortunate metaphor to have used, for, poor man, he was as thin as a skeleton, a permanent and gallant invalid, and with his enormous hat, his cloak, coats and mufflers he looked like an over-decorated scarecrow which was being swept away in a gale. Everything in his youth seemed to have been arranged by fate to make Dr. Channing into the cultured parson of Boston's richest and most cultured parish. And this he became. With a country place on the sea at Newport, with a rich wife and a large house in Boston, he was the proper person to have the cure of the souls of the merchant-princes. As a pulpit orator he was sufficiently distinguished to fear no rival. That says much for him; for not only was it the golden age of the sermon but his competitors were a highly trained set of men. He was as sure of his position when problems of philosophy, history and literature were being discussed as any tutor or professor of Harvard. He was the first really intelligent man to become a Unitarian; his insistence on the importance of the cultivation of the mind as the only means by which the freer and richer life of the spirit could be attained was a satisfying compliment when addressed to a professor-prince. He was as able a man in conference, on the platform and in the debating society, as he was in his own study or in the pulpit. His parishioners believed themselves very fortunate in their minister, which they indeed were. But it soon became apparent that his idea of his job and his parishioners' idea of his job were very different. If with his material wealth he thought it necessary to sleep in the attic to satisfy his conscience; if as the busiest man in Boston he found it necessary to find time for personal attention to those of his parishioners who were in sickness or in trouble, that was his affair. But it was perhaps regrettable that so cultured a man should take charity, meekness and service so seriously. Curates could attend to these.

Bostonians misjudged the character of their Dr. Channing. It was pleasant to them to have a parish priest who was the friend of Wordsworth and Samuel Taylor Coleridge. It flattered them that Channing's historical essays had given him an international reputation as a writer, short-lived though that reputation was to be. What was insufferable was that he told them quite plainly that it was not simply the enrichment of the spiritual lives of his well-to-do parishioners with which he was concerned but the lives of every man, woman and child in

America, however poor, however ignorant. It was not enough for a man to save his own soul; he must help the factory workers in Lowell to save theirs. He became America's first and most enlightened social-reformer and as a reward began to be "cut dead" in the street by many of his parishioners. Such treatment was, needless to say, of no importance whatsoever to Dr. Channing. It is astonishing that, hurrying through the street from this appointment to that, his poor bones rattling, he even noticed that he was being cut. Perhaps he did not; but was told.

What did make him unhappy was that, being the animater and inspirer of the young and intelligent men of the day, he felt himself responsible for their heresies. Views and opinions, of which he was only too willing to accept parentage, were taken by the younger generation and hybridized with their own. Dr. Channing was consequently left with an illegitimate grand-child—transcendentalism. His belief in the divinity of Christ was as absolute as his belief that social reform was a spiritual necessity for those who would save their souls. The Tran-scendentalists doubted the divinity of Christ and, except for shedding tears over the plight of a runaway slave, they did their slumming in their own parlors. By living like wise philosophers they inevitably became poor. It was their own poverty which inspired them. Channing's poor whites and sweated laborers, uneducated and boorish, left the intellectuals quite unmoved. Charity began at home.

From the great Dr. Channing Elizabeth Peabody no doubt learnt much—untiring industry, for example; but there were many lessons she did not learn. She was full of fervor for a cause; so was he. Her trouble was that she had too much fervor. She was always ready to enlist for a campaign in which, to give her her due, she was always in the vanguard. Channing was a valiant campaigner. He was steadfast; she was not. There was often some doubt on which front she might appear; and at least once in her life some doubt concerning which side she was on.

That the story of the rise and fall of Bronson Alcott as a Boston schoolmaster should be relevant to a biography of Hawthorne he himself would have denied. The Temple School and the scandal connected with it had nothing to do with him. He did not even meet the Peabodys or Bronson Alcott until some time after the whole affair was finished and done with. None the less, the improbable chain of circumstances is there which links Hawthorne to the Temple School. If Miss Elizabeth Peabody had not left the services of Dr. Channing and offered them to Bronson Alcott, if she had not deserted her leader when the big guns of Boston propriety began to open up on the Temple School and if she had not taken refuge in dull Salem with her family, Hawthorne would never have met his future wife. If he had not married Sophia, who, unlike her sister Elizabeth, had been kind to Bronson Alcott in trouble, he would never have gone to live at Concord and would never have been the Obstinate Wagoner.

Bronson Alcott because of these circumstances happened to become an intimate acquaintance of Hawthorne for a period of some twenty-five years. Hawthorne got to know him well, thought him to be possessed of the noblest soul he had ever known, thought nothing of his brain, and on occasions found him such an insufferable bore that he used his children to act as scouts so that he could escape by the back door before Alcott got in by the front.

Born into a family of farmers in the hills of Connecticut, Bronson Alcott received his education at the village school; and that, strangely enough in the light of his subsequent career, was all the schooling he ever received. He began in poverty, he lived in poverty, but he died in more comfortable circumstances, having become the father of the authoress of *Little Men* and *Little Women* and many other popular works of fiction. He once in his life made a profit—but only once, and then as a youth. His mother had relations who had raised themselves above the level of the standard of living of the average farmer. They had become schoolmasters and parsons. Young Alcott was sent to these relations to see whether he could be trained. The experiment was a failure for the very good reason that Bronson had made up his mind to become peddler and so to get rich quick. And a peddler he became, depositing his store of combs and trinkets—New England manufactures—in some Southern town and walking the countryside to sell them at back doors to servant girls. It was not a particularly honest way of earning a living; but it was a hard life, and a "gift of the gab" was essential to success.

Having made a complete failure of the peddling business, having nearly starved, and having nearly died of illness contracted on his journey, Alcott returned to the homestead, penniless and looking most peculiar, rigged out in fancy clothes bought on credit in New York.

How it happened that Alcott, the garishly dressed peddler, turned himself into a schoolmaster and an inspired reformer of educational methods, has never been satisfactorily explained. His infant pupils adored him. Not so the parents. What had been good enough for them must be good enough for their children. They were not interested in educational reform and saw no necessity for it. If it was praiseworthy of him to devote the larger portion of his small salary to providing materials for his school, it was intolerable that when his own funds ran out he should continue to make purchases by giving I.O.U.'s which could never be met. The parents were strict Calvinists and were consequently disinclined to believe, as he believed, that out of the mouths of innocent children words of great wisdom would come if the proper encouragement were given. Their children had been born in sin. It was clear to them that Mr. Alcott had heretical views, so that when, as he was sure to do sooner or later, he referred to the Son of God as Jesus the best of all schoolmasters, he found himself faced with empty benches next morning. Dismissed or deserted, young Alcott, always on the verge of starvation, always quite fearless and always talking, moved on and on. Yet there seems always to have been one member of every community who was prepared to testify not only to his absolute sincerity but to the admirable progress of the children put under him.

So he talked and taught; and so met and married Abigail May; and was persuaded to make for Boston, the Mecca of all educationalists in America.

Boston was Unitarian. Boston was liberal. But Boston was also a place where credentials were required and examined. And Alcott had no credentials with which to impress the Bostonians. His sincerity, however, impressed Dr. Channing, who introduced him to many eminent men of the day. Alcott pretended not to be impressed by the men he met but the truth was that he was immensely impressed by the amount of reading and learning they possessed. They all spoke and thought from the solid foundation of a sound education. Alcott was self-educated. He had read; but he had never been taught. Boston was interested in the man, recognized the derivation of some of his educational theories (in which recognition it was probably wrong), and was prepared to help him get a job of some sort in which his practice could be tested. Realizing for the first time the disadvantages of the position of the self-educated man, Alcott unnecessarily and unwisely tried to get even with them by hectic study.

It was a long time before Alcott, with Dr. Channing's blessing and Miss Elizabeth Peabody's assistance, was able to collect the funds and the pupils for that school which he was sure would be the prototype for the juvenile schools of the future. Alcott was never willing to do things by halves, and remembering his past extravagances for his pupils (never for himself) and his trust in the Almighty to provide petty cash, one is alarmed to read what he wrote in September, 1834: "I have obtained very fine rooms in the Temple and have made arrangements to fit up the interior in a style corresponding to the exterior. . . . I have spared no expense to surround the senses with appropriate emblems of intellectual and spiritual life. Paintings, busts, books, and not inelegant furniture have been deemed important." The school opened therefore heavily in debt. Alcott was optimistic. Those were boom times and a boom is infectious. The number of pupils was most satisfactory. By October he was teaching thirty-four pupils, of whom most were under ten years of age.

Alcott had not liked Miss Peabody on first acquaintance,

highly recommended though she was as Dr. Channing's friend and former secretary. Her manners were unnecessarily bad; she was opinionated, she was self-assertive. Yet he accepted her as his assistant. And she wholeheartedly accepted him. What Bronson Alcott's career might have been without Miss Elizabeth no one can possibly tell. Had her admiration for him been at the first more temperate, their association and the Temple School might have lasted longer. The school had been running for less than a year when Miss Peabody, with that impatience which was one of her permanent characteristics, published her *Records of a School*, in which she described in detail Alcott's methods. In January 1835 Alcott wrote in his diary, "Miss Peabody is now present every day and keeps a journal of the operations and spirit of the instruction. It bids fair to prove a faithful transcript of what passes in the schoolroom. This journal is to be published. . . ."

Alcott's methods were dialectical and analytical. He must remove obstructions to the growth of the mind, obstructions which lie in the appetites, passions, desires and will. Then he could reach the hearts of his pupils. He would have their affections, and where he had them, he could vivify the imagination and then take "direct intellectual action." In practice his methods approximated those of psychoanalysis. By the asking and answering of innumerable questions the barrier between himself and the pupils would disappear and truth would out. This cross-examination was kept up day after day. He began to get some very astonishing answers. Alcott, fascinated with the success of his method, confined himself more and more to moral and spiritual instruction. Miss Elizabeth and Miss Sophia Peabody, like press reporters, took down every word that these children said, though, as they were writing in longhand, they had to abridge the words of the master.

Not everyone approved of Miss Peabody's book. "We regard it," wrote a reviewer, "as a mingled mass of truth and error, of useful and useless and injurious principles and methods." Not everyone in Boston approved of what was passing in the Temple School. The venture had been initiated with the blessing of the Unitarians. But what faith was this in which Alcott was instructing his children? Not Unitarianism certainly. Dr. Channing warned him. But Alcott would not listen; for he was Channing's equal by now; his new friend Emerson had convinced him of that. Alcott had become the inspired missionary as well as inspired teacher, and a philosopher, too. He would be warned by no one.

The second edition of Miss Peabody's book (1836) made matters worse; for in attempting to explain that there was no truth in the rumor that Alcott was teaching the Oriental doctrine of preëxistence, she set forth the doctrine that he was teaching, one which had "come spontaneously from the children themselves." Meanwhile she and her sister continued to take down the Conversations. She prepared them for publication and wrote a preface. Then suddenly before Alcott had any idea that his ship was unsafe, she ratted on him. She resigned.

As was only natural, once having resigned, she was prepared, loyalty not being one of her good qualities, to listen to all the criticism which her Boston friends were only too anxious to pour into her ear. Surprised by its volume and violence, she remembered the considerable part which she had given to herself in the conversations about to be published. Her heart went down into her boots. She sat down and wrote Alcott a letter. It was, as Alcott's most recent biographer [3] has described it "a curious compound of fear, duplicity and chaotic language." She assures him that she has been *very wary* in what she said about his opinions in connection with the birth of Christ. She herself would have never gone so far, of course. As to the *Records* she feels the book (which she had prepared and to which she had written a preface) should not go to print unless the objectionable parts are left out; "at least they must be entirely disconnected with *me*." Her remarks upon circumcision must be omitted. She asks him to tell a deliberate lie, namely, to deny that it was she who recorded the remark of a little boy who said that the body was formed *"out of the naughtiness of other people."* Her letter was a peculiarly nasty document, and it is unfortunate for her that it has been preserved. But Alcott was a man entirely without fear. He published, though helping Miss Peabody as far as his conscience allowed, which was not very far. When the book received a hostile criticism from certain sections of the press, he promptly published a second series.

As a schoolmaster he was doomed, even though Emerson rushed into print to help him. His pupils one by one began to be withdrawn. The brokers came in and seized the books, the pictures and the plaster casts. All were put up to auction and sold. Nothing could have been more dignified than Alcott's behavior under these distressing circumstances. As a final gesture of independence and of belief in his own opinions Bronson Alcott invited a colored girl to join the class. And that was the end of the Temple School. Miss Peabody retired to join her

[3] Odell Shepard.

family in Salem, not without the satisfaction of knowing that the deserted ship had sunk. Little Sophia, however, felt differently from her sister. She wrote Alcott a charming letter.

It is difficult to see why Miss Peabody attached so much importance to Hawthorne and to his work. He had published but one book; and that she had not read. She had shown one of his stories to Emerson—the arbiter of her literary taste—and he had not liked it. That should have been enough to make Miss Peabody drop him at once. But she was worried at the time—worried by what such friends as the dangerous and versatile Margaret Fuller might be thinking of her. She was temporarily exiled from Boston and living with her parents in dull Salem. It looked as if by her disloyalty to Alcott she might lose the esteem of those new campaigners, the Transcendentalists, and might be refused as a recruit. She was out of a job and out of favor. She was restless. She had been thwarted. She would get even with those Hathorne women yet, even though Elizabeth Hathorne was proved not to be her author and even though little Louisa had caught her out. She summoned her mother and her sisters, Sophia and Mary, to assist her and organized the long drawn out siege of Herbert Street; at the same time she tempted the female defenders of that house with confidential notes, long letters, gifts of flowers and of books, and invitations. Elizabeth Peabody was pitted against Elizabeth Hathorne, and they were fighting for the control of Nathaniel's destiny.

Being quite without financial resources Elizabeth Peabody could not let the grass of the backyard grow under her feet. She had to try to get back into her intellectual *monde* and had to find a job. There were many occasions, therefore, when she had to leave matters concerning the Hathornes in the hands of her mother and sisters and direct operations by written instructions from afar.

Not only did the Peabody women become obsessed by the importance of gaining the confidence of the Hathornes but in their efforts to achieve results became jealous of each other in any minor success. Mrs. Peabody planted a hawthorn bush in her garden with some ceremony. She struck her standard. Sophia was detailed to get in touch with Louisa. The mother would tackle Elizabeth Hathorne. But nothing turned out according to plan, and it was Mary Peabody, later to marry that great educationalist, Horace Mann, who without effort attracted Elizabeth Hathorne from her lair. Every move was reported by them to Miss Elizabeth Peabody. Sophia wrote of a visit to Herbert Street, "Louisa came to the door and took me upstairs. As Elizabeth did not know I was coming I thought I should not see her. It would be an unprecedented honor if she should come. I asked for her immediately, and Louisa said she would be there in a few minutes! There now! Am I not a privileged mortal? She received me very affectionately, and seemed glad to see me; and I all at once fell in love with her." The Peabodys' obsession and consequent jealousies increased. When, for example, Elizabeth Hathorne called at the Peabody house to go for a walk with Mary, Mrs. Peabody put on her bonnet and whisked her away before informing her daughters. Presents were delivered maliciously to the wrong recipient. A piece of rock fished out of the sea by Elizabeth Hathorne on one of her nocturnal perambulations was given as a thing of exquisite beauty to Mary. Mary passed it on to Sophia, and she, unwilling to receive presents from Elizabeth via her sister, passed it on to her dying brother who had one look at it, said it was hideous and turned his face to the wall. Presents, such as a bunch of violets, sent in the opposite direction, that is to say from the Peabodys to the Hathornes, got diverted in transit by malice aforethought. Meanwhile Elizabeth, now back in Boston, bombared the Herbert Street house with her epistolary missiles. Two are worthy of quotation—the first because it is amusing, the second because it was dangerous.

The first began, "Dear Louisa,—You know I want to knit those little stockings and shoes,—I think I will do it in course of time *at your house.* . . ." Her underlining did not pass unnoticed. Miss Peabody would even knit with the despised Louisa in order to get seated in the Herbert Street house.

The second is a dangerous letter because it is a deliberate attempt by Miss Peabody, who knew of the political divergences between Elizabeth Hathorne and her brother—the one being ultra-conservative Whig and the other being poor man's Democrat—to separate Nathaniel Hawthorne from the small group of Bowdoin friends, loyalty to whom was one of his fixed principles. Elizabeth Peabody had found the window through which she might squeeze (there was never any question of a door) to gain entry to Elizabeth Hathorne's heart. The subject of this letter was Hawthorne's determination to seek a job other than that of writing fiction, a job which would in his opinion satisfy his anxiousness to prove to all that, scribbler though he was, he could do a day's work alongside any man, be paid for it and be worthy of his hire. Miss Peabody wrote, "If, as you say, he has been so long uneasy . . . perhaps he had better go; only, may he not bind himself *long,* only be free to return to freedom. In general, I think it is better for a man to be harnessed to a draycart to do his part in transporting 'the commodity' of the world; for man is weak, and needs labor to tame his passions and train his mind to order and method." Miss Hathorne cannot have received too well such advice from Miss Peabody. She then warns her correspondent of the dangers which may befall Hawthorne, the temptation, for instance, "*to fall to the level* of his associates. And I have felt more melancholy still at the thought of his owing anything to the patronage of men of such thoughtless character as has lately been made notorious. . . . I too would have him help govern this great people; but I would have him go to the *fountains* of greatness and power—the unsoiled souls—and weave for them his 'golden web,' as Miss Burnley calls it—it may be *the web of destiny* for this country. In every country *some one man* has done what has saved it. It was one Homer that made Greece, one Numa that made Rome, and one Wordsworth that has created the Poetry of Reflection. How my pen runs on—but I can write better than I can speak." In view of this amazing piece of prose one hopes that she must have meant she could speak better than she could write. But this letter is interesting for two reasons: it is the first record of an attempt by one of the intellectuals to separate Hawthorne from his Bowdoin friends, and it is the most complete abnegation of what she was about to do—to go to George Bancroft to get Hawthorne a job, the Democrats being in power, and to obtain work for him also on the *Democratic Review*. What happened, in point of fact, was that Bridge and Cilley had asked Bancroft for a political job for Hawthorne, and when Miss Peabody approached him, Bancroft remembered Hawthorne and recommended him to Washington because of his *in memoriam* eulogy of Cilley, a good

Democrat. So though Miss Peabody claimed the appointment, it was the dead Cilley, one of his Bowdoin friends, who really obtained it. And it was not to be a job for the obtaining of which any of them need have been proud.

Meanwhile in Salem Hawthorne himself, owing to the hysterical behavior of the two households, found himself for once in a very strong position. He could play off Miss Burnley against Miss Peabody (Miss Burnley also kept open house for famous men of letters); and he could play off Miss Helen Barstow against Sophia. He could always, of course, play off one of the Peabodys against another.

No one questions Nathaniel Hawthorne's pleasure at being lionized by Miss Peabody in the beginning. He himself has testified to it. Longfellow's praise of *Twice-Told Tales* in the *North American* was a press criticism and, though every young author is grateful for a good notice, after a few months the notice, the book and the gratefulness grow dim in everyone's memory. A year after the book was published Miss Peabody came and revived Hawthorne's interest in himself. She was already sufficiently well known so that her attentions were rather flattering.

What no one could have foreseen was that Nathaniel Hawthorne and Sophia Peabody were to fall in love with each other. In the summer and autumn of 1838 he made one of his long expeditions through New Hampshire, into Vermont, and round back again by way of Connecticut. In January 1839 he left Salem to take up his post in the Boston Custom House. Between those two events a far more important event has to be recorded: he became secretly engaged to Sophia. And a very long engagement it was to be.

The necessity for secrecy was not, unfortunately, the usual reason given—no money on which to live—though that reason might have been given. The necessity arose because Sophia was not considered, even by herself or by her future husband, to be in a fit state of physical health to enable her to contract a marriage with anyone. In the first months of 1839 both families would have objected to the union. Mrs. Peabody had, some time before, written a long and earnest letter to her youngest daughter, to whom she was quite devoted, a letter in which she warned her in the most tactful manner possible against allowing her heart to take flight, and praised and recommended a place by their own hearthstone as possibly the most comforting spot she could find. Sophia was on a visit. She must come home; settle down; and accept the inevitable, which was to be a spinster who, if her health permitted it, must do something to earn a dollar or two.

The courage and the brightness of her outlook were remarkable. Except when in pain she was probably far and away the most cheerful member of the family. She recognized the soundness of others' opinion—that she could not be guilty of putting her ill health on the shoulders of a husband. She was one of those invalids who never give themselves up for lost; and she was not lost; for having conquered her complaint, she married, made an excellent wife and bore her husband three children. She lived until she was sixty, and so outlived her virile Nathaniel.

Her physical debility, the symptoms of which were chronic headaches, may have been due to a dozen causes: it may have been neurotic, the justification for this suggestion being that

Nathaniel Hawthorne at the Age of Thirty-six

Nathaniel Hawthorne seems to have cured her, by his determination that she should marry him, by his insistence that she should cast all her pain upon him. And that worked: whereas the science of all her doctors did not work. She was eleven years old when the trouble began. Miss Peabody writes, ". . . the endurance of her physical condition defied all the poisons of the *materia medica*—mercury, arsenic, opium, hyoscyamus, and all. Her last allopathic physician was Dr. Walter Channing, who limited himself to fighting the pain without attempting a radical cure. In 1830, when she was living on hyoscyamus, which did her less harm than any other drug, she was able to come downstairs occasionally. . . ."

Is it to be wondered at that when Elizabeth and Louisa Hathorne heard that their beloved brother intended to marry Sophia Peabody, they did everything in their power to postpone and to prevent it?

As to her intellectual attainments it is very easy to make fun of them; very difficult to assess them fairly. At the time of her secret engagement she was a prig and an intellectual snob, not necessarily by nature, more probably because she was a Peabody and a girl of her epoch. Like so many other young people she was *bouleversée* by Mr. Emerson. She writes to Elizabeth, "Your slight account of Mr. Emerson's 'address' is enough to wake the dead, and I dont know what the original utterance must have done. I told Mary I thought Mr. Emerson was the Word. She exclaimed 'You blasphemer!' 'Do you really think it blasphemy?' said I. 'Oh, no,' she replied, 'It is the gospel *according to you.*'" Or again, "I think Mr. Emerson is the greatest man that ever lived. . . . He is indeed a 'Supernal Vision.' Mr. Emerson is Pure Tone." It is hardly surprising that Nathaniel Hawthorne, having listened to Sophia, came to the conclusion that however intelligent and charming a man Emerson might be, his influence over some was deplorable. And he said so.

As to her learning, she had obviously tried to learn too much. She made such remarks as, "I went to my hammock with Xenophon. Socrates was divinest, after Jesus Christ, I think. He lived up to his thoughts." Who, one wonders: Christ, Xenophon or Socrates? Sophia was reputed not only to be an artist but also to "know" French, German, Hebrew, Greek, Latin and mathematics. She would draw the leg of a horse and then, as the headaches came on, throw herself into the hammock and read a little Hebrew, which had the same effect as two aspirins. Like many girls of her own time and country, she was attempting to be a record-breaker. She had neither the health nor the brain to be one. And the standards of efficiency of her age were low, deplorably low. It was not an age of specialization but of diversity of interest and a delight in what we now know as a "smattering" of many subjects. It is to Hawthorne's great credit that he not only cured her physical complaint by autosuggestion but cured her, too, of her intellectual snobberies. She remained, however, in his eyes and in her own, an artist—which she was not. An efficient copyist we can believe her to have been. During their married life she behaved admirably. If after his death she convinced herself that her English—which had not until then appeared as one of her starred subjects—was more correct than that of her husband, one of the greatest writers in the English language, her folly can be attributed to grief.

In January 1839, Nathaniel went to Boston to take up his job. Nathaniel Hawthorne and Sophia Peabody were not married until 1842. And between those two dates much happened—to Hawthorne.

7

Boston

IF Hawthorne had been other than he was, if, that is to say, he had wished to meet the society of the intellectuals of the day, any job obtained for him by Miss Peabody and George Bancroft would have attracted him. To work with Bancroft, to lodge with Hillard—for this had been arranged—to be within walking distance of Longfellow, of whom he had seen much during the past year, and to be brought out in society by Miss Peabody would have seemed luck to anyone the least socially minded, if one liked that sort of society. What they none of them seemed to realize was that this desire for a job had never, as Bridge supposed, been a desire to get out of sleepy Salem or to earn money. But his strange experience of life had made him determined to show that he could earn his daily bread along with the rest of his compatriots.

He might have refused the job offered had he not got into conversation the year before with a man on a journey from Boston to Worcester. "An old gentle man," he writes in his journal, "Mr. Philips of Boston, got into conversation with me, and inquired very freely as to my character, tastes, habits and circumstances—a freedom sanctioned by his age, his kindly and beneficent spirit, and the wisdom of his advice. It is strange how little impertinence depends on what is actually said, but on the manner and motives of saying it. 'I want to do you good,' said he with warmth, after becoming, apparently, moved by our communications. 'Very well, Sir,' replied I, 'I wish you could for both our sakes; for I have no doubt it would be a great satisfaction to you.' *He told me by all means to act, in whatever way; observing that he himself would have no objection to be a servant, if no other mode of action presented itself.*" Hawthorne was impressed.

Writing to Longfellow, he tells him, "It has pleased Mr. Bancroft (knowing that what little ability I have is altogether adapted to *active* life) to offer me the post of Inspector in the Boston custom-house; and I am going to accept it with as much confidence in my suitableness for it as Sancho Panza had in his gubernatorial qualifications. I have no reason to doubt my capacity to fulfil the duties, for I do not know what they are. . . . They tell me that a considerable portion of my time will be unoccupied, the which I mean to employ in sketches of my new experiences."

It is easy to read the disappointment between these joking lines. It was to be a sinecure—so he believed. He had not asked for or expected a sinecure. It was also a job, he had been told, which the biggest fool in the world could do as creditably as he. Which was no doubt true; but the reason for putting men of intelligence into such jobs was not that they should do them better but that the party in power should help those of its supporters—or as many of them as it could—who happened to be financially embarrassed. What is surprising is that he showed no enthusiasm or even contentment that Bancroft was to be his chief. Hawthorne would have much preferred to work under a laborer than under the famous and popular historian, whose over-garnished prose style he disliked. One might have expected, however, that a man so passionately interested in the history of New England would have been pleased to associate, even in a custom house, with the great American historian. Was it just the first sign of his obstinate behavior in refusing to hitch his wagon to one of Miss Peabody's stars? Possibly.

George Bancroft was really worthy of anyone's attention. The son of a famous Unitarian minister of the days of the schism, he was intellectually precocious almost beyond belief. At the age of thirteen he entered Harvard with a reputation for "stumping" his elders and betters, which was as remarkable as it was no doubt tiresome. So impressed was the Faculty of Harvard with him as an undergraduate that when his time came to leave, every effort was made to secure his services for the future. He was sent to Europe at the expense of the university, and it was expected of him that he would return a most philosophic theologian. He went to Göttingen (Harvard was fast becoming a *dependence* of Göttingen), where he obtained the degree of Doctor of Philosophy. He went to Germany with two passports: the one, signed by the Secretary of State, opened frontiers; the other, signed by Ticknor, Everett and Norton, professor-princes, opened the front doors of the houses of the savants of Europe. He studied under Schleiermacher and Hegel. He knew both the von Humboldts. He met Lord Byron. He sat at the feet of two such incomparable human beings as Goethe and Pauline Borghese. He learned languages with fascinating facility. He returned to Harvard, full of his own importance, full of plans, and well pleased with himself.

Some time before his arrival a message had preceded him across the Atlantic from some correspondent in Europe advising the dons of Harvard that they must expect a surprise

when they saw their Bancroft once again. Professor Andrews
Norton—one of Bancroft's champions and friends, one of those
who had advised the employment of the university's funds for
the advancement of Bancroft's career—hearing this, promptly
wrote him a letter to reach him before he set sail. Did Bancroft
realize the sort of place Cambridge was? "There is no place," he
wrote warningly, ". . . where . . . anything like ostentation
or vanity, anything *outré* or *bizarre* (if I may use two French
words at once) is observed with a keener perception of ridicule,
or lends more to the disadvantage of him in whom it is discovered." Excellent advice—and a very true description of
Cambridge. When he arrived, the professors took one look at
George Bancroft and were not amused; for he had returned in
the strangest of clothes. His continental mannerisms were exaggerated, and unless one was proficient in German, French
and Italian, there was no understanding his "English." There
was no reason at all why Norton should have excused himself
for having used two French words in one sentence. Except to a
linguist, Bancroft's conversation was well nigh incomprehensible.

No sooner had he arrived than he perpetrated an outrage
the like of which had never been heard of before in Cambridge.
With arms outstretched, a gesture he had learnt in France no
doubt, he greeted his old friend Professor Norton, "*Mon cher
collègue,* etc." Norton smiled. And then Bancroft kissed him.
To kiss Professor Norton on one cheek was *outré,* to kiss him
on both cheeks was indeed *bizarre.* Norton was scandalized.
Cambridge wasn't; after the first shock was over, Cambridge
enjoyed the chance to ridicule. Pedagogues love ridicule. And
in this peacock of a professor they had an ideal object.

Bancroft and his reforms went down under the ridicule of professors and undergraduates. After a year of unhappy work as tutor in Greek, Bancroft resigned. Everyone heaved a sigh of relief. But when they bid him farewell and wished him success in his project of running a boy's school with Cogswell (another renegade in their opinion, another fancy professor), they all thought no doubt that they had seen and heard the last of George Bancroft. Within a decade Bancroft was to be acclaimed even at Harvard as the first great historian of the United States; later he was to become a member of the Cabinet; later still Minister Extraordinary and Plenipotentiary to the Court of St. James, and Minister in Berlin. He was to become as famous in the United States as Lord Macaulay in England, and was destined to live, with his laurels still bright, until the year 1891.

No one has ever been more thankful to leave a job than Bancroft. It was no doubt the making of him that the job he undertook was as little suited to his particular ability as had been that of the would-be reformer of university education. His boys disliked the little man. Yet his seven years at Round Hill School were not wasted; for it was during that time that his ideas of his great History of the United States, conceived at Göttingen, began to materialize. It was during those years, too, that his political opinions were formed. However satisfactory it would be to relate that George Bancroft, to spite the reactionary Whig professors of Harvard, had thrown in his lot with the detested Jacksonian Democrats, it would not be quite true. Democrats were socially ostracized in New England, and it would have been amusing, since he had already been ostracized by Cambridge society, to have joined the Democrats just to show that he, an ambitious man, did not care at all what the professors of Harvard thought of him. But that was not the case or the whole case. Certainly it pleased him, when he was a success, to think that he had irritated his university colleagues just as much by his politics as by his professional behavior. But all the philosophy and history he had studied in Germany, all his researches into the history of his own country, had made him a convinced supporter of democratic principles. He refused to believe, as Hawthorne and Orestes Brownson refused to believe, that the immense efforts of his own countrymen had been made to place a few hundred Hamiltonians, superior and rich men, in control of the destinies of his beloved United States. So he became a Democrat and with much eloquence did his best to further the Democratic cause.

Because he had married a Dwight, a Whig, and was engaged in collecting material for his great historical work, he was persuaded to refrain from seeking party preferment—which he could undoubtedly have got. He was neither a professor-prince nor an author-prince, but his work was planned on as ambitious a scale as that of Ticknor or of Prescott. He too had countless foreign correspondents searching the libraries of Europe for anything which would be of assistance to him in writing his great history. But when his wife died, he was left with children and little money. And the Democratic Party (President Martin Van Buren) came to his assistance. He was given the job of Collector of Boston Custom House and Port. He, in his turn, gave jobs to Orestes Brownson, the Socialist minister of many persuasions, and to Nathaniel Hawthorne, Cilley's eulogist, and the writer of historical tales. Strange trio of *douaniers!*

Bancroft had already published the first two volumes of his History of the United States, was already a famous man and had already married a second wife, with a large house in Boston, when Nathaniel Hawthorne received his summons to the custom house. Hawthorne was still the recluse at heart, and the name of Bancroft perhaps conveyed to his mind a picture of a man as socially inclined as any of those brilliant friends of whom Miss Peabody was continually speaking. Bancroft was no attraction, Boston was no attraction but, now that he was engaged to Miss Sophia, Salem was.

A dull place it might be; but for him it was the soil in which his family had grown. That he, haunted as he was by the thought of his ancestors, William and John, should have had to do his wooing in the house at the end of Charter Street which overlooked those ancestors' graves, was one of fate's more macabre jokes. He did not miss its sinister significance. In that posthumous work *Doctor Grimshawe's Secret* he described the house, but described the graveyard first. "Thus rippled and surged, with its hundreds of little billows, the old graveyard about the house which cornered upon it; it made the street gloomy, so that people did not altogether like to pass along the high wooden fence that shut it in; and the old house itself, covering ground which else had been sown thickly with buried bodies, partook of its dreariness, because it seemed hardly possible that the dead people should not get up out of their graves and steal in to warm themselves at this convenient fireside." Of the house he wrote, "So far as ever came to the present writer's knowledge, there was no whisper of Dr. Grimshawe's house being haunted. . . . The house itself, moreover, except for the convenience of its position close to the seldom-disturbed cemetery, was hardly worthy to be haunted. As I remember it, (and for aught I know it still exists in the same guise) it did not appear to be an ancient structure, nor one that would ever have been the abode of a very wealthy or prominent family;—a three-storey wooden house, perhaps a century old, low-studded, with a square front, standing right upon the street, and a small enclosed porch, containing the main entrance, affording a glimpse up and down the street through an oval window on each side, its characteristic was decent respectability, not sinking below the boundary of the genteel. It has often perplexed my mind to conjecture what sort of man he could have been who, having the means to build a pretty, spacious and comfortable residence, should have chosen to lay its foundations on the brink of so many graves. . . ."

To that house in Charter Street Nathaniel Hawthorne came to bid farewell to his Sophia. He went home, packed his trunks and left in the stagecoach for Boston. Arrived in Boston he carried his possessions up into George Hillard's attic.

He was not to get the post of Inspector. His job was to be anything but a sinecure. He was appointed Measurer, that is to say, measurer of coal and salt and the custom house's check-weighman, who must be on Long Wharf as long as a ship was there being unloaded. As dock hands were paid by piece-work, the amount they could earn depended upon the number of hours the Measurer was prepared to be on duty and the number of ships which arrived to be unloaded. No dock hand was ever to complain that his wages had been curtailed by the absence of the Measurer. Bancroft told Emerson, who retailed the news to Miss Peabody, that Hawthorne was the best man he had in the custom house. There was to be no time for serious writing. The love letters to Sophia, the three little volumes of *Grandfather's Chair* (a book for children, written to the order of Miss Peabody and published by her) and two or three stories were the literary output for his two years in Boston.

Weighing and gauging was a cold job in winter and a hot one in summer. In February he writes in his scrapbook,[1] "Yesterday and day before measuring a load of coal from the schooner Thomas Lowder, of St. John, N.B. A little black, dirty vessel. The coal stowed in the hold, so as to fill the schooner full, and make her a solid mass of mineral. . . . The first day, I walked the wharf, suffering not a little from cold; yesterday, I sat in the cabin whence I could look through the interstices of the bulkhead, or whatever they call it, into the hold. My eyes, what a cabin! Three paces would more than measure it in any direction, and it was filled with barrels, not clean and new, but black, and containing probably the provender of the vessel; jugs, firkins, the cook's utensils and kitchen furniture—everything grimy and sable with coal dust. There were two or three tiers of berths; and the blankets, etc. are not to be thought of." Follows a long description of life on board. "The bitter zero atmosphere came down the companionway, and threw its chill over me sometimes, but I was pretty comfortable—though on reaching home, I found that I had swaggered through several thronged streets with coal streaks on my visage." In the heat of summer he and the supercargo followed the shade cast by the mainmast. "This old man kept tally of the Alfred Tyler's cargo on behalf of the Captain [an old English sailor from Yorkshire in whom Hawthorne took consid-

[1] Now lost, withheld or destroyed.

erable interest] diligently marking all day long, and calling 'tally, Sir,' to me at every sixth tub. Often would he have to attend to some call of the stevedores, or wheelers, or shovelers —now for a piece of spun-yarn—now for a hand-spike—now for a hammer, or some nails—now for some of the ship's molasses, to sweeten water—the which the Captain afterwards reprehended him for giving. These calls would keep him in about enough movement to give variety to his tallying. . . . Then sitting down he would converse (though by no means forward to talk) about the weather, about his recent and former voyages, etc., etc., etc., we dodging the intense sun round the main mast." There were two principal cargoes which it was his duty to measure—coal and salt. A salt ship took nearly a fortnight to unload either for road transportation or for reshipment in flat-bottomed boats for the inland trade. "The salt is white and pure —there is something holy in salt." Sometimes a boatload of English factory girls arrived from the old country to work in the new mills at Lowell. With these we gather he had no truck, official or otherwise; though he was amused by the amount of leg displayed as they disembarked. There was nothing "holy" in that trade, which was as close to white slave traffic as anyone could wish.

For two years salt and coal and the quelling of small riots on the quays were his regular and uncongenial task. It was "tally, Sir, tally" day in, day out. To Sophia, who had described the delights of the country round Concord, where she was staying with the Emersons, he wrote, "My heart thirsts and languishes to be there, away from the hot sun, and the coal-dust, and the steaming docks, and the thick-pated, stubborn, contentious men, with whom I brawl from morning till night, and all the weary toil that quite engrosses me, and yet occupies only a small part of my being, which I did not know existed before I became a Measurer."

8

West Street and West Roxbury

THE West Street bookshop and lending library of modern foreign literature was the sort of business project which has sent not a few literary spinsters to the bankruptcy courts and more to hostels for gentlewomen in distress. Elizabeth Peabody and her mother succeeded where thousands have failed. As a money-making proposition the shop must have produced only meager profits, and it is difficult to believe that their hopes in that direction were ever very high. Such ventures start from a confidence that there is a need and from the ambition of the promoters to collect around them intelligent people. The rendezvous of the intelligentsia which pays is the most improbable of castles in the air; for the intelligentsia seldom accept the invitation and still less seldom leave their money behind. Yet the Peabodys did make enough to keep them all, and the shop did become for several years the gathering place of famous men and women.

No one knew better than Miss Peabody the greatness of the stake she was risking. There was not only the risk of financial failure—the lesser of the two evils since the Peabody family was accustomed to live from hand to mouth—there was the risk, in the event the bookshop went bankrupt, of her being removed from the society of brilliant men just at a time when their work was about to be recognized and their importance established. Those were stirring times in the intellectual life of New England. To be *au fait* with every new development it was essential to live in Boston or within a few miles of it. Miss Peabody had to keep herself. Though the family had a genius for managing on very little, prolonged idleness was out of the question. By profession—if she can be said to have had a profession—she was a school marm, the daughter of a school marm and the sister of one. She was no doubt an enlightened educationalist, one who would follow in the footsteps of her masters, Gerando and Pestalozzi; but the fact remained—a chilling fact— that, without a private income, were the scheme of the bookshop to fail, she might be offered a position in a school in Connecticut or in the wilds of Maine, an offer which she might have to accept. What was so important was to keep in with people, to be surrounded by people of the right sort. Some might say why not go to Concord, straight to her own Mount Olympus. Indeed the advice to get closer to Mr. Emerson was excellent. She attended most carefully to her friendship with him; and she was wise, for though Alcott bore her no grudge, their dealings cannot have done much to improve his opinion of her. Alcott and Miss Fuller, who had taken her place at Temple School, were very close to Emerson, much closer than she was. But the truth was that of all difficult places for an intelligent young woman who wanted to make a living, Concord was the most difficult. The gods of Olympus, with the exception of Emerson, were all on short rations. Nothing could be expected of them. Concord's principal business was unfortunately the breeding and exporting of school marms. To present one's self as a schoolmistress was to ship coals to Newcastle.

That Miss Elizabeth Peabody did solve all her problems with the opening of the West Street rendezvous, must be acknowledged as a very creditable fact. While Mary went out to work to keep herself in pin money and Dr. Peabody busied himself making up homeopathic doses on the ground floor, Mrs. and Miss Elizabeth Peabody attended to the lending library, the sales department, the lecture agency and, in the little back room, the printing press which was soon to be noisily thumping away, printing the pages of Hawthorne's *Grandfather's Chair*. They also had to take care, naturally, of the increasing numbers who came just to have a look, hoping during their visit to have a close view of the men and women who were making a stir in the literary world. For though with their Philistine sense of humor the Brahmins of Boston gave it the name of the Hospital of Incapables, even the Brahmins came. It was pleasant to turn over the pages of the latest volumes; and though many of them disapproved of the admittedly clever men, young and middle-aged, whose advanced views were receiving so much publicity, they found the bookshop a convenient neutral ground on which to meet them. It was here too that one found out when Mr. Emerson was going to lecture next and what his subject was to be. Or, if one wanted to, and strange to say quite a number of people did, one paid one's subscription to Mr. Alcott's "Conversations." Old Dr. Channing was often to be seen—embodiment of the highest respectability in the intellectual world. It was remembered now how closely in the confidence of the great old man Miss Elizabeth had been; and the youngest generation came to have a look at him. In these rooms, at midday, Miss Fuller gave to intelligent women those talks which made her famous. She was just as much the object of emotional veneration as is the film star of today, though necessarily her fame was known to hundreds instead of millions. The Peabodys lived in a whirl.

If the Symposium or Transcendental Club had had any permanent headquarters, the convenience of the Peabodys' as an agency and accommodation address would not have been so obvious to most of its members. But it was a rule of the club—not that it ever had anything approaching a book of rules—that the meetings should be held only when and where convenient to members. The first meeting was held at George Ripley's house, the second at Alcott's. Miss Peabody had great luck or great wisdom in opening her shop just when she did. The pioneering spirit which had brought the ancestors of so many of the members over to the United States, a spirit still to be seen in action in the trek to the West, became a force in intellectual society. Just as the members of the Bay Company had determined that, once arrived in America, they would lead their own life according to certain common ideas and free themselves from the hegemony of Europe, so a group of young New Englanders, most of them Unitarian ministers at one time or another, agreed that as intellectual pioneers they would build in their own country a new road, along which Americans might advance toward the goal of a purely native culture. They were determined that their ideas as well as their civil governors should cease to come from overseas. However praiseworthy their ambition may have been, there was, as they immediately realized, a scarcity of original and American philosophic thought upon which to build a new ideological structure. As long as they were content to be pioneers preparing the way for others, a few genuinely American ideas—most of which seemed to have originated in the mind of Bronson Alcott—gave the Transcendentalists an appearance of homogeneity. But once they stopped to consolidate and construct, which they did almost at once, their lack of system and unity became immediately apparent. Though so many of them had passed through the Harvard Divinity school, they were not even agreed on the changes they must make in religious opinion. Ripley, for example, thought Alcott an atheist. But the Transcendentalists were united—and here is the great paradox—in their enthusiasm for and knowledge of two foreign products, the English ideologies of Wordsworth, Coleridge and Carlyle, and the German idealistic philosophies of Kant, Herder and Schleiermacher. Not only were they acquainted with the works of these authors, but some were personally acquainted with their foreign masters. F. H. Hedge and George Ripley were actively engaged in propagating this knowledge in America by their editing of *Specimens of Foreign Standard Literature*—a Transcendentalist document, to which W. H. Channing, James Freeman Clarke and Margaret Fuller lent a hand with translation.

Meanwhile Emerson, the keenest intellect and the most spiritual man of his time in America, produced immediately for his admirers what he had hoped that some day someone would provide—an American system of philosophy, the product of an American mind. It was hardly a system and it was not very American, but its reception was enthusiastic among those who had read the Germans and the English and were bound to find in its pages what they were known to admire. The publication of *Nature* was certainly an event worthy to be recorded in the history of American literature. The esteem in which the author was already held was sufficiently increased to give him at least the appearance of being a leader. *Nature* was not, like most philosophic works, an end; it was a beginning. Taking immediate advantage of the interest which his name was exciting to expound his views to larger numbers Emerson delivered addresses to selected audiences and selected for each audience the particular theory most likely to shock his hearers into thinking for themselves. Though the impractical and even impossible Alcott had lost all chance of leadership, it is remarkable how Alcottian the shocks which Emerson delivered seem to us now. How very like Alcott, for example, to choose the "wrong" things to say to the "wrong" audience. His address on the American scholar in 1837 was a shock to academic smugness. It was mild, however, compared with the sensation he caused in the next year when he delivered an address to the Senior Class of the Divinity School in Cambridge. His hearers were young men about to be ordained, as he had been ordained shortly after leaving the school. "Go alone," he admonished them; "refuse good models, even those which are sacred in the imagination of men; and cast behind you all conformity. Do not be afraid of degrading the character of Jesus by representing him as a man. To do so is to indicate with sufficient clearness the falsity of our theology. God works through living men. Look for the new Teacher. Remember that it is not in Palestine only where great religious truths have been expounded for the first time."

He must have known what would happen: and it did happen. Orthodoxy could not allow such an heretical address to be delivered, without official denunciation, in the training college of what was in fact an Established Church. Pamphlet was answered by pamphlet, speech by speech. George Ripley and

Theodore Parker, both men with cures of souls, both ministers with pulpits, ranged themselves on either side of Emerson in his defense. Professors and Boston Brahmins attacked. Mr. Emerson was in the news. But the Renaissance of learning was in danger of becoming a Reformation; and that was not what the Transcendentalists wanted, for they knew full well the diversity of the religious opinion secretly held among them.

Even while his friends rallied around him, Emerson with his Divinity School address encouraged them to stress the importance of other items in the long Transcendental program of reform.

Ripley and W. H. Channing began to stress the importance of forming colonies within the old New England colonies, now states; of forming groups who would put into practice the ideal of community living—to reduce the hours of bread-winning and increase the hours of self-culture. Socialists though they called themselves, it is remarkable how few of them took an interest in the urgent sociological questions of the day. They talked of mankind and worked for the few. Orestes Brownson, the wild giant from Vermont, who must have created a record by the number of times he changed his allegiance to churches within the church of Christ and who found peace at last in the Roman Catholic fold, was perhaps nearer in mind than any other to the Socialist of today. Meanwhile figures such as Hedge, Margaret Fuller, and James Freeman Clarke worked on at their German grammars of philosophy, believing—as did Emerson—in the inner light of intuition and the ultimate revelation of Wisdom and Truth by instinct.

It cannot be denied that the absence of any acceptable program added to the excitement. Four years after the divinity address, Emerson delivered a lecture in Boston on the Transcendentalist. Describing Transcendentalism as the Saturnalia or excess of faith, admitting that it was wholly German in origin, and acknowledging that those who called themselves Transcendentalists were considered by the public to be bad citizens and worthless members of society—in that they did nothing to help any cause or to better the conditions of the unfortunate—he sang the praises of illumination and the *illuminati*. The address may have encouraged the more fanatical of his followers; but in furthering a cause, a selfish and intellectual cause, it did no good.

Inadequate as is this account of the beginning of Transcendentalism in America, it does perhaps explain why Miss Peabody's bookshop—the rendezvous—provided a stimulating atmosphere for those who did believe and an entertainment for those who did not.

For a man who attached such great importance to privacy, peace and quiet as did Nathaniel Hawthorne, the hurly-burly of No. 19 West Street, into which he had to force his way to see his Sophia, was much to bear with patience. To Miss Elizabeth Peabody he still had a debt to discharge. It was she who had suggested to him the only sort of work which as yet he had found possible in conjunction with the performance of his official duties. He had always wanted to write for children. He got on with children remarkably well. They were not so curious about his character as grown-ups. They did not find him mysterious or unforthcoming as did their parents. He might be doing hack work, but as hack work it was pleasant enough. And when the task was performed, there was no looking about for a publisher. Miss Elizabeth was publisher and printer. As a printing press, publishing office and bookshop, there was much to be said for No. 19 West Street. As a social center, as a place to visit Sophia and as an atmosphere for a semi-invalid, there was much to be said against it, though for once words seem to have failed Hawthorne.

Surroundings more uncongenial to him are difficult to imagine. The Transcendentalists were interested in Hawthorne for two reasons. He was a queer fellow, for one thing, with a great deal of reserve (not a transcendental quality) and a remarkable, melancholy beauty. He was the man, secondly, whom Sophia Peabody was intending to marry. They did not admire his writing to any great extent, and he was "one of them" only through their interest in Sophia. He on his part must be charged with an astonishing misreading of the Peabody character. Pity him under the circumstances, we can. Pity Sophia, as he did, we cannot. There were things about her he did not understand. We cannot believe that she considered herself a "persecuted little Dove" or that her dwelling place was "Babel." And though the Peabodys were to write unkindly things about Miss Margaret Fuller they could hardly have wished with Hawthorne that she would "lose her tongue," her conversations in West Street being one of that institution's most successful attractions.

Though the Peabodys admired Hawthorne, they must always have considered him a man with a sackload of false values. Their belief and trust in intellectuals may have been foolhardy, but it was genuine. Their disinterest in the "average" man, the "man in the street," was consequent upon their faith in intellect. Given the choice of making friends with an educated

man or a man with no education but much strange experience, Hawthorne invariably chose the latter. He must have
been an embarrassment at times to his future in-laws and more
than a little tiresome. When invited by George Bancroft to dinner to meet Margaret Fuller he wrote to Sophia jubilant that
at the last minute an urgent job had prevented his going. When
offered free tickets to one of Emerson's lectures he returned
them. He had better things to do. When called upon by Jones
Very, the mystical poet of Salem—a man whom the Emerson
group particularly admired—he wrote to Sophia complaining
that he could not get the bore out of his rooms.

Yet there was always time to be found for a man like Pike.
It was enough to make one despair. Pike was plebeian, hideous, hopeless, and so unintelligent that no one could possibly
bother with him—except Hawthorne who happened to be,
though the Peabodys sometimes forgot it, what is now known
as a novelist. They were both Salemites. They had a fund of
gossip in common. Pike's account of the Salem ghost was fascinating. Pike had seen the headless ghost. And Hawthorne remembered the digging up of a head; whether the head was the
one the ghost was looking for or someone's else could not, of
course, be determined. But far more interesting to Hawthorne
than Pike's ghost were Pike's fits, which prevented the poor
man from ever lying down flat on his back. "He has perfect
consciousness when flat," Hawthorne reports, "but is unable
to call for assistance or make any noise except by blowing
forcibly with his mouth and unless this brings help he must
die." What would happen to poor Pike, Hawthorne wonders,
if when he was staying in some hotel or boarding house, his

warning snortings were mistaken for snores? "A strong, stubborn, kindly nature this," he records in his journal. Here we are far from Transcendentalism and Miss Peabody's enlightened souls. And just as the *illuminati* were never to forgive him his friendship for President Pierce, so his family were never to be understanding about the unattractive and plebeian Pike.

Yet left to himself he could make friends with men as intelligent, if not as inspired, as the members of the Transcendental Club. His friendship with George Hillard—who knew both Longfellow and the Peabodys—and his wife was of the greatest value and comfort to him. The two men approached each other slowly and carefully. Who introduced them is not known, but someone suggested that on his arrival in Boston to undertake his duties at the custom house, Hawthorne should lodge with the Hillards, and for years afterwards he used the Hillards' as his Boston headquarters. By profession a lawyer, by inclination a literary scholar, and in moments of enthusiasm an eloquent political speaker, Hillard wore his culture like a comfortable cloak. There was no ostentation in his learning. He could be intimate with Longfellow and a member of what Boston called "Longfellow's Mutual Admiration Society," yet he could be as much at home with the Transcendentalists or with individualists such as Hawthorne. They had a common friend in Longfellow, who was still a young and amiable widower, still the lodger in Craigie House, not yet the owner of it, not yet the younger Boston Brahmin he became after his second marriage. They had in common too a love of long and rather silent walks and of sea bathing. On two occasions when Hawthorne was in trouble, Hillard without any fuss appeared to help him. Hillard could always be relied upon, which was more than Hawthorne could truthfully say of most of the intelligent men in whose company he was fated to live.

There now appeared in his life a woman who was later to cross his path less pleasantly. Margaret Fuller had one trait in common with Hawthorne: to both of them it was a complete impossibility to accept another man's word for the value of a thing, person or opinion. Only by personal experience could they attach value to anything or anybody. The introvert and the extrovert may find each other's behavior hard to bear; but they are often interested in each other. Margaret was interested in Hawthorne, and he, though he could use harsh words about her, was interested in Margaret. In what proportions a reader of the *Blithedale Romance* chooses to see Margaret Fuller and Fanny Kemble in the character of Zenobia is beside the point. The point is that without having observed Margaret closely it is difficult to believe he would ever have imagined such a character. Years later, years after she died, he would still puzzle over her—"a great humbug of course, with much talent and much moral reality, or else she could never have been so great a humbug." She was an influence in her day all the same. Had an artist of those times painted a Conversation Piece of the Transcendentalists, only one woman would have been depicted occupying a chair in the front row and looking as if her prominent position was hers by right. There would have been other women in the group. Miss Elizabeth Peabody might have been depicted shoving herself forward. But of all the women only Margaret could have assumed the throne. Did they not all call her Queen Margaret behind her back?

Margaret had had a strange childhood. She was the daughter of a Cambridgeport lawyer—a man with a large practice of small and tedious cases, a man with political ambitions and literary tastes. He had his vengeance on life in a curious way: he undertook the education of one of his daughters, Margaret, and attempted to turn her into an infant prodigy of learning. This fearsome taskmaster and almost maniacal Latinist succeeded at least in teaching her much Latin and inculcating in her not only a taste for classical literature but an ability easily to absorb the information of the driest kind. He also succeeded in ruining her constitution and her nervous system. It was an unhappy childhood. She was allowed no friends. Ovid, Molière and Shakespeare were her playmates, though Shakespeare was taboo on Sundays. Deprived of those social relations without which a child begins to invent imaginary playmates, Margaret no doubt developed her imagination very fully. Romantic dreams filled her head, and the inevitable day came when someone appeared in her life upon whom she immediately projected all her romanticism. Margaret fell in love with a young Englishwoman who was staying in the neighborhood. This young woman seems to have possessed in full quantity the infinite tact required to deal with the situation, and all went well until the day came when they must part. Margaret then collapsed.

Even her father now realized that there was something wrong with his educational system. Margaret was sent to school. One can hardly decide whether the school or Margaret was more to be pitied. For she was resolved that the whole school was to fall at her feet and adore her, just as she had adored the Englishwoman. They did not do so; in fact, they only giggled. Frustrated, she determined upon revenge. She would disunite; she would set girl against girl. Her tongue was glib, her mali-

cious inventions ready, and for a time she succeeded. Then
the worst happened. The whole school united together and,
before the mistresses, charged her with calumny and deceit.
Unable to defend herself she spectacularly collapsed, physically
and mentally. That was the end of her school days. The incident—the last of her failures—is properly recalled here because
of Emerson's criticism of her: that she did not sufficiently question the desirability of allowing members of her own sex, and
so many of them, to fall in love with her.

　After a period of rest and retirement Margaret next appeared
as a social excitement among the youth of Cambridge. She
was a plain girl and now knew it. But she surrounded herself
with youth and beauty, and she developed her exceptional
powers of conversation. Gaining a reputation as the Queen of
Cambridge, she appeared to begin and end her ambitions with
social entertainment. Then came the conversion. She had passed
from adolescence to adulthood, and her conversion was not less
adult because she failed to take up any particular denomina-
tion of Christianity. She turned rather to a belief in an idealistic
philosophy and surrendered her life to a cult. The return of
F. H. Hedge from Germany seems to have been the turning-
point in her career. She, Hedge and James Freeman Clarke
soon had their heads bent over books of German philosophy
and Italian literature. Removed from Cambridge because of
the retirement of her father and set down in Groton, which
seemed to her as remote from civilization as Lapland, the extraordinary young woman continued her studies alone and re-
galed her friends with reams of notes and criticisms sent
through the post. When the father died, as he did quite soon
(of cholera, an improbable disease to find in Groton), she came

to Boston where we have already seen her as successor to Elizabeth Peabody in Alcott's Temple School. She saw to it that
children should not have a training such as hers had been. A
well-known school in Providence desired her services, almost
on her own terms. The girls—and girls had loathed her when
she was younger—fell in love with her by flocks. Her self-
confidence was now more than restored: it was established.

Harriet Martineau, a somewhat sour critic of American talent, was so impressed with her that she advised Emerson to take
notice. He did. He has recorded their meeting. "Her extreme
plainness,—a trick of incessantly opening and shutting her eye-
lids,—the nasal tone of her voice,—all repelled; and I said to
myself, we shall never get far." Describing her arrogance of
mind, he writes, "She idealizes herself as a sovereign . . . she
spoke, in the quietest manner, of the girls she had formed, the
young men who owed everything to her, the fine companions
she had long ago exhausted. In the coolest way, she said to her
friends, 'I know all the people worth knowing in America, and
I find no intellect comparable to my own.'" How fond Emerson must have been of her really, and how much he must have
admired her, to have written those sentences in a *Memoir* to
be published just after her death! "She made me laugh," he
admits, "more than I liked; for I was, at that time, an eager
scholar of ethics and had tasted the sweets of solitude and
stoicism." And Emerson always believed in that solitude as
other men have believed in the oasis which is a mirage.

Margaret Fuller had "arrived," but her success was not hailed
with universal enthusiasm. That the Peabodys should have been
irritated with her success is only human. For five years her
Conversations in the Peabodys' bookshop were an autumnal

event in the lives of all the most intelligent women in Boston. But if there was a certain amount of truth in Hawthorne's description of her as a humbug, it must be remembered not only that was she an adept herself in spotting a humbug, but that she was at that time ever ready to hear criticism of herself, listen to it and deplore the inadequacy of an understanding which many should have envied. She was rude. She was ugly. But though Hawthorne's *Zenobia* was at times offensive, she was always beautiful.

When the end of the year came, Hawthorne resigned his position in the custom house. It is almost certain that he would have been discharged, not of course because he was inefficient but because the presidential election had put the Whigs in and the Democrats out. Much as in theory at least the Whigs disapproved of the spoils system—the replacement by order of the President and with the approval of the Senate of thousands of men holding positions in the Civil Service from the highest to the lowest—the system had become such an important driving-belt in the mechanism of party politics that even the Whigs were at a loss to see how the machine could run without it. Like Bancroft, Hawthorne might have been left drawing his salary for many months. Unlike Bancroft he was only too ready to quit.

What he did next, and immediately, was so inconsistent with what we would have supposed him likely to do that his decision cannot be glossed over. Though Hawthorne had perhaps attended as a guest one or two meetings of the Transcendental Club, he continued to show none of that appreciation of German idealistic philosophy which was the *raison d'être* of the club and a qualification for membership. Many of the members of the club were remarkable men, and remarkable for their goodness. Longfellow had been insistent on the quality of goodness which as a group they exhibited, and this Hawthorne was willing to concede. Yet he distrusted them. Being, as Van Wyck Brooks has described him, "the most deeply planted of American writers," one who "indicated more than any other the subterranean history of the American character," he doubted the necessity of going either to Königsberg or Göttingen for the fuel with which to kindle the fire of American genius. It is surprising, to say the least, therefore, to find him one of the very first to throw in his lot with George Ripley in the latter's venture of Brook Farm. It is still more surprising that a man who, as we have shown, demanded privacy as he demanded bread, who was the least gregarious of all men and who became mum when more than three people were collected together in one room, should have been eager to join a community in which a large number of men and women were to sacrifice privacy by living together and working cooperatively. Of all unlikely communitarians Nathaniel Hawthorne was the most unlikely. And Brook Farm, that camp of Socialists and Conscience-Whigs, where even Margaret Fuller complained that she was taken for a conservative, was hardly the place for a Democrat.

To understand Hawthorne's presence at Brook Farm it is necessary to look back on the immediate past and consider his immediate expectations. Forgotten now were the compulsions which made him seek a job. He had proved to his own satisfaction that both in quantity and quality he could show himself efficient when working alongside men who had not spent twelve years writing short stories in an upper room. Hours on Long Wharf in the icy blasts of a wintry North American gale and equally long hours on the burning hot decks of a collier in summer had proved this conclusively. What was not forgotten was the disappointment with which he had heard the false rumor that the Custom House job was to be a sinecure. It was then that he had written Longfellow saying that he would make the best of things in that the insecurity of earning money by writing would be compensated by security of income. His post in the custom house provided security of income for a short term of years at best; but the job of Measurer left him no surplus of energy which would enable him to write imaginative prose. Consequently on leaving the custom house he was looking for some job, however ill-paid, which would satisfy the conditions under which his work as an author could continue. Ripley with his eloquence and with his strong character, convinced Hawthorne that in the community of Brook Farm—where at most they intended to work four hours a day (Coleridge had hoped to have to work only two hours a day when he contemplated emigrating to the banks of the Susquehanna)—he would find that combination for which he was seeking.

There was another reason, however, and a more personal one. Romance and gallantry can be discovered even in a subscription list. Ripley's venture suggested to Hawthorne's mind the possibility of removing Sophia from No. 13 West Street and from that atmosphere which he so much deplored. It was part of the Brook Farm plan of living (though impractical at first) to allow approved married couples to build their own cottages on the estate and live apart, though they could still share the spirit and work of community life. Hawthorne had been engaged to be married now for two years. He cannot have looked favorably upon the chances of an improvement in Sophia's health if she were to remain in Boston. Her health was one of the obstacles to their marriage. Gallantly, therefore, he risked what we have every reason to believe were his entire savings; and he bought a married man's share in Ripley's syndicate. A bachelor in whom the coöperative spirit had been singularly lacking and for whom fraternization was a painful experience, he nevertheless went off to work at Brook Farm as a laborer and to dwell among those for whom the "community" was an end in itself. The prospect cannot have been inviting; but he went to prepare a way for his Sophia.

Ripley's reputation among the Transcendentalists was high and well established. But it must not be thought that all the members of the symposium approved. It was an interesting experiment, and they wished Ripley well. All were prepared to encourage a man to combine physical labor with intellectual pursuits. But couldn't that be achieved by the ownership of a small holding, some pigs, some chickens and a cow or two? Critics such as these did not seem to realize that even two cows keep a man to a rigid time-schedule. They could not, in fact, see how a community would run a farm better or how the group system would further those idealistic theories of life they had in common. In this respect Ripley was more practical than his critics. He had at least understood that if hours of labor were to be reduced there must be a rigid system by which, at all times of the day, workers would be available. Alcott noticed an initial mistake in the original organization of Brook Farm—he of all men who was to make such a ridiculous failure of his own venture. Alcott could not see why men and women should forever sacrifice privacy and plenty and combine to make a venture succeed unless they all had so strong a faith— whatever it might be—that it would coördinate the community and allow the essential development of an *esprit de corps*. Ripley did not see this necessity because he believed that men and women, of any political or philosophic opinion and of any religious or antireligious views, would be willing to live in peace and to work for the common good provided that the scheme secured maximum hours of leisure for intellectual pursuits with minimum hours of practical duties. Ripley promised them complete liberty of thought and no hieratical control, if only they would do what they were told to do at the time when they were told to do it. Neither cows nor cabbages, he thought, could wait indefinitely. But Alcott was right, and Ripley, as he was later to discover, was wrong. To Emerson and Margaret Fuller, Brook Farm was an experiment—a premature experiment. They were prepared to give it their blessing, but they asked whether, in order to live a more spiritual life, it was really necessary to "herd together."

No one understood better than Hawthorne that before the Arcadian existence could be realized, Arcadia must be prepared with more than words. He became a full-time farm hand. Like other American farm laborers he worked for fourteen hours a day, or as long as light lasted. His body might ache —and being that of a townsman it did—but at the end of the day came such perfect sleep as he had never in his life experienced. To that extent he was happy. New to the job of agriculture, he was well aware that he and his friends might even, though they had a tutor, be making embarrassing mistakes. Looking back on that period of his life, Hawthorne wrote in the *Blithedale Romance*, "To be sure, our next door neighbours pretended to be incredulous as to our real proficiency in the business which we had taken in hand. They told slanderous fables about our inability to yoke our own oxen, or to drive them afield when yoked, or to release the poor brutes from their conjugal bond at nightfall. They had the face to say, too, that the cows laughed at our awkwardness at milking time, and invariably kicked over the pails; partly in consequence of our putting the stool on the wrong side, and partly because, taking offence at the whisking of their tails, we were in the habit of holding these natural fly-flappers with one hand, and milking with the other. They further averred that we hoed up whole acres of Indian corn and other crops, and drew the earth carefully about the weeds; and that we raised five hundred tufts of burdock, mistaking them for cabbages; and that, by dint of unskilful planting, few of our seeds ever came up at all, or, if they did come up, it was stern-foremost; and that we spent the better part of the month of June in reversing a field of beans which had thrust themselves up in this unseemly way. . . . But this was pure envy and malice. The peril of our new way of life was not lest we should fail in becoming practical agriculturists, but that we should probably cease to become anything else."

It would seem possible that apart from relying on liberty, equality and fraternity as coördinating principles, Ripley made another initial mistake. The nearness of Boston to the site chosen for the colony had certain obvious disadvantages. Though some of the communitarians believed that they were living in the depths of the country, Brook Farm was only eight miles from the center of the city. Discourage visits to Boston they might, but the nearness of Beethoven symphony concerts, the Athenaeum, the theaters and Miss Peabody's lending library of foreign literature must have been a comforting and at the same time a disturbing thought to those who did not take the venture as seriously as did the founders of it. It was difficult to settle down to a new way of life so close to the old haunts. The "Combined Order of Life," as Emerson called it, necessitates—unless the members are to be rigorously controlled—a removal from familiar surroundings and local society. Coleridge understood this when he wished to exchange not Grasmere for Ullswater, or Highgate for Barnet, but wherever he might be in England for the banks of the river Susquehanna. Ripley chose the banks of the Charles, a river closely bound up with the life of Boston. It was no grave, irretrievable step for girls or boys, who had not quite made up their minds what to do with their lives, to put up five hundred dollars and go out for a time to Brook Farm. The average age decreased; and the numbers of curious sightseers and relations who came out from Boston increased. It was not to coöperate with such as these that Hawthorne had sacrificed his privacy and invested his savings.

There were, however, many visitors who were welcomed by the Ripleys. The advice and the encouragement of men such as Emerson and W. H. Channing, the Christian Socialist, were invaluable. So keen were the Ripleys to secure Margaret Fuller as a member that they invited her to stay whenever and as long as she wished. It was at Brook Farm that Hawthorne was able to study her so closely. Her first visit, which lasted some ten days, did not leave her with a favorable impression. On arrival she felt desolate. No one took any interest in her or troubled about her. Then on Saturday evening she opened one of her Conversations, on Education. Her audience "showed a good deal of the *sans-culotte* tendency in their manners—throwing themselves on the floor yawning, and going out when they had heard enough." This would not do at all. She was quite unaccustomed to rudeness. Bravely she told herself that on second thought this lack of deference would do her good. Then on Monday afternoon she had another objectionable experience. "Out with the drawing party; I felt the evils of want of conventional refinement, in the impudence with which one of the girls treated me." Margaret's magic did not seem to be working. It must have been a nervous strain, consequently, to open the next Conversation, the subject of which, Impulse, she had chosen because she thought it would do them good. "It was a much better conversation than the one before. None yawned, for none came, this time, from mere curiosity. There were about thirty-five present, which is a large enough circle." This was better. Even the impudent girl made up to her before she left. She had already exerted her strange influence over the married women and was made almost ill by the number of confessions to which she had to listen.

Another visit of Margaret to Brook Farm was recorded by Hawthorne. He found her in the woods—those woods which were so precious to him as a lonely retreat—surrounded by young communitarians dressed in motley for the occasion of Frank Dana's birthday. How insufferable at times this gregarious existence must have been to him, cooped up with what seems to have been a mixture of coeducational postgraduates and idealistic reformers! Yet he never complained of their company. His complaint was of a different kind. "While our enterprise lay all in theory, we had pleased ourselves with delectable visions of the spiritualisation of labour. It was to be our form of prayer and ceremonial of worship. Each stroke of the hoe was to uncover some aromatic root of wisdom, heretofor hidden from the sun. . . . The clods of earth, which we so constantly belaboured and turned over and over, were etherealised into thought. Our thoughts, on the contrary, were fast becoming cloddish. Our labour symbolized nothing, and left us mentally sluggish in the dusk of evening. Intellectual activity is incompatible with any large amount of bodily exercise. The yeoman and the scholar . . . are two distinct individuals, and can never be melted or welded into one substance."

Late in the summer of 1841 he left Brook Farm, returning to it in the autumn. His own family had not needed to remind him that he was a writer and not a yokel. He returned as a boarder—one, that is to say, who was only to do Ripley's minimum of hours in the fields or in the stables. He was still keen to make a success of the experiment; still saw in the woods and fields on the banks of the Charles River sites for the home he would build for Sophia. He even became a Trustee and the Chairman of the Committee of Finance—a strange appointment. But if Ripley was trying to bind him to the venture more closely, it was too late. Six months before, Sophia had visited him. Even then she was concerned about him. "Since I saw you at the Farm, I wish far more than ever to have a home for you to come to, after associating with men at the Farm all day. A sacred retreat you should have, of all men. . . . I could see very plainly that you were not leading an ideal life. Never upon the face of any mortal was there such a divine expression of sweetness and kindliness as I saw upon yours during the transactions and witticisms of the excellent fraternity. Yet it was also the expression of a witness and hearer, rather than of comradeship."

Exactly when the break came no one seems to know. It should still be discoverable, though the date is not a matter of real importance. While Ripley would not have let Hawthorne go without a struggle, one can be fairly sure the battle was not conducted on the terms described in the *Blithedale Romance*. In that excellent and dramatic chapter called "Crisis," Coverdale, the narrator, renounces the ideals of Hollingsworth and refuses to follow him further on the ground that he is bent on turning the community into an impossible philanthropic venture. Ripley, however, did not turn Brook Farm to any new purposes until 1845, and then rather against his own judgment. The chapter cannot, therefore, be accepted as entirely autobiographical, though it is more than probable that concerning the purchase of land Ripley did have rows with his chairman of finance.

It had been an unpretentious castle in the air, but now it had vanished utterly. Meanwhile there were more tangible evidences of the future. The Peabody-Emerson clan gathered. And with the appearance of the second series of *Twice-Told Tales*, Hawthorne's zest for literary work returned. But he had also to deal with the problems raised by Sophia: he had to win over his sisters to the idea of his marriage and he had to break to his mother the news of an engagement which was already a year old. The sisters were fighting a losing battle. But the mother, as mothers sometimes do, had known all along, and when she gave her blessing, the defense of the sisters Hathorne collapsed.

One day in July, 1842, Nathaniel Hawthorne sat down before the writing table in George Hillard's sitting-room in Boston. He had to write a letter to the Rev. James Freeman Clarke—Margaret Fuller's great friend.

My dear Sir,—Though personally a stranger to you, I am about to request you the greatest favor which I can receive from any man. I am to be married to Miss Sophia Peabody; and it is our mutual desire that you should perform the ceremony. Unless it should be decidedly a rainy day, a carriage will call for you at half-past eleven o'clock in the forenoon.

Very respectfully yours,
Nathaniel Hawthorne.

What Hawthorne intended to do had it rained, history does not reveal. But it does reveal this very curious coincidence, that though James Freeman Clarke was intimate with the Peabody and Emerson households, he only set eyes on Hawthorne twice: the first time when he married him; the second time when the coffin was opened and he gazed on the dead Hawthorne whom he was about to commit to the grave.

Sophia and Nathaniel were married in the Peabody bookshop. They left it to take up their residence in the Manse—Emerson's old home in Concord. Hawthorne was in his thirty-ninth year.

9

Concord

AT no period of his life was Hawthorne more happy than during the first two of the three years at Concord—that is to say, from July, 1842, when he married, until the end of 1844. His state was something of an achievement; for long consecutive months of happiness are rare in the life of so sensitive a man; and though the inward attunes itself easily to felicity, it responds infrequently enough in most men. Only in retrospect does the continuity become apparent. "How happy I was," a man may reflect, "during those two or three years, every day of them." But to record that everything is rosy day after day, week after week, is quite another thing; and in the *Notebooks* of 1842–1843 Hawthorne accomplished an admittedly difficult feat. He wrote thousands of words about himself in which he expressed temporary happiness, perhaps as well as it has ever been expressed in the language. He not only expressed it over and over again without annoying the reader (in itself something of an accomplishment), but in a variety of ways he indicated as he had never done and was never to do again, his zest for life and his appreciation of the simple things which life was giving him. Without this document, now as nearly restored as we shall probably ever have it (though missing pages have a habit of turning up), we would have to take on trust one whole aspect of Hawthorne's character—his power of enjoyment. Again and again we have been told that Hawthorne was inhibited from feeling extremes of emotion. The truth is more probably this, that after his experience of the first two years at the Old Manse, he was conscious of his inability to experience happiness so deeply again.

Yet no one but Sophia could have suspected at the time how gay was the song which his heart was singing. He remained outwardly much as he had always been—a somber and shy man. To friends he would express contentment; but not the thrill of newly experienced joy. Sophia could do this. Without reticence or reserve she wrote letters to her mother and to her great friend (Mary Caleb Foote of Salem) singing his praises and her own felicity.

None the less, on the plane of human relationships there were many adjustments to be made; and it is to their credit that they made them without friction. Sophia would not be able to see so many of her Concord friends or so frequently as her former social habits had encouraged. He in his turn, though still allowed his old tricks of shunning society, must not lock himself away from her; must do many menial jobs until a country girl could be trained as a servant; might curse the stove, curse the kettle and overboil the potatoes, but must not let these little irritations interfere with his work. For by his work the butcher, the baker and the rest were to be paid. So admirable at this time was his temper that he could even "pug" clay for Sophia's amateurish modeling; and pugging clay for someone's else use is a soul-destroying job, as anyone who has tried it knows.

Middle-aged already in manner if not in heart, he had married at last and had for the first time in his life a home of his own. The house to which he had come was an old house. It had great charm and was placed in surroundings of peaceful, agricultural beauty. Concord's famous nonagenarian parson, Dr. Ezra Ripley, had died the year before. His heirs, the Samuel Ripleys, not wishing to take over their inheritance immediately, had let the Manse to the Hawthornes. The Old Manse, the old parsonage, stood on the rising ground above the water meadows of the Concord River. It was a sleepy and sluggish river, the current of which was so slow that Hawthorne spent weeks there before he understood which way it flowed.

The house constituted a visible sign of the importance of the Ripley and Emerson families in local affairs. It had been built in 1765 for William Emerson—Ralph Waldo's grandfather—who had watched from the study window the first engagement in the Revolution, when the local farmers fired at British redcoats across the Concord Bridge. William Emerson died and the next incumbent of the living, Ezra Ripley, married his widow. And now at last Ripley had died, too—an old, old man. Concord mourned and missed her famous "squarson"—a local priest and squire of autocratic behavior. In his time he had been considered a modernist, and his time had been a long one. He had welcomed the early reforms of Dr. Channing. But the ball which Dr. Channing had set rolling had long since got out of control and was now spinning towards damnation, kicked by his own stepgrandson and other Trancendentalists. Over these young men and their generation Ezra Ripley had no authority. He knew it, and told Dr. Channing so. Over the rest of the flock he continued to rule as an autocrat until his dying day. Woe betide the Sabbath-breaker. Woe betide the slacker who lay abed when the town's fire bell rang in the middle of the night, and did not, as the doctor did, get up, saddle his horse, sling fire buckets over his arm and gallop off down the road. Ripley was a man who had no small opinion of his powers of intercession with the Almighty. What, he questioned, was the use of the curate's praying for rain—especially as the curate's garden was down by the river and was not suffering from the drought? So he lifted up his hands and prayed in a loud voice. His congregation were all drenched to the skin before they got home. Emerson had many such anecdotes to relate concerning Dr. Ripley.

Now the old man was dead, and the Hawthornes were redecorating the Manse. No lay occupant had ever profaned that house "until that memorable summer afternoon" writes Hawthorne, "when I entered it as my home. A priest built it; a priest had succeeded to it; other priestly men, from time to time, had dwelt in it; and children born in its chambers had grown up to assume the priestly character. It was awful to reflect how many sermons must have been written there. The latest inhabitant alone—he, by whose translation to Paradise the dwelling was left vacant—had penned nearly three thousand discourses, besides the better, if not the greater, number that gushed living from his lips."

Old stone gateposts—there was no gate—made a formal beginning to the avenue of black ash trees which reached from the road to the house. On one side of that avenue lay the plots of kitchen garden which were for three years to be the object of Hawthorne's attention. The garden was of "precisely the right extent. An hour or two of morning labor was all that it required. But I used to visit and revisit it a dozen times a-day, and stand deep in contemplation over my vegetable progeny, with a love that nobody could share or conceive of, who had

The Old Manse

never taken part in the process of creation. It was one of the most bewitching sights in the world to observe a hill of beans thrusting aside the soil, or a row of early peas just peeping forth sufficiently to trace a line of delicate green. Later in the season, the humming-birds were attracted by a peculiar variety of bean; and they were a joy to me. . . ." At the back of the house was the old orchard, the planting of which had amused Ripley's parishioners, who did not know he was going to live to the age of ninety. Now past its prime it still produced masses of fruit but of poor quality. "In the stillest afternoon, if I listened, the thump of a great apple was audible, falling without a breath of wind, from the mere necessity of perfect ripeness. And besides, there were pear trees, that flung down bushels of heavy pears; and peach trees, which in a good year torment me with peaches, neither to be eaten nor kept, nor without per-plexity and labour, to be given away." The house—too large for them and in a bad state of repair—appealed to Hawthorne's romantic tastes. Once painted white, it was now old in appear-ance beyond its years. Thick and luxuriant moss grew on its timbers wherever the moist northeast wind struck it; creepers that love the sun grew over the rest. It was a creaking, rather ghostly house with many more rooms than they required. It was so cold in winter that the servant bending over a washtub full of boiling water was reputed to have hoar-frost on her hair. But it was a comfortable house to which he became during his all too short tenancy very genuinely devoted. And when spring came to the Concord vale, or summer, or best of all, autumn, there was for him no place like it.

"My life at this time, is more like that of a boy, externally, than it has been since I was really a boy. It is usually supposed that the cares of life come with matrimony; but I seem to have cast off all care, and live on with as much easy trust in Providence, as Adam could possibly have felt, before he had learned that there was a world beyond his Paradise. My chief anxiety consists in watching the prosperity of my vegetables—in observing how they are affected by the rain or sunshine—in lamenting the blight of one squash, and rejoicing at the luxurious growth of another. . . . The fight with the world—the struggle of a man amongst men—the agony of the universal effort to wrench the means of life from a host of greedy competitors—all this seems like a dream to me. My business is merely to live and to enjoy; and whatever is essential to life and enjoyment will come as naturally as the dew from Heaven. This is—practically at least—my faith. . . . True, it might be a sin and shame, in such a world as ours, to spend a lifetime in this manner; but, for a few summer weeks, it is good to live in this world as if it were Heaven. And so it is, and so it shall be; although in a little while, a flitting shadow of earthly care and toil will mingle itself with our realities."

The peace and seclusion of their honeymoon were soon disturbed. George and Susan Hillard, on their way to far-off Niagara, came to stay from Saturday to Monday. The visit gave Hawthorne pleasure. There was something in the sound of the coach rumbling up the avenue to the front door which was eminently satisfactory. In that sound was an immediate realization that at long last he had achieved part at least of what was essential to happiness. He was a man now with a wife and a household. He was a man "having a tangible existence and locality in the world;" and though he had no wish to entertain often, the first occasion was unique and very pleasant. He was a host; and with charming simplicity he records in his journal the splendid breakfast he gave them in the morning—flapjacks and whortleberries, which he had picked on the hillside, and a dish of perch, bream and pouts, which he had hooked out of the river the evening before.

The visit is remarkable also because of what happened on that Sunday morning. The incident was in itself trivial enough, but it marked the beginning of a new phase in Hawthorne's life. It was the first of Emerson's efforts to become intimate with a man of whose writings he thought nothing but whose personality magnetically attracted him.

Hillard and Hawthorne set out for a long Sunday walk. They wanted to walk to Walden Pond—a place-name later made famous by Thoreau's writings—but did not know the way. So they walked through Concord and called on Emerson to ask him the right path to take through his woods. Emerson was eager to accompany them. But it happened to be churchgoing time, and the Rev. Ralph Waldo Emerson did not wish to be seen breaking the Sabbath by going for a walk when others were walking to church. So for a time Hillard and Hawthorne had to wait until Emerson could say that "the road was clear." Hawthorne, a quick observer of men and their behavior, did not let this incident pass without record. When it came to a matter of parochial propriety, Emerson, the author of *Nature*, the sensational lecturer of theological students, was apparently no very adventurous spirit. The hour of service having passed, Emerson, Hillard and Hawthorne set out. On their way they came upon a famous Concord character walking in his fields, and fell into conversation with him. He was Edmund Hosmer, Concord's renowned yeoman farmer and rustic philosopher, a man much admired and cultivated by Emerson. With little hesitation Hosmer began to give his opinion on world affairs and domestic politics. Hawthorne knew that Emerson had put Hosmer's sayings in the *Dial*, the journal of the Transcendentalists then being edited by Margaret Fuller, all of which he thought very bad indeed for Hosmer. He listened with interest. There it was—the oracular manner! Emerson's influence again. Why could not Emerson leave people alone, letting them be, as they should be, "themselves"? Though Hawthorne underestimated Hosmer and overestimated Emerson's effect on him, one can understand how it must have shocked him, with his constant abhorrence of enslaving influences, to see the farmer's natural simplicity suffer from the impression he might be making in intellectual circles.

Emerson's influence over many of his friends was magical and, in Hawthorne's opinion, pernicious. Good and clever though Emerson unquestionably was, there was something unpleasant in the spectacle presented by those of his intimates who came so much under his influence that in manner, speech and even in looks they closely, and apparently quite unconsciously, imitated the "master." It would be difficult to find men of more marked individuality than Alcott, Ellery Channing and Henry Thoreau. Yet many have testified to the fact that all three were at times ridiculous in their imitations of Emerson. Young Ellery Channing who was the least talented of the three was the worst offender. Alcott had bad lapses; closing one's eyes when listening to him, one would have supposed that it was Emerson speaking. Thoreau, in appearance like a thin Aberdeen terrier, could be trusted to mimic Emerson regularly and he adopted a handwriting which was like a forgery of the master's. It is admittedly unpleasant to witness admiration becoming mimicry. Individuality is profaned by the professional imitator, who makes another's face and voice his own. The armor which Hawthorne put on to protect his spiritual virginity against the seductive assaults of Mr. Emerson was perhaps excessive. But Emerson, quite unconscious of Hawthorne's fears, pursued him for the rest of his life. Hawthorne might stop to utter an occasional rebuke, but for the most part he kept his distance and marched on, deaf to all endearments.

The stage was now set for Emerson, for Ellery Channing, and for Henry Thoreau, but the drama opened with the entrance of Margaret Fuller. She arrived at the Manse when Hawthorne was out and cornered Sophia. The Friend, as W. H. Channing called her, came with one of those propositions which is sincerely meant to be a help to everybody. It was that her sister and her husband, young Ellery Channing, should come to live in the Manse as paying guests. Margaret in torrential conversation explained it all to a flustered Sophia. The house was absurdly big for them alone. It would be so nice for them and economical, too, to have the dear Channings, such very sensitive people. And their presence would compensate Nathaniel for his inability to persuade the saintly George Bradford, his Brook Farm friend, to live with them. Young Ellery and his wife would do very well in Mr. Bradford's place. Sophia weakly said yes; and Margaret left.

When Sophia told her husband of this interview his brows knit, and with great solemnity he sat down at his writing-table. The Ellery Channings were *not* coming to stay at the Manse.

It could have all been so simply done on half a sheet of writing-paper; but no; nothing less than several folios sufficed in his opinion to put this proposition out of court once and for all. The pomposity of the style and the serious treatment of his argument make the letter a ridiculous and at the same time a very human document. He begins by making it quite clear that it is he, not Sophia, who is turning down her proposal, and he begs Margaret not to think for one moment that he has anything against the "social qualities of Mr. and Mrs. Channing"— which was slightly impertinent. The Garden of Eden was meant for two, not for four. That is his main argument. "Boarding-out," he explains, is, essentially and inevitably, an unnatural relation. "The Channings ought not to seek for delicacy of character and nice tact and sensitive feelings in their hosts . . . those characteristics should never exist on more than one side." Sophia, he explained, was as yet a most inexperienced housekeeper. He was afraid that with the Channings in the Manse, it would "take but a trifle to render their whole common life diseased and intolerable"—which was putting it rather strongly. As for Mr. Bradford (there Margaret had nearly got him) it must be remembered that "his negative qualities seem to take away his personality: and leave his excellent characteristic to be fully and fearlessly enjoyed. I doubt whether he be not precisely the rarest man in the world." Bradford may have been rare enough, but how Hawthorne had sighed with relief when he received his refusal of the invitation.

When he was nervous or put in a difficult position, Hawthorne's style in letter writing became deplorable. An even more unfortunate letter which we will consider later was one written to Edgar Allan Poe. Without meaning to, he could give offense in his letters, for when the letter to all intents and purposes was finished, he had the habit of adding a paragraph of stark frankness at the end—which was not valor but honesty gone riotous. To maintain a high standard of honesty in a letter is easy for the writer. It is less easy for the recipient to feel pleased with the letter and its author.

Ellery Channing and his wife were not coming to stay at the Manse. That was now decided. Ellery took a house down the road with an acre of vegetable garden which he intended and was expected to cultivate. Ellery Channing's visible means of support were small. The house he took was sufficiently close to the Manse for him to wander up at all the most inconvenient hours. He was the kind of visitor who arrives five minutes after a most frugal luncheon has been served, and refusing to divide two meager portions into three, wanders out into the sitting-room to await the return of his hosts. The unfortunate hosts gobble their meal in order to entertain the unfed man who is such an embarrassment to them. They find that he has left, taking with him the books which his hosts were in the midst of reading, or that he has forgotten to take away the books which he had brought with him under his arm. This Ellery Channing had always been "difficult." As Sophia knew, he had been difficult as a boy. His family knew how difficult he had been as a Harvard undergraduate: he had disappeared and gone west just at the time he was about to take his degree. And now Concord was finding him difficult. He was "agin" all authority and all tradition. By turns moody, irascible, and charming, he could be friendly and unfriendly to the same man in the same day. He anchored his life to Emerson and so, floating like a boat in the sluggish Concord River, he came quietly alongside another boat tied to the same anchor: the friendship between him and Henry Thoreau was the only satisfying element in both their lives.

Hawthorne wrote in his journal, "There is nothing very peculiar about him—some originality and self-inspiration in his character, but none, or very little, in his intellect. Nevertheless the lad himself seems to feel as if he were a genius; and, ridiculously enough, looks upon his own verses as too sacred to be sold for money. Prose he will sell to the highest bidder; but measured feet and jingling lines are not to be exchanged for gold—which, indeed, is not very likely to be offered for them. I like him well enough, however; but after all, these originals in a small way after one has seen a few of them, become more dull and commonplace than even those who keep the ordinary pathway of life. They have a rule and a routine, which they follow with as little variety as other people do *their* rule and routine; and when once we have fathomed this mystery, nothing can be more wearisome." A wise observation. It is fair criticism even if underlying it there is an annoyance with Emerson and with Ellery's sister-in-law, the editress of the *Dial*, Margaret Fuller, because of what to Hawthorne seemed an unjustifiable recommendation of him as a poet of distinction. But of contemporary poetry Hawthorne was no judge. And that he came to be very fond of Ellery Channing we know. What perhaps—or almost certainly—Hawthorne did not know was the nature of the shadow over Ellery's head. Ellery Channing was a poet and a severe critic of poetry. So severe was he that he apparently convinced himself that to confine one's self to the writing of minor poetry was like committing the crime against the Holy Ghost. Integrity and self-deprecation pushed to extremes can be very tiresome to others. There is little doubt that Ellery Channing could be most tiresome concerning the value of his own production as a poet, particularly to a man such as Hawthorne, who was sceptical of the value of all the rhymed verse of his time. Several memorable lines and a few stanzas of beauty are no small accomplishment; but they were no accomplishment at all in the opinion of their author. In fairness to Channing we must remember that fear he had of the cloud over his shoulder. And he was quite right about its existence. He *was* a minor poet—a very minor one. He was one of those poets whom later generations know largely between the limits of quotation marks.

Hawthorne, liking the youth, did his best to give his name some small publicity in the preface to *The Old Manse*. The passage is a long one—too long to quote in its entirety—but it gives a sketch of incidents which reveal the character of both men. Hawthorne writes of himself and Ellery Channing rowing their boat against the current of the Concord River and turning off into the Assabeth: "A more lonely stream than this, for a mile above its junction with the Concord, has never flowed on earth." Up stream they rowed, they fished, and eventually they came to a place in the woods where they landed in order to make a fire on which to cook their meal. "It was the very spot in which to utter the extremest nonsense, or the profoundest wisdom. . . . So, amid sunshine and shadow, rustling leaves, and sighing waters, up gushed our talk, like the babble of a fountain. The evanescent spray was Ellery's, and his, too, the lump of golden thought, that lay glimmering in the fountain's bed, and brightened both our faces by reflection. Could he have drawn out that virgin gold, and stamped it with the mint-mark that alone gives currency, the world might have had the profit, and he the fame. My mind was the richer, merely by the knowledge that it was there. But the chief profit of those wild days, to him and to me, lay—not in any definite idea—not in any angular or rounded stuff—but in the freedom which we thereby won from all custom and conventionalism, and fettering influences of man on men." The leaves of the trees which overhung the Assabeth had whispered to them, "Be free! Be free!" and they liked to think that the ashes of their camp-fires marked their daily progress towards freedom.

With what interest Mrs. Hawthorne watched her husband and Mr. Emerson together can be imagined. Her spiritual home, she had believed, was in Emerson's soul; her whole heart and being now belonged to Nathaniel, her husband. Emerson's interest in Hawthorne was the best of all testaments to the correctness of her judgment. Would that they could be friends—intimates. She watched them. Her husband had not yet grown that moustache which was to hide the severity and the sculptural beauty of his upper lip. At forty years of age his great good looks were probably never more remarkable. He was physically fit, strong and healthy. Emerson was, physically, as different from Hawthorne as can be imagined. His anatomic structure was so much too long for its breadth that when he bent forward he looked as if he might break, like a match stick. He who spent so much of his life glorifying physical labor could not have been built to a scale more unsuited to it. He was in fact quite unsuited to it. Though he was once known to wield an axe, it was not his axe which brought down the tree. Climatic conditions were probably responsible for the prevalence of big noses, but Emerson's was such an outsize, such a tomahawk of a nose, that the adjective "emersonian" was coined to describe such strange structures. The bony brow was large but also rather misshapen; and his hair was thin and nondescript in color. But what all have testified to was the keen and immediately reactive expression, ever changing, ever alive and always astonishingly spiritual. Sophia observed and occasionally recorded. She watched them skating over the ice of the Concord River and its water meadows—her husband sweeping on and on, apparently tireless; Emerson in pursuit, weary, breathless, his nose stuck out in front, breathing the cold air and complaining bitterly of Hawthorne's strength and endurance. Meanwhile, Thoreau—an inefficient ballet dancer on skates—was performing the most absurd and the ugliest antics all on his own. At another time she would record the most flattering observation. "Mr. Emerson delights in him; he talks to him all the time, and Mr. Hawthorne's looks answer. He seems to fascinate Mr. Emerson. Whenever he comes to see him, he takes him away, so that no one may interrupt him in his close and dead-set attack upon his ear. Miss Hoar says that persons about Mr. Emerson so generally echo him, that it is refreshing to him to find this perfect individual, all himself and nobody else." A true and charmingly ingenuous observation. Hawthorne himself noticed and was amused by Emerson's deference to his wishes. "By the by, Mr. Emerson gave me an invitation to dinner today, to be complied with or not, as might suit my convenience at the time; it happens not to suit." There was no conceit in this passage from his journal, only a record that he was not going to be pursued by Emerson. "The mystic, stretching his hand out of cloud-land in vain searches for something real. . . . Mr. Emerson is a great searcher for facts;

but they seemed to melt away and become unsubstantial in his grasp." Hawthorne liked him and admired his poetry; but he was not going to be an Emersonian. He was not going to be hooked and landed, as Ellery Channing had been, by that "everlasting rejecter of all that is, and seeker for he knows not what."

In October, 1842, Emerson persuaded Hawthorne to leave his wife for one night and to walk with him to a Shaker village in New Hampshire. Hawthorne knew the Shaker communities of old and had long been interested in their way of life. "Mr. Emerson held a theological discussion with two of the Shaker brethren; but the particulars of it have faded from my memory so that I cannot adequately recall them. Wherefore let them rest untold. I recollect nothing so well as the aspect of some fringed gentians, which we saw growing by the roadside, and which were so beautiful that I longed to turn back. . . ." Turning to Emerson's journal we find Emerson admitting that his talk had not been a great success. "I doubt not we should have had our way with them to a good extent if we could have stayed twenty-four hours; although my powers of persuasion were crippled by a barking cold, and Hawthorne inclined to play Jove more than Mercurias." Emerson attributes some of his failure to Hawthorne, but in their strange relations there was one difficulty Emerson could never overcome. Hawthorne's impressive silences and his humility in argument (he seems seldom to have lost his temper with Emerson, though when he did "humility" hardly describes his words) goaded Emerson into excesses of verbosity. Plaintively Emerson admitted at the end, "He said so little that I talked too much, and stopped only because, as he gave no indications, I feared to exceed." In Hawthorne's eyes Emerson exceeded the limits often and in all kinds of tests, and he recorded his opinion not in secret diaries but in published work—work which at that time, one should remember, was considered topical comment. In *The Celestial Railroad* (1843) Hawthorne was attacking Transcendentalism; he was condemning a theory of life and behavior which was held sacred not only by his wife's family but by those, almost without exception, with whom he was in daily or weekly social intercourse. After nearly a century has passed and without a guiding sign from his biographers, it is difficult for the reader of today, picking up either *The Celestial Railroad* or *The Old Manse*, to realize the "snub direct" which in those two works Hawthorne gave to the very men who, though not professing to admire him as a writer, were so interested in him that they importuned him with their attentions. Hawthorne was known to be kindly and perfectly honest; he had been a "Brook Farmer;" and his ridicule probably did something to detract from the vogue of Transcendentalism and to dim the luster of the word. The openness with which he wrote of his friend Emerson, and especially of his followers, in *The Old Manse* is altogether surprising, for Emerson was still the rage.

"There were circumstances around me [at the Old Manse] which made it difficult to view the world precisely as it exists; for, severe and sober as was the Old Manse, it was necessary to go but a little way beyond its threshold, before meeting with stranger moral shapes of men than might have been encountered elsewhere, in a circuit of a thousand miles. These hobgoblins of flesh and blood were attracted thither by the wide-spreading influence of a great and original Thinker, who had his earthly abode at the opposite extremity of our village. . . . They came to Emerson, as the finder of a glittery gem hastens to a lapidary, to ascertain its quality and value. Uncertain, troubled, earnest wanderers, through the midnight of the moral world, beheld his intellectual fire, as a beacon burning on a hilltop . . . it attracted bats and owls, and a whole host of night birds, which flapped their dusky wings against the gazer's eyes, and sometimes were mistaken for fowls of angelic feather. . . .

"For myself, there had been epochs in my life, when I, too, might have asked of this prophet the master-word that should solve me the riddle of the universe. But now, being happy, I felt as if there was no question to be put, and therefore admired Emerson as a poet of deep beauty and austere tenderness, but sought nothing of him as a philosopher.

"Never was a poor little country village infested with such a variety of queer, strangely dressed, oddly behaved mortals, most of whom took upon themselves to be the important angels of the world's destinies, yet were simply bores of a very intense water."

This was strong medicine for those he had just left behind in Concord on his return to Salem. Yet it is possible that his prestige among them went up, not down, because of it.

There was one who could claim to be exempt from any charge of following Emerson to Concord and that was Henry Thoreau; for he had managed somehow to be born in Concord. But as the years passed the influence of Emerson over him became more and more apparent. Even his friend Frank Sanborn (whose life of Thoreau is chronologically perhaps the most upside-down biography ever written) recorded in his diary,[1] "In his tones and gestures he seemed to me to imitate Emerson,

[1] *Henry D. Thoreau.* American Men of Letters series.

Emerson's Home in Concord, Massachusetts

so that it was annoying to listen to him, though he said many good things. He looks like Emerson, too—coarser, but with something of that serenity (*sic*) and sagacity E. has. He dresses plainly, wears a beard in his throat, and has a brown complexion. . . . He is a little under size, with a huge Emersonian nose, bluish gray eyes, brown hair, and a ruddy weather-beaten face, which reminds me of some shrewd and honest animal's—some retired philosophical woodchuck or magnanimous fox." Even the shape of his collars was that of Mr. Emerson's unique pattern.

Henry Thoreau, like Alcott, can be judged not by what he accomplished but by his uniqueness as a person and by the steadfastness with which he maintained his ideals. "Thoreau, acid and obstinate, but of an absolute integrity." [2] That is a good description. Thoreau considered that certain fixed ideas were precious, so precious that nothing else mattered, so precious that he was blind to the fact that they did not together make a pattern of life or of behavior. "Whatever question there may be of his talent, there can be none, I think, of his genius. It was a slim and crooked one; but it was eminently personal. He was imperfect, unfinished, inartistic;"—the writer of these lines will be recognized as Henry James—"he was worse than provincial—he was parochial; it is only at his best that he is readable. But at his best he has an extreme natural charm. . . ." Though he was not of an old Concord family, Dr. Ripley and young Emerson had brought Thoreau to the especial notice of the authorities of Harvard when he was an undergraduate. And the authorities listened. Poor old Dr. Ripley was not to forget that sponsorship when he heard the crazy young man telling everyone that God could be worshiped with more sincerity in

[2] *Times Literary Supplement*, December 12, 1936.

the woods and the fields than in the pews of the church.

After he left college, schoolmastering was the obvious career for this son of Concord—son of Concord by chance, for his family came from the Channel Islands and had only arrived in America in recent times. And Thoreau did occasionally do a job of work as schoolmaster or tutor. His theory that one had to preserve complete independence whether from man or job —a theory which in some strange way he had to reconcile with his ideals of the beauty of labor and the necessity of friendship —and his notion that the Almighty could well have created the world on the first day and rested from all manufacture for the other six days did not recommend him to employers. He trained himself to reduce his requirements to a minimum. His clothes were serviceable according to his standards, though their appearance struck others at times as queer. He took no alcohol. He did not use tobacco. Even so, but for that room at the top of Emerson's stairs, but for the heroic efforts of his friends to find him publishers, but for the pencil-maker's bench at home, Henry Thoreau would have been hard put to it at times to earn his daily bread.

Poet and philosopher (he was an arch-Transcendentalist), pencil-maker and pedagogue, he had a knowledge of Greek and the classics superior to that of anyone in Concord. His name was to survive, however, not because of anything he learned from books but because he observed the life in the fields, hedge-rows, brooks and woods of his own countryside and understood the animals, birds, fishes, and flowers that inhabited them. There was no money in that, unless he were to turn catcher of vermin. But there was a dollar or two always to be earned as a hedger, ditcher, local surveyor. Someone was always wanting a tree cut

down, some firewood chopped or fruit trees pruned. He became a minute observer of nature; but he was a bird-watcher
rather than a bird-killer, and while he knew all the living inhabitants of the Concord River, he did not want to kill any of
them. Certainly Thoreau was no sportsman, nor was he a zo-
ologist or a scientific historian of nature. He was rather an
authority on local lore. He knew what he knew but had no wish
to tabulate or classify it, as the great Agassiz was to find out.
Professor Agassiz, later the friend of Hawthorne, an eminent
Swiss scientist, and one of the first distinguished foreigners to
vivify scientific research in the United States, was soon put on
to Thoreau. And Thoreau enchanted him. But the fact soon
came out that Thoreau was a very "natural" natural historian;
he would watch and send by the coach to Cambridge a rare
mudturtle without wishing to know how the Professor would
classify it or where he would place it in the scheme of the universe. He would catch a pout and had less than no interest in
what Agassiz discovered when he dissected it. But heaven help
anyone who tried to teach the wiry, bearded Thoreau how to
chop a tree to fall in the required direction or how to erect the
uprights for a frame house. These things he *knew;* just as he
knew Greek, just as he knew how to make the best pencils.
Emerson delighted in him. He was Emerson's odd man about
the place, and his natural man, made flesh. He could of course
be very tiresome, most irritating; but he was something of a
discovery.

Hawthorne liked his "Mr. Thorow": he liked his music box,
too, and was loath to return it. Thoreau had one possession
which was of far more importance in his life than the music
box; and this, too, he gave up—or sold—to Hawthorne. Thoreau

had been an early visitor to the Manse. Hawthorne had asked him to dinner and had liked the young man. "He is as ugly as sin, long-nosed, queer-mouthed, and with uncouth and somewhat rustic, although courteous, manners, corresponding very well with such an exterior. . . . On the whole, I find him a healthy and wholesome Man to know." After dinner they walked up the river. Thoreau shouted for his boat (the famous canoe, The Musketaquid) and a boy paddled it over. They got in so that Thoreau could show off his skill with the paddles. Hawthorne was amazed. He bought The Musketaquid for seven dollars and regretted that with another seven he could not purchase Thoreau's aquatic skill too. So Thoreau parted with his most precious possession. He had built it himself with the aid of his brother John, whose death created so profound a void in Henry's heart that even his friendship with Ellery Channing—the other most certain value in his life—only partly filled it. In this small craft the brothers Thoreau had made that expedition known as *A Week on the Concord and Merrimac Rivers*. Renamed by Hawthorne, it was to appear once again as the *Pond Lily*. But all the instruction which Thoreau gave Hawthorne was of no avail, and nothing could persuade the boat to obey its new master as it had its old. This disobedience Hawthorne found understandable, for he had developed a respect for Thoreau's craftsmanship. About to leave Concord to take a job as tutor to the Emersons of Staten Island, Thoreau came back to the Manse one day. Could he take out the old boat just once more? They went down together to the river, which had swollen to the size of a muddy sea. They emptied her out and set forth to get a view of the floods from a neighboring hill. It was quite an adventure. For on the return journey, at Thoreau's insistence, they jumped from the canoe on to a great block of ice and were "borne by it directly to our own landing place, with the boat towing behind." Thoreau so often did the unexpected.

Money? Money in small sums was forever leaving the pocket. What money was coming in? Very little. During the winter months of those years in Concord Hawthorne worked hard enough, though the attractions and distractions of summer at the Manse brought all writing to a standstill in hot weather. There was a brisk demand for his stories. Edgar Allan Poe, about to produce a new magazine, wrote to young Lowell (also engaged upon a similar enterprise) asking him whether he could get anything out of Hawthorne. The answer would probably be no; for he supposed that Hawthorne's output must be fully booked up. It probably was booked up ahead. Hawthorne was by no means prolific. The best of what he had would go to O'Sullivan of the *Democratic Review* and the rest to other publications which had taken his work before. Unfortunately it was one thing to place work and another thing to get paid for it. The number of periodicals issued in the Eastern States was far in excess of the demand, and competition for the best authors was keen. Though the terms offered were attractive, editors seemed always in arrears with their payments. And the mortality rate for periodicals was high—which meant often no payment at all. So that while on paper Hawthorne's position was sound, his purse was often empty. What avails the balance sheet of a poor man when the till is empty? The standard of living declined, yet could never, it was hoped, become so low as to prejudice the health of Sophia and the baby. Neighbors arrived with wonderful cakes, and Dr. Ripley's garden and orchard supplied a rich abundance of vegetables and fruits. The fare was richer in the summer than in the winter.

By 1845 Hawthorne considered his position desperate. And though because of his editing of Bridge's *Journal of an African Cruise* he had already received something which by rights he considered Bridge's, he had to write to him for another one hundred and fifty dollars in September. He received one hundred dollars. The Samuel Ripleys wished to return to the Manse and, according to Hawthorne, announced their intentions not by direct information but by the unexpected appearance of carpenters, "making a tremendous racket among the outbuildings, strewing green grass with pine shavings and chips of chestnut joists, and vexing the whole antiquity of the place with their discordant renovations. Soon, moreover, they divested our abode of the veil of woodbine which had crept over a large portion of its southern face. All the aged mosses were cleared unsparingly away; and there were horrible whispers about brushing up the external walls with a coat of paint—a purpose as little to my taste as might be that of rouging the venerable cheeks of one's grandmother." Hawthorne, rightly or wrongly, was much offended by the Ripleys' behavior. Concord, however, had come to know and to love the Hawthornes. Emerson told Sophia not to let her husband worry about his debts—ridiculously small in any case—and advising him to let the creditors whistle for their payment, he reminded him that he was not the only man in Concord who owed money to shopkeepers. But debts, however small, did worry Hawthorne unmercifully. If he could pay up he would "clear out," in spite of entreaties to stay in the neighborhood.

Meanwhile the fortunes of the Peabodys in Boston were equally unhealthy. The novelty of the bookshop had worn off. They had been silly. By harboring young men of genius and providing them with free board and lodging, they had earned for the shop the name of the "Hospital for Incapables." Sophia in her anxiety had written to her mother asking what their true position was. "God takes care of us," she replied. "It has become an imperative duty for us no longer, as heretofore, to invite almost strangers to stay day after day and week after week. My feelings would impel me to say to all the good and to all the unfortunate, 'Come and find an asylum here.'" It was the old story of the Ladies' Teashop that tries to feed the unemployed: the charity is satisfactory to the unemployed but disastrous for the ladies. In another letter she expressed the natural but at that time unfortunate sentiment that the "bairns" might keep their parents in comfort in their old age. It was all most untimely, because the bairns, too, were trusting in God for another miracle of loaves and fishes. She followed up this unfortunate hint with a bit of mother-in-law's advice for Nathaniel. If he wanted a smashing success as an author he must listen to her. He must write a biographical sketch of her grandfather Palmer. ". . . he would feel a holy joy in tracing the character of the incorruptible patriot, the ardent lover of freedom, the unwearied doer of public duties, the devoted husband and father, the indulgent master, the saint-like follower of his Divine Teacher, of whose spirit he was full." There was a subject for him!

It was at about this time that Hawthorne began to show a marked disinclination to have anything whatever to do with Peabodys.

They must return not to Boston but to Salem. By September 1845 they were reduced almost to penury. Mrs. Peabody suggested that her daughter should return to her, but Sophia refused. "Unceiled rafters and walls, and a pine table, chair and bed would be far more preferable with him" than marble halls without him. She had, she told her mother, been in negotiation with the Mannings, through Louisa, for the rental of the old kitchen of the Herbert Street house; but finding that the Mannings wanted as much for the kitchen as for the parlor, she had taken the parlor and was now happy. She thanked heaven for those years at the Manse, but not unnaturally she added that if George Ripley of Brook Farm and others, who owed her Nathaniel three times the amount of his debts, had paid up, this catastrophe would never have come to pass. "It is wholly new to him to be in debt, and he cannot 'whistle for it,' as Mr. Emerson advised him to do." [3]

With remarkable and admirable promptitude Frank Pierce and Horatio Bridge came up to Concord to see their old friend and to inquire what could be done for him. Is it to be wondered that in later times Hawthorne stood by the hated ex-President Pierce and snapped his fingers at the intellectuals? Though Pierce and Bridge were men of very limited wisdom, they were the most steadfast friends one could wish for.

The Democrats were in; the Whigs out. Polk, the most feeble president of Democratic views with the possible exception of Pierce (both were men of no recognizable personality), was in Washington preparing his list. Bancroft had got into the Cab-

[3] An obvious misquotation. It was the creditors, not Hawthorne, who were to do the whistling.

inet; and O'Sullivan of the *Democratic Review,* who owed
Hawthorne money, could be expected to worry both Bancroft
and the President into working the Spoils System in Hawthorne's favor. It must be remembered that in the days at the
Custom House in Boston Hawthorne had done nothing to
endear himself to Bancroft. Polk had possibly never heard of
him. Bridge, seeing that in order to gain the attention of the
party Hawthorne would have to leave Concord, asked him to
come to stay with him in order that he might introduce him to
Democrats of importance. Hawthorne obediently went, and
he enjoyed himself. For once in his life he knew exactly
what he wanted; he wanted to be made Postmaster of Salem.
O'Sullivan in Washington, however, discovered that Bancroft
thought the existing postmaster too good a fellow to be ousted
by the Spoils System. Wouldn't it be an admirable plan for
Hawthorne to go to China as a consul? And for some days at
least Hawthorne thought he was China bound. But all plans
went awry for a time, and Hawthorne returned, penniless and
despondent, to the Manning house in Salem.

Behind the scenes there was working on Hawthorne's behalf
a man who was to become famous later as a member of Lincoln's
party; a man, however, whom Lincoln had no cause to love;
a man who held in contempt such men as Bridge and Pierce,
not only because he was then a Conscience Whig and they
were Democrats, but because he had a natural and simple superiority over such men. The man was Charles Sumner. He
knew perfectly well that he was inviting a snub when he wrote
Bancroft's wife his appeal on Hawthorne's behalf, but he had
no hesitation in making the magnanimous gesture. The letter
will be quoted almost in full, partly because Hawthorne's biog-

raphers have either ignored or made light of Sumner's generosity, partly because he should be given credit for doing what his conscience prompted him to do.

To Mrs. Bancroft

Boston. Jan 9th 1846.

You will think that I never appear, except as a *beggar*. Very well. I never beg for myself. But I do beg now most earnestly for another; for a friend of mine, and of your husband's, for a man of letters, of gentleness.

I have heard today of the poverty of Hawthorne. He is very poor indeed. He has already broken up the humble and inexpensive house which he had established in Concord, because it was too expensive. You know how simply he lived. He lived almost on nothings; but even that nothing has gone.

Some of his savings were lent to Mr. Ripley at Brook Farm; but he is not able to repay them, and poor Hawthorne (that sweet, gentle, true nature) has not the wherewithal to live. I need not speak of his genius to you. He is an ornament of the country; nor is there a person of any party who would not hear with delight that the author of such Goldsmithian prose as he writes, had received honour and office from his country. I plead for him earnestly, and count upon your interference to keep his name present to the mind of your husband, so that it may not be pushed out of sight by the intrusive legion of clamorous office-seekers or by other public cares.

Some post office, some custom house, something that will yield daily bread—anything in the gift of your husband—or that his potent influence might command—will confer great happiness upon Hawthorne; and I believe, dear Mrs. Bancroft, it will confer greater upon you; feeling as I do, that all true kindness blesses him that bestows it more even than it blesses the receiver.

I wish I could have some assurance from your husband that Hawthorne will be cared for. . . .

I wrote to your husband lately on peace; but he will not heed my words.

Believe me, dear Mrs. Bancroft

Yours sincerely $\begin{cases} \text{providing you do not} \\ \text{forget Hawthorne} \end{cases}$

Charles Sumner.[4]

(The reference to peace had to do with Sumner's opposition to the Mexican War and to the policy of the new "war-hawks" such as Bancroft.)

Bancroft—brilliant but flamboyant—with Sumner's letter before him, could not resist the obvious temptation. Here was Sumner of all men—a Conscience Whig, one who put down much of the unhappiness of the state of affairs in America to the Jacksonian Spoils System—pleading to get a Democrat into a job! "I am so glad," he wrote sarcastically, "you go for the good rule of dismissing wicked Whigs and putting in Democrats." It was a cheap joke; but he did get Hawthorne his job as Surveyor to the Port of Salem. Hawthorne, however, had to wait for it.

[4] *Life and Letters of George Bancroft,* by M. A. De Wolfe Howe. Scribners, 1908.

10

Decline and Ascent

THE Concord period was over. Not even the difficulties of the last year there could diminish the wonderful peace and happiness of the other three years. Hawthorne had fallen on bad times. Viewed from the darkness of mental and domestic poverty which he was now experiencing, the golden sunshine of Concord appeared in exaggerated brightness.

When he returned to Salem, his first task was to prepare a collection of the pieces he had written at the Manse; he added one or two older ones, wrote a preface, and sent the whole off to his publishers. *Mosses from an Old Manse* was to be his third volume of short stories—his third and, as he stated publicly, his last. He changed his mind later about that. The statement is important only because it shows that Hawthorne, then one of America's most successful writers in that genre, intended to turn mind and hand to some other form.

That he enjoyed writing the preface, so very interesting as autobiography, is clear. It is far and away the best of the whole book. The excitement over Transcendentalism was dying down. The fire was not as bright as it had been, though the ardor of each individual member of the Club remained, of course, as strong as ever. To find a dig at Mr. Emerson and his friends would be amusing to many of his New England readers. His publishers, therefore, might well have been pleased with these topical and personal *obiter dicta*. But it must be doubted whether they were equally well pleased with his self-criticism at the end of that preface or with the disparaging things he found to say of the book which he was inviting the public to buy and which his publishers had agreed to publish at their own expense. As a writer of what would now be called "blurbs" for his own books Hawthorne was unique. We can like him very much for his honesty—sorry though we may feel for his publishers. But wasn't Hawthorne carrying his honesty a little too far? Some of his friends, competent critics, thought that he was. Their complaint was that he took his readers much too much into his confidence and so, being a writer of fiction, exposed the artificial limb, which he had made, without its trouser. He exposed his own deficiency as a craftsman. The intimacy which he tried to create between himself and his readers was of precisely the wrong kind. Over and over again he tells the reader: "I had the material; I am a trained workman; but what I have produced is not as good as either you or I had expected."

The roots of this false attitude toward the reading public are to be found in the biographical facts. Hawthorne was a teller of tales, and in the days of his complete obscurity in the upper room in the Manning house he imagined that he would read the tales to a few selected friends. No such friends existed. Later when his work began to appear in magazines he liked to think that some few of the buyers of those magazines would read his particular contributions. His circle of invisible friends widened. But when his work appeared in book form, his readers seemed to become fewer; their scarcity was evinced by what Hawthorne wrongly considered the poor sales of his collected short stories. He knew he had done good work. He refused to realize the smallness of the New England market. And he could not, poor man, have imagined that his *Twice-Told Tales* would have a steady if slow sale for more than a century and would continue to sell to this day. He was humiliated by his lack of success. And he consequently addressed all too intimately the unknown who were known to like his work. That this position was fast deteriorating into a literary trick must be admitted.

One may doubt too whether he was wise to confess to his limited public that at Concord he had achieved nothing more than in the past. It was quite true; but they might have been left to find it out. Without those last paragraphs of the preface the book would have been accepted as an interesting if not particularly promising indication of the author's development. What had been expected of him was a novel. And there was no novel. "These fitful sketches, with so little of external life about them, yet claiming no profundity of purpose,—so reserved, even while they sometimes seem so frank,—often but half in earnest, and never, when most so, expressing satisfactorily the thoughts which they profess to image—such trifles, I truly feel, afford no solid basis for a literary reputation."

There was another and even more unfortunate last paragraph in a letter written immediately after the publication of the new book. Hawthorne addressed his letter to Mr. Edgar Allan Poe, whom he did not know personally, and invited him to give the book a notice. He began well enough: he just mentioned the fact that the book was out and then wrote a paragraph of adequate and effective praise of Poe's work as a writer of tales. (No one at the time was talking of Poe's poetry.) Then came that disastrously honest last paragraph: he had to warn

Poe that he thought very little of him as a critic. The result was inevitable.

Poe happened to be the best-known professional critic of contemporary literature in America. He had invented a style, tabloid in its compactness, which has been imitated in America ever since. Poe recognized Hawthorne's genius and was constantly asking young James Russell Lowell (who acted as his intelligence officer in New England) about Hawthorne's work and what he had for sale. Hawthorne's letter seemed to be an invitation to say what he thought of the new book. And he said it. "Let him mend his pen, get a bottle of visible ink, come out from the Old Manse, cut Mr. Alcott, hang (if possible) the editor of the *Dial* and throw out of the window to the pigs all the old numbers of the *North American Review*. Let him beware of becoming an imitation Tieck." Parenthetically it must be admitted that the comment was not original: Poe himself had been accused of imitating Tieck; and as *Feathertop*, which is indeed something of a crib, was not published until 1852, Poe probably relied on a story—the gossip of Lowell perhaps—that Hawthorne was trying to learn German with the aid of primer, phrase book, dictionary, and *Die Vogelscheule*.[1] Let him above all remember, said Poe, that *The Pilgrim's Progress*, an overrated piece of literature, was as a literary form quite fatal to imitators. To employ allegory as Hawthorne was employing it was nothing more than an attempt to hint at a meaning which he himself was unable to express in plain English.

Poe when he hit a nail on the head hit it very hard. His aim was sure, his hand strong. Yet in all probability such criticism

[1] See Randall Stewart, p. 321.

does less harm to an author's reputation than the unfortunate hyperbole of an over-enthusiastic Herman Melville.[2] Exaggerated praise can make both its author and its recipient look very silly.

Hawthorne was in a very difficult position. While his important friends were pulling strings in Washington, the local committee of the Democratic Party had been going quietly about its business, and having completed its list of applicants, had sent it on to the Senate. There was therefore no hope at all of Hawthorne's getting employment in Salem unless one of the applicants were to retire in his favor. As all were poor men, this was much to ask. If Hawthorne were to get the surveyorship of the Salem Custom House, then a man called Lindsay must retire. Lindsay at first refused but eventually a Mr. Mullet (the hero of the hour) persuaded him that they should both withdraw. They were both employed by Hawthorne afterwards as his inspectors. It had been a complicated bit of local political jobbing, so that when Mrs. Hawthorne wrote to her mother (March 23, 1846), "This morning we had authentic intelligence that my husband is nominated, by the President himself, for Surveyor of the Custom House," she was either ignorant of what had been going on or was using her vivid imagination to satisfy her pride. Not a word about poor generous Mr. Mullet who had to wait thirty-seven years for anyone to come to ask him for his story and fifty years before his generous action was recorded in print.

Hawthorne was now secure for three years or, as he thought,

[2] Herman Melville, who did not know Hawthorne at that time, conceived an exaggerated admiration for him because of *Mosses from an Old Manse*.

Nathaniel Hawthorne, 1846. From a Crayon Drawing by Eastman
Johnson in the Longfellow House, Cambridge

for as long as he liked. The work was uninteresting, but it was light, for the Surveyor was only expected to do half a day's work. His companions in the custom house, with the exception of poor Pike, were depressingly uncongenial. But security of income meant much to him. If he were to write to the best of his abilities, he must be relieved of the tension of earning the price of the baby's milk and their own meat and vegetables by his pen. Or so he believed. Yet the truth was that something always prevented Hawthorne from combining the salaried job with successful creative work as an author. To add to his difficulties the housing problem became acute. As soon as his post in the custom house had been secured, the Hawthornes left the chill atmosphere of the old Manning house and went to live in Boston. This plan no doubt suited his wife who had the Peabody homing instinct, but it added two journeys a day to his working hours. Returning home in the afternoon he had little inclination to do more than attend to a few domestic duties and play with the children.

They moved again, back to Salem, where they took a house so small that Hawthorne's own writing desk had to be in the nursery and consequently was never opened. He became a nursery maid and rather liked it. Next they moved to No. 14 Mall Street, an enviably large house, all the windows of which faced south, a house with a shaded yard or garden in which Julian's carriage could be left with complete security and in which Una could play. Hawthorne's mother and two sisters, the three recluses, came to live with them but caused no inconvenience. They had their own rooms and remained in them.

Yet even here the custom house officer could do no work on his return from the office until he had taken time to become thoroughly familiar with his surroundings. He took on the duties of organizing the lectures for the local lyceum, which would seem to have caused him considerable trouble. The lyceum or lecture society movement then some twenty-five years old was in its heyday. Lyceums existed in every small town of the Northern States and in many of the Southern States too. The system was typically American, democratic and admirable. Just as distinguished members of the medical profession of today are called upon to give their services to hospitals, so in the middle of the last century men with any claim to intellectual superiority were expected to give addresses to the lyceums. They were a severe tax on the powers of the old, but they provided the young with an excellent chance to be heard and known. James Russell Lowell and Oliver Wendell Holmes traveled far and wide as coming young men; they received their expenses and a small fee and they got to know their country well. Emerson, it is said, had he accepted all the invitations to address the members of lyceums, would have had to make an address every day of the year. The members of these clubs wished to hear all sides to all questions; consequently Alcott was received and listened to in towns where the collegiate and religious authorities would have liked to pillory him. Since they were not debating societies, a member who disapproved of what he had listened to could go home and grumble alone but could not engage the speaker in a controversy; for the speaker was the guest of the lyceum. A wide variety of subjects was essential to a lively interest among the members. Lowell on the poetry of Keats suited some. The colossal Webster on the Constitution pleased others. The job of organizing these lectures in Salem fell upon Nathaniel Hawthorne. It was the only volunteer work he was ever known to undertake, and it was no sinecure; but it did in all probability widen his understanding of human nature. In a small way, too, it was good publicity for him. To that, however, he would never have given a thought.

Came the year 1849 and more elections. The Democrats were out. The Whigs were in. A certain amount of apprehension among Democrats holding small offices was only natural. Whatever the Whigs might say about the Spoils System, the fact remained that a great many Democrats did go out whenever the Whigs came in. Hawthorne, however, considered himself perfectly safe. It was known that he had not got his surveyorship as a reward for past services to his party but because of his services to American literature. Though it had been the gift of a Democratic government, it had been obtained largely because of the plea of Whigs—such Whigs as Sumner. He must, he told himself, be perfectly safe because Zachary Taylor, twelfth President of the United States, a distinguished general of the Indian campaigns and latterly one of the two army commanders of the Mexican War, had definitely stated that he would not dismiss Democrats from the Civil Service unless they had either been found incompetent or had used their official position to assist the Democratic Party machine in the elections. General Taylor was a Whig, it was true; as a party man he was not much more ardent than Hawthorne. Or so Hawthorne thought. He was doubly safe in his surveyorship, he considered, because he had found out that quite a number of Whigs in Salem were for him. So Hawthorne continued to go down to the custom house as usual, did his three-and-a-half-hours work, returned home for luncheon, played with the children, and then went upstairs to write.

It never seems to have occurred to him that the local committee of the Whig Party in Salem might do what the local committee of the Democratic Party had done three years before: prepare their list of recommendations for appointments to put up to the Senate and ignore the very existence of Nathaniel Hawthorne. Among the offices for which they recommended their followers was the surveyorship of the custom house. It was undoubtedly sly of them not to mention who the existing Surveyor was. Had Washington been told, Hawthorne would probably never have been removed. But since they were not told, the Senate had no grounds for objecting to the Whig nominee.

When Hawthorne heard the rumor that he was possibly going to be turned out of his office, his indignation was of that righteous kind which burns into a man's soul and inflames his mind. And at that fever pitch he began to fight a desperate rear-guard action. There were many of both parties who rallied to him. But once again Time and the Party Machine were working to the tactical advantage of the enemy. Why did they wish to turn out such a distinguished son of Salem from a position which he so obviously needed? And how could they justify their attempt to get rid of him when the whole nation had read President Taylor's conditions for removal, without the proof of which no Democrat was to be displaced by a Whig? Such were the questions his friends put to the local committee. And unwisely certain members of the committee, though there was no need for them to do so, answered those questions. They said that his close association with the *Salem Advertiser* was proof of his activity as a political propagandist and that his political bias could be shown by his dismissal of two inspectors because of their unwillingness to support the party with subscriptions. Hawthorne's work for the *Salem Advertiser* had in fact consisted almost entirely of literary criticism. The two inspectors were suspended (not dismissed) because of seasonal inactivity in the port. Hearing of this, Hawthorne, with no court to appeal to, fired his already overheated mind with ideas of revenge. To Longfellow he wrote: "If they succeed in getting me out of my office, I will surely immolate some of them." Longfellow may have remembered how the young Hathorne of Bowdoin days was considered a dangerous youth when angered. Perhaps, Hawthorne wrote, it was his notice of *Evangeline* [3] in the *Salem Advertiser* which these blockheads of county politicians had read as political propaganda? To his wife's brother-in-law, Horace Mann, he wrote a letter of appeal and explanation, most of it pompous and official, in which, however, there occurs a most un-Hawthornian threat: "I shall do my best to kill and scalp him in the public prints; and I think I shall succeed." The man in question was a Mr. Upham.

For long months hope alternated with despair. And then at last one day the new Surveyor came down to the custom house, carrying his commission in his hand. The early hour at which Nathaniel returned to his house was a sign which Sophia understood: he had been sacked. The blow had fallen. She said that she was glad—happy that it was all over at last. She showed him a few dollars she had been able to save out of his salary. She told him not to worry; to go up to his workroom, put on the

---

[3] The story of which Hawthorne had given to Longfellow.

Moscow green dressing gown with the penwiper she had made for him attached to the lining, and write.

And he wrote as he had never written before. He had two children and a wife to keep. O'Sullivan who had failed him at the last crisis now came forward with one hundred dollars on account. And Hillard began to go round with a hat collecting donations for a distinguished man of letters in distress.

It was just at this time—in July, 1849—when his difficulties appeared to have reached their height, that his mother became suddenly and desperately ill; and he realized that she was about to die. So to a mind already overwrought with the tempers and disillusionments of political squabble and laden with the uncertainty of the economic future, there was added the emotional strain of a deathbed scene. Even more distracting perhaps was his attempt to find in his own mind an excuse for the life his mother had lived and to understand the love that he still had for her. A more worthless and useless life, except that it produced Nathaniel, is difficult to imagine. By her example her two daughters, Elizabeth and Louisa, the former a very keen intellect, had shut themselves off from all social and practical relationships with the rest of mankind. That her son had not followed suit was in no way attributable to the mother's realization that her ways of life were wrong. She had allowed him, too, to hibernate for twelve long years—years which now horrified him when he looked back on them. Would he now admit, at the hour of his mother's death, the unhappiness her perversity had brought to the lives of others?

He came near to it, worked round it, but could not bring himself to any definite expression of criticism. He was deeply

moved by the condition of his mother. He had not expected
to be; for there had always been, he says, a sort of coldness
between them, ever since he was a small boy. But looking down
upon her, now that she was about to pass out of his life forever, he was reminded of the sort of life she had lived. "I kept
filling up, till for a few moments, I shook with sobs." She could
not have been brought into the world for this, only for the
experience which she had had. There must be a rebirth; "otherwise it would have been a fiend that created us, and measured
out our existence, and not God. It would be something beyond
wrong—it would be an insult—to be thrust out of life into an-
nihilation in this miserable way." His mother's life and death
only confirmed his belief in what may be called his *looking-
glass* philosophy; he believed that what we call reality is only
an image of an image, and that in a future life or lives we will
come directly face to face with reality, and so understand.

During these long days of his mother's illness, so unaccustomed had he been to visit her, that he seems to have gone into
the sickroom only three times. Not so Sophia, who, because of
the hopelessness and helplessness of her two sisters-in-law, Elizabeth and Louisa, was on duty night and day for the best part of
a week. The two recluses could only stand and stare. But
Sophia, whom these two women had a few years before considered physically unfitted to contract marriage with their beloved brother, now had to support their mother's body with
one arm and with the other whisk away the buzzing flies from
the dying woman's face.

Meanwhile downstairs on the ground floor Hawthorne was
left to look after and amuse the children. A more macabre scene

is difficult to imagine. It must be explained that though the mother and the sisters had maintained no daily contact with Nathaniel and Sophia during their residence in Mall Street, the children had been received into the rooms of the recluses and were welcome. They therefore knew their aunts and grandmother better than might be supposed. There came a day, however, when Nathaniel refused to allow his children to visit those rooms, because he considered that the three recluses were physically unhealthy and that it was unhygienic for young children to be with them. This order had so outraged Elizabeth that she was never seen again as long as it remained in force. The order was rescinded when Madame Hathorne first became ill but had to be reimposed when their grandmother's condition became critical. Their interest in all that was happening in the sickroom was increased by their being forbidden to enter it. They seem to have had not only phenomenal memories for dialogue overheard, but vivid imaginations concerning what was being done in the sickroom. Unable to take part in the drama upstairs, they acted it as a theatrical performance downstairs for their own, rather serious, amusement. Una was now dying grandmamma, now the doctor. The parts had to be interchangeable, for each child thought that he or she could play it better. And they acted before their father. It is not difficult to imagine how the strain of this play added to his already hyperemotional condition. He sat in the corner and recorded their words and actions in his journal. He must not reprove them. To do so would be to besmirch their innocence by making an ugly reality of the struggle upstairs; he knew, but they should not, that death was anything but a peaceful passage from Earth to Heaven.

Fate had been unkind. It is difficult to imagine a more inopportune moment for Hawthorne to undergo this additional and almost insufferable strain. It so happened that at that time he was engaged upon two works both of which by their nature were emotionally disturbing and both of which became, owing to his mother's death, topically significant: *The Scarlet Letter* and *The Custom House*. Both were intimate documents though of a very different kind. Both were family documents in different ways. *The Scarlet Letter*, the writing of which upset him more than that of any of his other works, was fiction; but it was also an attempt to solve the problem of conscience posited two centuries before by his ancestor William Hathorne—the problem of the Puritan suppression of all opposition. Hawthorne was the direct descendant of the principal persecutor of the Quakers, he was hypersensitive to the idea of the decline and fall of the Hathorne family, and he was never really able to dismiss the story of the witches' curse. The death of his mother —the last of the Hathornes—occurring when it did, only added a dreadful poignancy to what he had been writing. At this time too he was either writing or turning over in his mind that revenge he was going to have on his native town for his removal from the surveyorship. The family of Hathorne had lived in Salem for two centuries, almost since its foundation, and now he, Nathaniel, was about to shake the dust of Salem from his shoes. He was to renounce his townsmen as he believed they had renounced him and leave his native place forever. There before him on the bed, breathing heavily as death approached, lay his mother. When death should come to her the last link with Salem would be broken.

Madame Hathorne died on July 31, 1849. Nathaniel was so

upset that he retired from the view of his family. He was distraught, unnerved.

The date of his mother's death marked the lowest point to which the graph line of his fortune was to fall. For several months it remained at that low level. Though depressed he was industrious, remaining within his workroom many hours of each day. Then suddenly the graph line took an upward turn, then soared, climbing to the peak of his career. Within six months he was acclaimed in America; within two years his name was as well known in England as it was in his own country. If ever an author was saved by a publisher, hooked out of a slough of despond, it was Hawthorne. And the name of the publisher was James Fields, junior partner in the firm of Ticknor, Reed & Fields, known for short as Ticknor & Co.

James T. Fields was a publisher of genius. Born the son of a sea captain, he had entered the famous Old Corner Book Store, on Washington Street, Boston, as the youngest assistant. Rising to a junior partnership in the firm, he not only added luster to its already lustrous name but enlarged its activities so that it became the most famous publishing firm in America. He did more. He may be said to have introduced into the United States what seems to us today a *sine qua non* of publishing: he secured for the firm the loyalty of a number of young authors, printing their books at the firm's risk and loyally supporting their reputations and fortunes both at home and abroad. All this was entirely new to America. An author wishing to publish anything more serious than sentimental or exciting fiction was expected either to pay the printer's bill or to raise money by subscription to cover it. The publisher was primarily a bookseller—a wholesale bookseller perhaps. His list consisted

James T. Fields, Nathaniel Hawthorne, and William Ticknor.
Copyright by Harper and Brothers

mainly of reprints, pirated editions and works published at author's risk. The great burly, cheerful young son of a Portsmouth sailor changed all that. His firm must pay royalties or a cash sum down to distinguished foreign authors; for he argued that otherwise his chosen group of brilliant young Americans could never expect to be paid in England. His senior partner Ticknor, who was known just as well in England as he was in New England, retained the bookselling mind, which was probably a very good thing for the fortunes of the firm. James Fields was more versatile. An article written by Fields was always sound and always original, and the activity of publishing and selling never damped his ardor for literature. He could make men read because of his love of reading. And he could make men write their best because of his love of good writing. The Old Corner Book Store had been famous before his time, but in his time it achieved a genuinely international reputation. There, behind the green curtains, Fields used to sit—a big, happy man dressed in tweeds with a bushy beard. With apparently no difficulty at all he gained the sympathy of the useful and yet without insult or offense managed to keep the useless away. Works submitted were handed over to Whipple, the firm's senior reader. And Whipple's judgment was, if more severe than that of the firm, very sound.

As one writes of Ticknor and Fields welcoming the elite of the English-speaking literary world at the Old Corner Book Store, it is impossible not to think with some compassion of Elizabeth Peabody who by now was welcoming all the cranks who could not get a hearing in Washington Street. The Old Corner Book Store and its clientele constituted a grave temptation for the Peabodys to break the Tenth Commandment.

When Emerson visited West Street he found adulation. When he went to look at the books or have a talk with Fields in Washington Street, he found that he was a very considerable man in the eyes of those who knew personally the giants of literature of their day. Which was the greater compliment or the more attractive atmosphere? As Ellery Channing had told Hawthorne when he came unexpectedly to see him in Salem, Emerson was now a man of the world, was worldly wise as well as full of spiritual wisdom. The dotty and the disorientated were no longer as welcome as before.

When Fields, the intimate friend of both Thackeray and Dickens, called upon Hawthorne (he happened to be in Salem with an hour or two to spare), he was well aware of what he was doing. He had known Hawthorne's work for some years and had met him. He had done something at least to protest against the removal of Hawthorne from his office. More important, he had made up his mind that Hawthorne's name should now be included in Ticknor & Co's list; and he had come after manuscripts which he believed must exist. He found Hawthorne in his workroom crouching over the stove. He found him, as he had expected to find him, depressed. He told Hawthorne that now if ever, was the time to publish, and Hawthorne drearily asked who would publish; for he believed himself to be the most unpopular author in the United States. Fields was prompt in his answer. He would.

Still huddling over the stove, Hawthorne told Fields that he had written nothing worth publishing; in fact he had written hardly anything at all. Fields pointed to a cabinet, telling Hawthorne that he believed there was a manuscript within it which he should see. Looking at his watch he found that he had only just time to catch his train for Boston. Further argument and persuasion were impossible, and Fields took his departure. Two seconds later Hawthorne went running after him with a packet of manuscript in his hand. "How did you know?" he asked Fields. So Fields went scurrying to catch his train with *The Scarlet Letter* under his arm. He read it in the train. He read it all night. And next morning he was back in Salem. So began that happy association and that friendship with both Ticknor and Fields which was to last throughout Hawthorne's life.

The enthusiasm of James Fields for *The Scarlet Letter* was beyond the belief of the author. Seldom can an author accept a publisher's advice for alteration of a work already complete, not because he does not see the publisher's point, but because the relief of finishing a piece of creative work brings with it a powerful, an almost physical, deterrent to remaking something which bears the stamp of finality. Yet this James Fields was able to make Hawthorne do. He was able to prevent Hawthorne from publishing *The Scarlet Letter* as a long "short" in a collection of shorts. Here was a manuscript which with some enlarging and development could and must stand alone. Such was the enthusiasm of Fields for the manuscript in his hands that for a moment Hawthorne could not believe him. Realizing then that Fields meant what he said, he agreed to do as he was bid and to get on with the alterations; for both were anxious to advance the date of publication as much as possible. He pleaded for the retention of his introduction and, surprising though it may seem to us, Fields agreed. The introduction was *The Custom House*. It stands today without alteration as it was written for quite another book, that volume of short stories of which the first version of *The Scarlet Letter* was to be one.

As an introduction it makes nonsense; it is saved from the ridicule of the reader only because the great strength of the work which follows so overpowers it that its very existence is forgotten when the tragic tale of *The Scarlet Letter* is finished.

But to the people of Salem, and especially to the Salemites employed in the custom house it was difficult to get beyond the introduction, difficult to bother even with the first page of *The Scarlet Letter*. For by then they were so enraged with the author that it was more satisfactory to go back to page one and get the full flavor of the insult. Hawthorne had had his revenge. He had smitten the Salemites—or at any rate a few of them. It is really questionable, however, whether he made any serious effort to hit those who had harmed him; for he singled out for attack only the very effete old gentlemen who had been his associates in the custom house and left untouched the Salem Committee of the Whig Party who had turned him out of his office. However that may be, the very urbanity of his prose, the explanations to the reader that what he was writing must not be taken for fiction but as autobiography, and the control which he maintained over his sentences so that no one outside the borough of Salem would suspect his malignity—all this only added to the exasperating effect on those readers who "knew."

And this he attached to what is perhaps the most remarkable book he ever wrote. The success it received was deserved; for it always has been and probably always will be considered one of the greatest works of fiction of its period. Its one technical fault, which is immediately recognizable—that of overstressing the symbolism of the letter *A*—may have been caused by the known difficulties of enlarging a finished work. Once the pattern is formed, one may elaborate but one cannot really alter.

In spite of minor faults of construction, however, *The Scarlet Letter* clearly bears the stamp of genius. The continuous drive of Hawthorne's plot, for one thing, is an example to all those who would emulate him in his profession. And he achieves supremely the inevitability of great fiction—that quality which, according to Henry James, elicits the reader's unhesitating assent when he closes a book. James Fields' opinion—there was no time to consult Whipple or his partner—was once again proved sound. With the firm of Ticknor & Co. behind him, Hawthorne was a new man.

11

Lenox

WHILE still remaining within the Commonwealth of Massachusetts, the Hawthornes were to go as far away from Salem as was geographically possible. In October they had begun to look for a house somewhere in the Berkshires, preferably in the neighborhood of Lenox; but it was not until six months later that they discovered the little Red House on the Stockbridge Bowl. They moved in during the month of May, 1850. The delay which Hawthorne, eager to be away from Salem, had found so tiresome, was a blessing in disguise. Had he moved westward in October, he would have arrived at his new abode a disgruntled man still sorely injured by the treachery of his fellow Salemites, an author of short stories who must wearily sit for hours at his writing table in order to earn the dollars required for the maintenance of his family, a writer appreciated by a discerning few but ignored by the wider public. During the delay in finding a suitable house a great change had come over his fortunes and an equally great change had been made in him as a man. *The Scarlet Letter* had been published; he had an excellent firm of publishers supporting him; and the work which he had written had so touched the hearts of many of its readers that the author of it received something more than good notices—the sympathetic and friendly approach of unknown men and women in considerable numbers to express

Nathaniel Hawthorne, 1850. From a Painting by C. G. Thompson

their thanks and to do simple homage. Hawthorne was surprised and touched. He warmed to the enthusiasm of others, though he could not recognize his likeness in the gloomy and conscience-stricken man of his unknown correspondents' imaginings. So unrecognizable did he find their "portrait of the author" that he came to the conclusion that *The Scarlet Letter* was not "his" sort of book at all—an opinion he only changed late in life. He did not feel at all like the tragic figure conceived by those who did not know him but who read what he wrote. There must be something, therefore, very wrong with the writing—or so in his new mood of self-confidence he was prepared to argue. On the whole it was stimulating to reach so many and to stir them so profoundly; one got such queer letters —many of them written by lunatics and not a few by criminals bent on confession. All these he promptly destroyed. It is inconceivable, however, that he did not answer most if not all of them.

The little Red House on the slopes of the Stockbridge Bowl contained more rooms than its primitive architecture seemed to make possible from an outside view. Sophia and the children liked it at once. Hawthorne never pretended to be more than relieved that at last he had a roof over his head. It was all very well for Sophia, writing an enthusiastic account of it to her mother, to describe the boudoir, the parlor and the dining room and all the bedrooms. The number of rooms was sufficient. It was their size that failed to come up to his requirements. But it was summertime. Until the cold weather came again he would be unlikely to engage upon any very serious literary task, he being a cold weather writer. The smallness of the rooms would not trouble him for some months to come. He would devote himself to what was fast becoming his favorite occupation—to play with his children, to observe and record their every action. For weeks he led a happy, indolent, open-air life. Though the summer climate of the Berkshires did not come up to his expectation (it was either hot and sultry or damp and chilly; there was not the baking heat of the Boston-Salem seaboard to which he was accustomed), it had to be admitted that the humidity caused those ever-changing atmospheric effects which made the panorama from the Red House so attractive. The lake was beautiful and an excellent place to take the children to play; but it was not, of course, the sea. It hadn't the right smell at all. The neighborhood, however, had great advantages over most others—the lake, the woods, the view southwards to Rattlesnake Hill and Monument Mountain, with occasional glimpses of the Taconic Range; and there was for Hawthorne the ever attractive idea that within a few miles of where they lived the country looked as wild as he could wish. Wild it was to the west, but only the west; for at all other points of the compass the countryside might be expected to harbor the residence of a contemporary celebrity. Sophia had not buried herself in the country. Her neighbors were just as enthusiastic over Flaxman's drawings as ever she was.

During the summer months that part of the Berkshires which lies between the Housatonic River and the hills, from Pittsfield on the north, through Lenox, to Stockbridge on the south, was the home of a remarkable number of literary men and women, all of them eminently sane. The great distance from the cities of the seacoast preserved the district and its celebrities from the attention of cranks. Anyone like a crank or anything cranky was frowned upon in the land of the Sedgwicks, and the Berkshires were Sedgwick country; of that there was no doubt at all. There were Sedgwicks in Lenox and Sedgwicks in Stockbridge. Miss Catherine Sedgwick, the daughter of a Theodore, the sister of a Theodore and the aunt of a Theodore Sedgwick was the *grande dame* of the Berkshires. She was a woman of greater intelligence than the reader of her novels of New England life, so very popular in their day, might suppose. Living in New York during the winter months, she moved to the Berkshires in the summer; and many moved with her. It was she who introduced her great friend, Fanny Kemble, to the district, and the impulsive Fanny fell in love with the town of Lenox and its neighborhood; while Lenox, though shocked by her manly behavior and her manly trousers, fell in love with her. Then there was Sam Ward, the New York banker and patron of letters, now a near neighbor of the Hawthornes. Ward was the common denominator of Lenox, Concord, Cambridge and New York. He was the intimate friend of Longfellow; he was the "friend" to whom Emerson had addressed his *Letters to a Friend;* he had paid for and in part edited Ellery Channing's poems; and with his simple habits and friendly ways he had become an indispensable member of society in Berkshire county. Sam Ward must be on every picnic. The children adored him.

Pittsfield, the county town, had at one time belonged entirely to the Wendells (it had once been called Wendellboro); and it was not surprising to find there in the long vacation Dr. Oliver Wendell Holmes, who had built himself a house on what was left of the family property. For seven happy summers Holmes lived at Canoe Meadow, planted a hundred trees a year, and became a familiar figure in the local towns on market days. To

Pittsfield too, came Longfellow and Charles Sumner. They stayed at the old Melville house which was now a guest house. At Arrowhead Herman Melville, combining agriculture with intensive literary production, was still willing to entertain his guests with stories of the South Seas—stories told and mimed. But in industry no one could rival the Englishman, G. P. R. James, whose output of fiction and other literature has perhaps never been equaled—one hundred novels, twenty-six volumes of history and an unknown number of pamphlets and articles. He had arrived in America to take up the position of British Consul in Massachusetts, and, in spite of his rather dull wife, when he came to the Berkshires the Sedgwick group accepted him as one of themselves. He soon got to know Hawthorne. One day, in the midst of a terrific storm, when Sophia was away and Hawthorne was alone at the Red House with Julian and Mrs. Peters (the colored servant), the Jameses paid an unexpected visit. Thundering knocks on the door announced the arrival of Mr. James, Mrs. James, two sons, a daughter, a maid and a coachman, all seeking shelter. To this large party Hawthorne was forced to play host, which he seems to have done with admirable grace. Though he sincerely hoped that this sort of thing would never happen again when Sophia was away (luckily Mrs. James was so frightened by the storm that she was speechless), Hawthorne warmed to James. Not so his young son, who took an instant dislike to the English novelist and wrote disparagingly of him when he grew to manhood. Hawthorne became almost welcoming in his attitude to strangers and acquaintances. To entertain was still a great strain; but he could do it now.

To no one in Berkshire did the coming of Hawthorne mean so much as it did to young Herman Melville. Melville was thirty years of age: Hawthorne was forty-six. Though the story that it needed a storm which sent both of them to take shelter in a cave to make conversation between them possible is almost certainly apocryphal, it illustrates well enough how the eagerness of the younger man may at first have been frustrated by the technique of the older man's reserve. Melville had to run Hawthorne to ground and corner him in a cave before he would make friends.

That Hawthorne meant more to Melville than Melville meant to Hawthorne cannot be denied. Melville had been one of his greatest admirers for some time; had written most eulogistic criticisms of his work—even ridiculous eulogies, some thought; and had expressed the fear that he might never have the luck to meet him. The news that Hawthorne had come to live at the Red House on the Stockbridge Bowl, an easy ride or drive from Arrowhead, excited him. And it so happened that he was not in the least disappointed in his author when he met him. The quiet charm, the lovable nature, the somber beauty of the expression and even the reticence of the man attracted Melville as he had been attracted only by one other.

Having met him, Melville warned Hawthorne that there was not the slightest use in trying to prevent him from coming over occasionally to the Red House or from talking when he got there, or from writing letters to him when he had returned to Arrowhead. The talk could be all one-sided, and the letters need not be answered. But talk and write he would and must; and did. Difference in age, differences in temperament precluded the possibility of complete friendship. But Melville was a dear fellow, told the most amazing stories of his adventures, and was so simple in his ways that he was no trouble about the house at all; the children adored him and on a picnic or excursion there was no man like him. And what a prose style the young man had! Melville need not worry. He was most welcome.

The careers of two authors living at the same time in the same country could not have been more strongly differentiated. Melville was fifteen years younger than Hawthorne, had already gained all his practical experience, and for the past six years had been climbing high on the ladder of literary success. Melville was cramming all his experience and his literary work into the first thirty to thirty-five years of his life. He was at this time writing *Moby Dick*, his supreme achievement. Hawthorne had done little but write since he was a child. His experience was not practical but observational. He did not write a full-length work of fiction until he was a middle-aged man, and the wider knowledge of men and affairs only came to him after his belated success. He continued to write until within two years of his death. The graph lines of their literary experiences make interesting comparisons. Hawthorne's line was long and it rose very gradually during a long twenty years. Climbing suddenly with the publication of *The Scarlet Letter*, it remained for a number of years at its apex. It was non-existent during his years in England and Italy, but with *The Marble Faun* it appeared again slightly below the top mark, continued there for two years, and then suddenly dropped to zero. Melville's line was a short and brave curve, like the curve of a great wave, and like a wave it broke and spread out flat, never to rise again. Melville and Hawthorne had this in common, that both based their fiction on a reserve of specialized knowledge. Melville's was practical, visual and exotic: Hawthorne's was obsessional, observative and narrow. And both were much affected by the early death of a father, a loss which was not compensated by transference of affection to a mother.

Nearly forty years of life remained to Melville. He became as reticent as Hawthorne was in his youth. He did not choose to talk of his South Seas experiences. He found refuge at last in a custom house where he spent nineteen years, forgotten by all except a few friends. And when he died he was almost as obscure a literary figure as was the Hawthorne who had been "backed" by Bridge and "discovered" by Miss Elizabeth Peabody.

When the summer was over the more distinguished of their neighbors packed up and went back to the cities of the coast. Oliver Wendell Holmes took a last look round Canoe Meadow, a last jaunt to the local market, just one more walk along the banks of the Housatonic River and then boarded the train for Boston. Soon the students of the Harvard Medical School would hear his asthmatic wheezings as he came up the stairs to lecture on the bits and pieces of a body they had just cut up; they would wait for the new joke or for the repetition of an old favorite and soon forget their tiredness and the unhealthy atmosphere in which they worked, as they listened to Holmes on anatomy. No one was a more popular lecturer either in the classroom or in the lyceum. Too tender-hearted to make a successful general practitioner (because excesses of distress brought on his inability to relieve the suffering of his patients) Holmes was happy as Dean of the Faculty and Lec-turer on Anatomy. He was passionately interested in his subject. He was known of course to be an amateur of letters. What more natural than that a man so witty and so happy in making the adroit comment should amuse himself and others by writing occasional verses and occasional articles. That he could write admirably for scientific journals would have been expected of a man so excellent as a lecturer and so keen on his work. But that he was to have a second career and a great success as an author—as the "Autocrat"—was as little in his mind as in those of his literary contemporaries.

The country squires and the holiday-makers retired. Melville and Hawthorne sat down before their writing tables. Melville had got in his crops, and Hawthorne had that autumnal feeling which meant work. He was engaged on the longest and per-haps the most popular book he was ever to write. In November he reported to his publisher and friend Fields, "I write dili-gently, but not so rapidly as I had hoped. I find the book re-quires more care and thought than *The Scarlet Letter;* also I have to wait oftener for a mood. *The Scarlet Letter* being all in one tone, I had only to get my pitch, and could then go on interminably. Many passages of this book ought to be finished with the minuteness of a Dutch picture, in order to give them their proper effect. Sometimes, when tired of it, it strikes me that the whole is an absurdity, from beginning to end; but the fact is, in writing a romance, a man is always, or always ought to be, careering on the utmost verge of a precipitous absurdity, and the skill lies in coming as close as possible, without actually tumbling over."

The last sentences are too important as criticism to be passed

over without comment. It may seem a strange ambition to
finish with the "minuteness of a Dutch picture" a work written
while one is "careering on the utmost verge of a precipitous
absurdity," but this is precisely the nature of Hawthorne's
genius. When we talk of the "three American *novels*," we must
remember that he never considered himself a novelist, though,
strangely enough, he would have liked to be one. Anthony
Trollope was a novelist. "Have you ever read the novels of
Anthony Trollope?" he asks Fields. "They precisely suit my
taste: solid and substantial, written on the strength of beef and
through the inspiration of ale, and just as real as if some giant
had hewn a great lump out of the earth, and put it under a glass
case, with all its inhabitants going about their daily business,
and not suspecting that they were made a show of." Hawthorne
was a romancer, and what he wrote were not novels but
romances. The word *romance* presents certain difficulties to us
because of its modern association with sentimentality and the
happy ending. Nothing ever turned out completely well in
Hawthorne's fiction. His inherited Calvinism could be trusted
in long works to keep in hand any tendency toward sentimentality.

Anthony Trollope returned Hawthorne's admiration in full
measure and found it hard to understand how he turned the
trick; how, that is, he could write fiction so impressive yet so
weak in construction and so far removed from the logic of
reality. Hawthorne's finished work might well be called ingenuous. But somehow it was original, inimitable, moving. His
naïveté of vision combined with the high polish of his prose to
produce a strange subtlety. And the slices of realism, with all
the "minuteness of a Dutch picture," were lifted from the

Notebooks and made to serve the purpose; they lent the solidity of granite to a construction all lightness and purity in its conception. The construction was imaginative and it stood solid.

The writing of the *Seven Gables* went on apace. By January 12, 1851, he reports that it is "so to speak, finished; only I am hammering away a little on the roof, and doing up a few odd jobs, that were left incomplete." By the end of the month the precious manuscript had been put into the hands of the expressman at Lenox, and Hawthorne was writing to Fields warning him that it had been dispatched and reminding him that there was no copy of it. "If you do not receive it, you may conclude that it has miscarried; in which case, I shall not consent to the universe existing a moment longer." He was very pleased with what he had written. Of that there seems no doubt. But he was afraid that "it has undoubtedly one disadvantage in being brought so close to the present time; whereby its romantic improbabilities become more glaring." The book pleased his publishers and it pleased the public—or all but a few. Of those few one became a source of persistent irritation to him. This man wrote sorrowfully to Hawthorne accusing him of defaming the name of his grandfather, whose name happened to have been Pyncheon, who happened to have been a judge, and who had lived at the time of the Revolution. "The joke of the matter is, that I never heard of his grandfather, nor knew that any Pyncheons had ever lived in Salem, but took the name because it suits the tone of my book, and was as much my property, for fictitious purposes, as that of Smith. I have pacified him by a very polite and gentlemanly letter." Or so he thought. Others claimed that their relations had either been libeled or made

The House of Seven Gables, Salem, Massachusetts. Copyrighted by the Brooklyn Institute of Arts and Sciences, 1913

ridiculous. There was a squabble even about the house of the seven gables. Salem, in spite of Hawthorne's great success with *The Scarlet Letter*, had not forgotten *The Custom House*. The Salemites—and it is not altogether surprising—were still suspicious.

The completion of *The House of the Seven Gables* was a memorable event in his life, not only because he had finished his first long work, but because in doing so he had used up material which had been on the table for many long years. The inevitable fall of all proud families—a theory of history proved by his own family—had now provided the subject for one of his major works. The story of the curse on the Hawthornes had been used, too. Finally in his portrait of Judge Pyncheon he wreaked that revenge on Mr. Upham of Salem which he had intended to take but which he had been unable to fit into *The Custom House*. Other old themes and theories too, were given a place in the new romance. He would now start afresh—if that in fact is ever possible.

Meanwhile Mrs. Hawthorne had given birth to another daughter, Rose, her third child.

Another summer came. The children wanted amusing. He was only too glad to amuse them, for the shores of the lake were very pleasant, and he never expected to do any serious work in the hot weather. But he did. Playing with Julian and Una inspired him. He wrote the *Wonder Book* for them in a month. If this successful and almost forgotten book for children had a subject which was not inspired, namely the tales from Greek mythology twice-told in the Hawthorne manner, it did happen to have great topical significance. For the mothers and fathers who would buy the book for their children were at the time much interested not only in the classics as literature but in the lives and local conditions of those who had written them. Flaxman's drawings in reproduction were the rage. Plaster casts were in demand. The intellectuals were diverting the attention of the educated New Englander from exclusively Christian and Renaissance writings and iconography, and introducing Greek mythology as a subject which, considered afresh and with sympathy, would throw light upon the nature of the spiritual world. But in this "movement" Hawthorne, needless to say, had no part whatsoever. He had noticed how young Herman Melville could rivet the attention of children by telling them tales of his personal experiences (which Hawthorne could not do) and had wondered whether in fact the experiences of gods and goddesses and of all those who had suffered because of their peculiar behavior would not interest children as much as Melville's tales of the South Seas. The *Wonder Book* was such a success that only the fact that Hawthorne repeated the form in the larger *Tanglewood Tales* explains the obscurity in which it now rests.

He was also to write at this time another manuscript in which he displayed his interest in children. *Twenty Days with Julian* was never meant for publication. It began no doubt as a father's accurate account of a child's behavior during his mother's absence. Mrs. Hawthorne and her two daughters left him to visit her mother, Mrs. Peabody. When she came back she would want to know how Julian had behaved. She would have a full record of their doings. He became determined to identify his thoughts and behavior for twenty days with those of his son. He became an accurate observer and recorder of the daily life of a child and consequently wrote an interesting manuscript. Alone with Julian for many hours a day (the colored servant slept out and attended only to household work), he put him to bed in a cot alongside his own, he got him up and washed him, he tried to keep him amused during the long summer hours of daylight. At night he stayed awake wondering whether Julian was asleep. He paid no attention to what the boy ate, except when the rumblings of his stomach, coming from the cot, warned him that he had unwisely eaten a lot of unripe fruit. But this was of no importance beside the fact, immediately recorded, that on waking, the frightened Julian was quite unaware of the source of the noises. Hawthorne was as surprised at this as he was to discover that Julian was much more anxious over the prospects of their pet rabbit, which they were about to give away because he made too many messes on the carpet. The effort to participate fully in the daily habits and thoughts of his son was not perhaps entirely successful, but it resulted in some interesting pages of observation, many of which have recently been restored to their original state after the expurgations of Mrs. Hawthorne.

After he had been left alone so long with Julian, the return of Mrs. Hawthorne and his daughters made Hawthorne aware, painfully aware, of the smallness of the little Red House. It would not do at all. Pike had been asked to look out for a small property on the coast (for Hawthorne had a hankering for the sea) but had found nothing to suit. Fanny Kemble's suggestion that they should move into her house—which had the same number of rooms but larger—had been considered and turned down. The truth was he detested the climate of the Berkshires, so damp and uncertain in summer, so arctic in winter. The work which he must soon begin (*The Blithedale Romance*) was already prepared and he must get settled somewhere—anywhere but in the Red House—before the winter set in. For this reason he agreed, in desperation, to move his family to the house in West Newton, vacated because Horace Mann and his wife (Sophia's sister) had taken up their residence in Washington in order to attend to governmental duties.

12

West Newton

No one had a good word to say about West Newton. It was Boston's most unpopular suburb. Whereas several suburbs could be described as being "by the Charles River" there was only one way to describe West Newton: it was "by the railroad"; and well did the inhabitants know it. The unattractiveness of the suburb to which he had come was of no serious importance to Hawthorne. He was only occupying the Mann house while he looked for a place to buy in the country—no one in New England would wish to move house in the winter —and while he wrote *The Blithedale Romance*. The winter's work was well in hand even before he decided to move to the Boston suburb. He had begun by borrowing from Mr. Tappan of Tanglewood, the landlord of the Red House, a collected edition of the works of Fourier—a strange set of volumes to find in a farm in Berkshire, but the winters up there were conducive to endurance tests in reading. That Hawthorne read these books from cover to cover is beyond the realm of possibility. No one "got stuck" sooner than did he when he attempted to read even a famous work of literature. No one ever was more honest in his refusal to continue with a book which irritated him. And Fourier's writing irritated him beyond endurance.

That he should have thought it necessary to consult the

works of Fourier before writing *The Blithedale Romance* seems strange. Brook Farm only became a Fourierist Phalanstery after he left. The new book was to be based on his own experiences at Brook Farm. Why then bring in Fourier? One reason may have been that, determined as he was to show his disapproval of Ripley's institution and of all institutions which resembled it, he found that the Phalanstery, as an exaggerated type, lent itself well to satirical treatment. But though the references to Fourier in *The Blithedale Romance* had their place in the finished work, they were of small importance. The outline of the story was conceived at the Red House; the writing was done at West Newton. Between the two events many changes had to be made.

Topographically he was well located in West Newton. For if he wanted to rub up his memory of scenes and places Brook Farm was within walking distance—a long walk admittedly.

During the actual writing of *The Blithedale Romance* two women and one man—Margaret Fuller, Fanny Kemble and Ripley—were for some obvious reasons and for some intimate and private reasons very much to the fore of his mind. It would have been impossible to have used the community of Brook Farm as material for a novel without thinking of Ripley and Margaret. And at the time he imagined the character of Zenobia, it would have been difficult for him not to think of Fanny Kemble. *The Blithedale Romance* might have been written in her house in Lenox. Hawthorne's circle of female acquaintances was small; and even if it had been large, Margaret Fuller and Fanny Kemble were women of such strong personality that they would have made their mark. That Fanny Kemble had no connection whatsoever with Brook Farm or with the lives of

Ripley or Margaret was of no importance. She had become one of the most vivid presences in his imagination.

To some the revisiting of Brook Farm, the deserted colony to which he in small degree and others so strongly had pinned their faith, might have been a dismal experience. But not to Hawthorne. The passages in *The Blithedale Romance* which directly refer to community life as he knew it at Brook Farm are written amusingly and with evident enjoyment; knowing what had befallen Ripley, Margaret Fuller and the community, he would hardly have found such pleasure in the work if he had not considered it completely fictional. And no doubt it was. For though many of the discussions and the arguments are realistic and some of the incidents are transcribed from his note-books, the story is entertaining and in large part fantastic.

Fortune had seemed to smile benignly on Ripley, but it was only a passing glance. When he sacrificed security of income and popularity as a preacher to undertake the foundation of the colony of Brook Farm his thoughts were wholly absorbed by one idea. Had he been the "man of adamant" whom Hawthorne describes at Blithedale he would never have met failure in the manner he did. With the strongest possible views on equality and broad-minded opinions in matters of religion, he found all ideas of leadership, dictatorship and censorship foreign to his mind. Ripley and his devoted wife could advise, persuade and recommend. They could not and would not command, order or ordain. Strongly though he held his own views, as a true and peace-loving democrat he was always prepared to admit that others might hold views antithetical "to his own and to respect them so long as they were truly democratic." Consequently when an energetic group of his members were anxious and even resolute, to the point of threatening secession, to turn his colony into a Fourierist Phalanstery, he agreed that this should be done, though he doubted its advisability. What had been initiated as a novel scheme of American living became an unaffiliated branch of the Frenchman's group movement; it was democratic, but political and foreign. Ripley was thereupon deserted by some of the finest characters who had believed in him and had come to live around him.

From that moment a series of disasters overtook the Ripleys. The Phalanstery was burnt down. Brook Farm went bankrupt. The Ripleys were penniless. For a time Sarah, the dear, good and much beloved Sarah, managed to keep the two of them alive by teaching school. Then Sarah died of an incurable disease, and Ripley went to work for Greeley on the *New York Tribune*, for him who had been one of Boston's most popular preachers, this was the dreariest of bread-winning drudgery. He was, however, to succeed at last as a journalist and to become one of the founders of *Harper's Monthly*.

What Hawthorne was thinking of Margaret Fuller just then it is impossible to say. It is unfair to him to interpolate here, as others have done, those opinions of Margaret which he wrote years later when in Italy. At the time when Hawthorne was writing *The Blithedale Romance*, her friends, notably James Freeman Clarke and Emerson, were compiling her three-volume memorial. Living in West Newton, he was in and out of Boston all the time, and in correspondence with her friends in Concord; so that he must have known all or almost all that others then knew concerning her strange life in Europe. Margaret was dead. And she died not as Margaret Fuller but as the Marchesa Ossoli. She was drowned within a few yards of the American coast on her homeward journey, and her boy and her husband were drowned too. When the news of the disaster came to Concord, Thoreau had been sent off post haste to see if anything could be done. Nothing but the burial of a boy was of any importance by then.

Margaret Fuller had landed at Liverpool in August '46 and, chaperoned by a married couple, had set out to see the sights of the Old Country. The sights were all human ones. She did not want a guidebook to the most picturesque views in the Lake District; she wanted to see and talk with Wordsworth—which she did. And so on to Edinburgh where she had the fortune to have a conversation with De Quincey. In London Carlyle waited upon her. It was gallant of him to call upon the lady who had once been associated with that man Alcott—Alcott who had physically and economically shocked Carlyle by mixing boiled and buttered potatoes with the fresh strawberries he had bought for his vegetarian guest. After this incident Alcott became America's bogus *penseur*. There must have been something in Margaret Fuller that Carlyle really liked. He shouted her down, of course, which was no mean feat; for she herself had by then developed a technique of entering a conversation which had the metallic efficiency of a can-opener. Her other friend in London was Mazzini. On her last night in London— "I wish the last night had been more melodious"—she, Carlyle and Mazzini were alone together. In the presence of a Transcendentalist and a liberal liberator, Carlyle, who was then at the height of what we should call his Fascist-Nazi mood, was at his rudest. He called their liberal reforms "rose water imbecilities," praised the virtue of power, and advocated the use of dog collars for those who did not know how to behave.

Over to Paris. It was odd of the French not to understand her when she spoke their language, for she had taught French in America and was considered in America something of an authority on French literature. But they didn't. And she did not understand them very well either. So with that admirable perseverance which gained for her such success as she had in life, she took French lessons—she who had given them. But the lion-hunting spirit, which was by now very evident, could not be curbed by linguistic difficulties. She must meet George Sand. She wrote to her, and Madame Sand replied that she would see her. But such was Margaret's inefficiency in pronouncing her own name in French that George Sand said she had never heard of such a woman. The woman, being Margaret Fuller, refused to leave. George Sand opened a door, had one look at her and decided it could only be "the American." After that they got on very well together in their interviews. She was introduced to Chopin and he played for her and talked to her, both of which she enjoyed immensely. Being a feminist, she naturally directed most of her interest to George Sand, of whom she wrote ingenuously.

Only by a mistake of destiny had she been born to middle-class parents in New England. For it was perfectly obvious in her own mind that she should first have seen the light in some magnificent Italian palace. Her soul was Italian. She felt it; she had always felt it. Her meeting with Mazzini had confirmed it. Mazzini she found what quite obviously she had needed for many years. Emerson had been spiritual, good, impractical; but though he could shock a divinity school to the core, he saw no

reason why he should lead the whole of America to a better life.
Mazzini was more: he was a liberal with a national point of
view and a program of liberation. With her "Italian soul" and
her friendship for Mazzini, Margaret was in grave danger of
becoming mixed up in Italian politics.

And now at last she was off to Italy. After a brief sight-seeing
tour she settled in rooms in Rome, a spinster unprotected. But
already she had been picked up—there is no other word for it,
however gallantly it may have been done—in St. Peter's by a
young Italian. Him she secretly married and, more difficult still,
secretly had a child by him in a village in the mountains. And
so Margaret Fuller became Italian both in body and soul. She
was now the Marchesa Ossoli.

Mazzini's arrival in Rome in the spring of 1849 was an event
in her life of the greatest importance. What Mazzini thought of
Ossoli is not known. No man was, however, quite immune to
Margaret's enthusiasm, and that she was privileged to share the
secrets of Mazzini at this critical period of his career is a safe
assumption. One must admit that they were both quite ruthless
in using Ossoli, whose family was employed by the papal authority, as a spy. Suborned from his natural allegiance and
consequently ruined—if an Ossoli could be ruined—Margaret's
husband too became a liberator, and while Margaret tended the
wounded during the siege of Rome, he was at his post on the
ramparts. But at bottom Ossoli was fatuous, and in spite of
being a Marchese, he was bourgeois. It is, in fact, highly improbable that Mazzini knew or suspected that the young man
he met at Margaret Fuller's was her husband and the father of
her child, for it would have been inconceivable to him that the
brilliant Margaret should have married a man so stupid and so

commonplace. Only two people were supposed to have known her secret—one an American friend, the other the American Consul in Rome (whom she did not know); and she had told them because she thought that the parents of the child, then farmed out at Rieti, might be killed in the war.

It was time to escape, if she could, with husband and child. It was therefore necessary to write to her mother and sister, telling them that she was a married woman and that she was the mother of a child. She warned them that her husband was younger than she, that intellectually they had nothing whatsoever in common, that they would not be able to converse with him, that he had no money and could earn no money. But she added that *deo volente* they were coming home.

It was not easy to get Ossoli to go to America. The more violent a liberator she became—a defeated one, to be sure—the more excellent a Catholic he became. But at last they arrived at Leghorn and took passage in the *Elizabeth*, a cargo vessel which would be two months at sea. Ossoli was terrified. The terror spread to Margaret; but they sailed.

The crossing was fair, and then in sight of Fire Island a gale sprang up and the *Elizabeth* went aground. She carried, it is said, quantities of marble for the palace of a *nouveau riche*, and though she was a new ship, the cargo soon went through her bottom. After the twelve-hour agony which followed, only the body of Nino, the child, dead but still warm, was recovered. Of Margaret and her husband no traces were found.

It would have been almost impossible for Hawthorne in any event to keep all traces of Margaret from appearing in the character of Zenobia. If his work necessitated—as indeed it did —a female character who was a feminist, who would argue with

men on equal terms and who was a match for them in her learning—then Margaret was one of the two women he had known
who served the turn. And if Zenobia was to be clearly feminine
—in order that the inequalities of sex and then love might bring
her to disaster—he had seen the same tragedies in Margaret. But
that Zenobia committed suicide by drowning had little to do
with the facts of Margaret's life. For he had already stored up
in his notebook the record of a gruesome search for a body in
a river, and this, quite properly, he was determined to use.

But to make Zenobia complete he needed the experience of a
woman of charm, of beauty and of mature confidence in herself; above all she must be a healthy woman, exuberant in spirit
and in body. He had had such an experience in his brief friendship with Fanny Kemble. Released at last from her Irish-
American slave-owning husband, Pierce Butler—a narrow-
minded bully, who had suffered shame and embarrassment from
her love of life and her anti-slavery propaganda—Fanny Kemble was now "Mrs. Kemble." She was a great artist in her own
genre. By reading Shakespeare's plays to large audiences she
made them feel that the plays had been faultlessly acted before
them. She had in fact that rare power—the power of dominating
any audience and yet making herself loved. She was entirely
careless of what others thought of her. And though she broke
every rule of decorum, she could always prove that her way
of doing things was more sensible than other people's. She
proved, for instance, that to wear trousers in a boat when fishing was decent, by pointing out how very indecent the summer
costumes of the ladies of 1850 were after they had been im-
mersed in a lake. Americans took to her—all but Mr. Pierce
Butler. And she was one of the great money-makers of her time.

She made money and spent it. She hurried to make more; and gave much of it away.

When at Stockbridge Fanny Kemble had ridden up to the Red House and claimed Hawthorne as her friend. She had taken up his son before her on her saddle, had given him a good time, given everyone a good time, and then, entirely unimpressed by Hawthorne's reputation as a genius or as a recluse, she had ridden away. And when she went back to England she wrote to him. She wrote him that the pirated editions of his works were best sellers. She thought he would like to know that he was as popular as the Brontës.

Fanny Kemble meant well. But it was not very pleasant or very satisfactory to be reminded that after one had spent some twenty years at work with pen in hand, foreign publishers were gathering the fruits of that industry without so much as a word of thanks to the laborer. For until Fields arranged the simultaneous publication of *The Blithedale Romance* in England and in the United States, Hawthorne had not received sixpence from English publishers, whose practice was to buy a book in America and set it up in type in England, without at any time paying a commission to the author.

It seems possible or even probable that Hawthorne was surprised, on his return to the coast, to find the keen interest taken there in the career of Margaret Fuller. The death of an intelligent young woman under such tragic circumstances may possibly have been the talk of the Berkshires for a few weeks. But by the time Hawthorne went to live at West Newton, interest in Margaret had greatly revived in those circles he knew so well

—in Concord and Cambridge—because of the preparation of the three-volume memorial.

Though Zenobia was the most striking and original character he was to create, it may possibly have occurred to him that he was sailing a little too close to the wind. Some of the conversation was obviously Margaret's, some of the views held by Zenobia were clearly Margaret's, and it was unfortunate that Zenobia had in the story to be drowned. She had to be drowned if only because on re-reading his notebooks or journals he had found a stirring description of a search for the body of a girl who had committed suicide by throwing herself into the Concord River. This appeared, rewritten, in *The Blithedale Romance:*

"Come, then," said Silas, "but I doubt whether I can touch bottom with this hay-rake, if it's as deep as you say. Mr. Hollingsworth, I think you'll be the lucky man to-night, such luck as it is."

We floated past the stump. Silas Foster plied his rake manfully, poking it as far as he could into the water, and immersing the whole length of his own arm besides. Hollingsworth at first sat motionless, with the hooked pole elevated in the air. But by and by, with a nervous and jerky movement, he began to plunge it into the blackness that upbore us, setting his teeth, and making precisely such thrusts, methought, as if he were stabbing at a deadly enemy. I bent over the side of the boat. So obscure, however, so awfully mysterious, was that dark stream, that—and the thought made me shiver like a leaf—I might as well have tried to look into the enigma of the eternal world, to discover what had become of Zenobia's soul, as into the river's depths, to find her body. And there, perhaps, she lay, with her face upwards, while the shadow of the boat, and my own pale face peering downward, passed slowly betwixt her and the sky!

Once, twice, thrice, I paddled the boat up stream, and again suffered it to glide, with the river's slow, funereal motion, downward. Silas Foster had raked up a large mass of stuff, which, as it came towards the surface, looked somewhat like a flowing garment, but proved to be a monstrous tuft of water-weeds. Hollingsworth, with a gigantic effort, upheaved a sunken log. When once free of the bottom, it rose partly out of the water,—all weedy and slimy, a devilish-looking object, which the moon had not shone upon for half a hundred years,—then plunged again, and sullenly returned to its old resting-place, for the remnant of the century.

"That looked ugly!" quoth Silas. "I half thought it was the evil one, on the same errand as ourselves,—searching for Zenobia."

Though he had by now a number of already recognized portraits in his fiction, there was every reason for him, having imagined his incomparable Zenobia, to absolve himself in the eyes of his readers from any charge of using his friendship with Margaret Fuller as material for the new book. It may be said that he prided himself on his ability to hoodwink the public. No one could see into his mind. No one could suspect that his opinion of such and such a person would be revealed by reading his fiction, and he was indignant when anyone suggested that it could. With a rag soaked in aniseed he could divert the hounds from following the line of his fox. Bring Margaret's name into the book—and his friends would say that he had paid his respects to the memory of his dead friend. It was all a little too obvious to be convincing. One of the principal characters in *The Blithedale Romance* is Priscilla, a hollow-chested, frail and mentally undeveloped sewing girl who has mysteriously appeared at Blithedale from some workroom of sweated labor in Boston. "She reminded me of plants that one sometimes observes doing their best to vegetate among the bricks of an enclosed court, where there is scanty soil and never any sun-shine." And it was on this slip of a girl that Hawthorne was to hang the label of Margaret Fuller, Marchesa Ossoli, feminist, lecturer, friend of Mazzini, Emerson and Carlyle.

". . . it forcibly struck me that her air, though not her figure, and the expression of her face, but not its features, had a resemblance to what I had often seen in a friend of mine, one of the most gifted women of the age. I cannot describe it. The points easiest to convey to the reader were, a certain curve of the shoulders, and a partial closing of the eyes, which seemed to look more penetratingly into my own eyes, through the nar-rowed apertures, than if they had been opened at full width." Emerson would have recognized Margaret Fuller in the last sentence; but the reader does not recognize Priscilla. " 'Did you ever see Miss Margaret Fuller? . . . Because,' said I, 'you reminded me of her just now.' 'How,' asks Priscilla petulantly, 'could I possibly make myself resemble this lady. . . .' " How indeed?

Surprised though Hawthorne's readers must have been to discover that a sixteen-year-old seamstress had so forcibly re-minded him of Margaret Fuller, the reader of today, who buys *The Blithedale Romance* in a cheap edition, is even more mysti-fied to find Priscilla compared with a woman who to him is little more than the shadow of a shade.

By using material which was not yet a decade old, Haw-thorne set himself a problem, the difficulty of which he knew well enough. Since he had chosen Brook Farm as the *venue* of his characters, his readers might justifiably expect a satirical novel of contemporary manners. He had great gifts for satire, which are indicated in much of his shorter work. Those who knew the plan of the new book looked forward to an amusing account, by a writer of genius who had been at Brook Farm, of the cruel blows of fortune and the ridiculous and thoroughly impracticable experiments in agriculture carried on in that short-lived Utopia. The story of the romance would have to be controlled by the probability of what, even at Brook Farm, might have happened—which gave him latitude enough; and it would have to convince the reader that the author, from his own special knowledge, had seen men and women behaving and thinking in such a way at Brook Farm; which, again, would give him wide scope for idiosyncratic characterization.

To write such a book Hawthorne was adequately equipped and thoroughly competent. It was not, however, from Brook Farm that the essence of his work must come; but from himself. And while this honesty of creative effort gave him his greatest strength, it also produced the gravest disappointment among those contemporaries who were looking for the satiric thrust. For though in Zenobia he had imagined a character so personal and so individual that no reader could question the possibility of meeting her in the flesh, she was yet so exotic and strange in her thought and behavior that she was not at all out of place among the purely imaginative characters of his invention. For his wisdom and honesty in choosing to be himself and not a Brook Farmer throughout the pages of *The Blithedale Romance* we are thankful now. Those of his contemporary readers who knew nothing of Brook Farm—his English readers for example—could never know the temptations he avoided.

And though as time passed and the Brook Farmers were forgotten, the book received its due praise, Hawthorne's contemporaries in New England had certainly not got what they expected. Henry James (too close to those times and too close to the society in which Hawthorne lived) expresses this disappointment admirably. "I should have liked to see the story concern itself more with the little community in which its earlier scenes are laid, and avail itself of so excellent an opportunity for describing unhackneyed specimens of human nature." This personal regret is very natural. Being the son of his father, Henry James was keenly interested in the people of that place and time and consequently regrets that *The Blithedale Romance* is not more autobiographical. In this we can sympathize with James, though we may feel that Hawthorne's prestige as a novelist is raised by the very absence of the qualities he misses. "I have already spoken of the absence of satire in the novel, of its not aiming in the least at satire, and of its offering no grounds for complaint as an invidious picture. Indeed the brethren of Brook Farm should have held themselves slighted rather than misrepresented, and have regretted that the admirable genius who for a while was numbered among them should have treated their institution mainly as a perch for starting upon an imaginative flight." Brook Farm was indeed only a perch for an imaginative flight to Blithedale, and it would be hard to better James's description of the course of Hawthorne's mind as he wrote his third important work of fiction in a room of Horace Mann's house in the smoky suburb of West Newton.

James Fields, on a visit to England, sold the English rights of *The Blithedale Romance* to Smith, Elder & Co. for some two hundred and fifty pounds. Hawthorne as an author had passed into that select company whose works had to be paid for on both sides of the Atlantic, and in advance.

He was house hunting. Sophia wished to return to Concord. Well and good. There was no possible reason why Emerson, Ellery Channing and Thoreau should now admire him as an author more than they did when he had last resided in Concord. It was not unsatisfactory, however, to remember that when he had left the Manse he had been turned out of the place as much because of his penniless state as because the Ripleys wanted to return to their house. He did not expect to be any more appreciated in Concord, if he were to return there, because he happened to be at that time the author most esteemed by the public as a writer of American fiction. It was as unnecessary for him to praise Ellery Channing's poems *now* as it was for Ellery to praise his prose—even though Ellery was beginning to show some sneaking affection for it. To the highbrows of Concord, his success would remain inexplicable. But James Fields was collecting for him pirated editions of his work published in Europe; he had been advised that Hawthorne had already received Routledge's edition of *The Scarlet Letter, The Mosses* and *Twice-Told Tales;* Bohn's edition of *The House of the Seven Gables, The Snow Image* and the *Wonder Book;* and Bogue's edition of *The Scarlet Letter.* James Fields was asked to buy examples of the rest, particularly translations. For these pirated editions Hawthorne had not received one cent. They were, however, proof of his popularity. He returned to Concord, not a rich man, alas, but with money enough to buy a modest property and with an international reputation.

It was Ellery Channing whom Hawthorne asked to find him a house in or near Concord. Ellery replied that he was glad to note that Hawthorne had evacuated "that ice-plant of the Sedgwicks" (no love lost between Berkshire and Concord); he told him to come *instanter* because he was alone, because he had a good cook and some drinks; and he gave Hawthorne what he knew would be good news: "Emerson is gone, and nobody here to bore you." How pleased Hawthorne must have been that one of Emerson's greatest friends recognized that Emerson bored him! Channing was an even older friend of Sophia and would stand no nonsense; he did not care whether Sophia did read his letter—which she probably did. "The skating is damned good," and finally, "N.B. Pipes and old tobac no end." This was another "dig" at Sophia who so hated tobacco that for years Hawthorne had to go into the shrubbery to smoke. But times were changing: within two years of this letter a guest of Hawthorne suffered from a swimming head because of the strength of the cigar his host gave him.

Hawthorne because of literary work could not accept Ellery Channing's invitation. So a few days later he again wrote to him complaining that Hawthorne's refusal had gone astray; everything had been made ready and now all the fun was spoilt; he had countermanded his orders to the butcher and had had a row with his cook. Ellery was thoroughly put out. "But as you are sweating Romances, and have got that execrable bore, a small family, it is all right. I am glad *now* you did not come. . . . For my own part, I would infinitely rather settle on the icy peak of Mt. Ararat than in this village. It is absolutely the worst spot in the world. There are so many things against it, that it would be useless to enumerate the first. Amongst others, day before yesterday, at six A. M., the thermometre was ten degrees below nothing. That is enough." Why, Ellery asks, not go to live in Venice, Cuba, Málaga, Greece, or that almost incredibly faraway place, California? Why come back to Concord? And why, of all places, think of buying Alcott's "Hillside"? Could he conceive anything more awful than to be a member of Alcott's household when the temperature was below zero, sustained bodily by Alcott's idea of what a human being should eat and warmed by what Alcott believed to be a fire? But how Alcott, dear man, chose to live, was none of Hawthorne's business. The purchase of the Hillside might alter the Alcott standard of living. He would buy the Hillside and rename it the Wayside; but he would remain where he was until the late New England spring had thawed the ground. The climate must be kindly and comforting before he came to live in Concord again.

13

The "Wayside"

TAKING one child with her Sophia preceded Nathaniel to Concord; he was to remain in West Newton with the other two until the new house was in order. She put up at the Manchester Hotel and walked back and forth to the Wayside. The weather was, fortunately, extremely hot. "The cartman had tumbled all the wet matresses in a heap in the farthest corner of the barn, and I had them all pulled out to dry." That first day she worked hard and late. She was compensated however. "We set forth slowly village-ward, and met Mr. Emerson and Mr. Thoreau. Mr. Emerson was most cordial, and his beautiful smile added to the wonderful beauty of the sunset."

The quotation is from a letter written by Sophia to her mother, a letter from one "fan" to another. Hawthorne was not one to appreciate the glories of Mr. Emerson's smile; it may have had its magical influence, but not somehow on sunsets.

Nor were Sophia's judgments in other matters above reproach. "The carpet on the study floor," she wrote, "looks like rich velvet. It has a ground of *lapis lazuli* blue, and upon that is an acanthus figure of fine wood-color; and then, once in a while is a lovely rose and rosebud and green leaf." Taste in carpeting changes rapidly, as we know, but it is difficult to believe that her taste was good even for those times.

Then Hawthorne himself arrived and was delighted with the

change which had been made in the house since he had last seen it—when it was covered with snow and full of Alcott squalor. He pottered about, gave his approval to the hill behind and his piece of wood up there, and lazily considered problems of horticulture. The only field of any value was, somewhat disappointingly, on the other side of the road. But Sophia liked the road. Friends came in from it for a chat. Hawthorne detested chats, for most of the chattering community wanted to see *him*. The house, however, was most conveniently provided with a bunk-hole out of the back door and up the hill. The meadow when the grass was long was another hiding place. Sitting there one afternoon with James Fields and seeing one of the Concord celebrities passing by, Hawthorne said peremptorily, "Duck!" and forthwith spread himself on the ground. And the two of them lay there prone, shaking with laughter, until the celebrity's footsteps sounded faint and they dared to show themselves again.

If there are passages in Mrs. Hawthorne's letters to her mother which are hard to bear, it must be said in her defense that the approaches which Emerson made to her husband and the more than fulsome praise given to her son were enough to turn her head. We have to remember in Emerson's defense that the accounts of those conversations came not from Emerson but from her and that they were expressed in letters written by a daughter to her mother. Emerson's great love of children, though occasionally expressed in exaggerated terms, was no pose. His *Threnody*, his song of lamentation on the death of his first-born, a boy he greatly loved, is certainly the most moving and possibly the greatest poem he ever wrote. That the same man could have talked to Mrs. Hawthorne about chil-

Hawthorne's Home in Concord, Massachusetts

dren in the way she recounts and yet could have written the quiet and dignified words of the *Threnody* shows at least how much more expansive in everyday relationships the leader of American Transcendentalism had become.

There were many inconveniences in being the novelist of the moment in America, particularly for a man so shy; but they were in no small part counterbalanced by the paucity of admirers in Concord, even among Hawthorne's friends. But now that his reputation was so firmly established he would be able to live quite comfortably among the Transcendentalists. If he was much importuned by the visits of complete strangers there was quiet amusement to be got from the knowledge that Emerson had been importuned by a complete stranger, who begged him to obtain an autograph from his distinguished neighbor, Nathaniel Hawthorne. The future in fact seemed to be full of easy relationships. But that was not to be.

For the unexpected did occur. It was an event with which no stretch of the imagination would ever have connected the life and career of Nathaniel Hawthorne. On the twelfth of June, 1852, the Democratic national convention met at Baltimore to choose a presidential candidate for the November elections. In January of that year the committee of the Democratic Party in New Hampshire had approached Franklin Pierce to obtain his assent as a possible nominee. Let us not misunderstand this offer. It was a compliment to Pierce who had worked hard in and for his own state. He had been named a "favorite son" of New Hampshire by the Democratic delegates of that state. He thanked them from his heart but stated categorically that the *use* of his name "would be utterly repugnant to my taste and wishes." Pierce was an honest fellow and had given up politics for good. He did not therefore want to appear, even to please his local caucus, as an "also-ran" at the Baltimore convention; for he could not have believed that under any circumstances his name would command much of a following. Any votes he might hope for would be mere tactical moves in some major strategy, and he would be little more than a pawn. He preferred —and it was typical of him—to remain on the political chessboard of his own state. But as the time of the convention drew near, he had to admit that there was something to be said for entering a New England name in an election in which slavery and constitutional questions must be discussed. So the name of Franklin Pierce went down on the list.

Nothing went right in that convention from the first moment. Looking back upon those times it is easy enough to see that, though the two-party system must survive, those great problems of conscience which were to force Civil War upon the country ten years later were already breaking up old party loyalties and preparing for the new alignment of principles which was to result in what we now know as the Republican Party. But Whig was still competing with Democrat. And the Whigs were in as great a difficulty in their own camp as were the Democrats in theirs at Baltimore in June, 1852. Both conventions achieved a record in the number of ballots taken, the Democrats with 49 and the Whigs with 53. Because of sheer exhaustion of voice and body the delegates to a national convention must eventually agree on a candidate. More than thirty ballots were taken at Baltimore and nothing was proved, except that the favorites were out of the running. It was not until the thirty-sixth ballot that Pierce's name was so much as mentioned;

and then it was put forward by the Virginian delegation. Thirteen more ballots were taken, with Pierce, the unknown, gaining little by little, until at last the Dark Horse had won with 282 votes to 11. "Within an hour," Hawthorne wrote, "he grew to be illustrious." To this generous statement one can hardly give unqualified assent.

Having been nominated as the Democratic candidate "for the high trust of the President of the United States," Pierce handed himself over to his party organization for the duration of the campaign. Every device known to the publicity experts of the day was needed if this man, so patently honest but so remarkably colorless, were to make any impression on those who must choose in November between him and General Scott. Among the many set pieces of propaganda in a presidential campaign there had to be a life of the candidate, published at the party's expense and sold to those who would buy, given away to those who would not. The writing of such a life could best be entrusted to a political journalist; for, at least in the case of Pierce, a vivid imagination was required to cast a semblance of greatness or popular appeal around the life story of the Democratic candidate. It was to Hawthorne, however, that Pierce entrusted his work. A man more unsuited to the task it would have been impossible to find in America; a task more uncongenial to the author it is impossible to imagine. Though Hawthorne protested his unsuitability, Pierce insisted; and he could insist, for Hawthorne was sure to respond loyally and warmly to any appeal from one who had been his friend since the days at Bowdoin, when he was still Nathaniel Hathorne, the son of an obscure sea captain. Pierce had the mind of an insensitive lawyer (though he was known in polite New Hamp-

shire society as "the General"), and it would never have occurred to him that in commissioning Hawthorne to write this
biography, he was asking an author of genius to debase his
talents for political purposes. Nor does it seem to have entered
the mind of this Dark Horse politician, who was destined to
become President of the United States, that the publication of
the life would estrange Hawthorne's literary friends, complicate his domestic life, and embarrass him in his day to day meetings with the inhabitants of Concord.

Having undertaken the task against his own judgment and
will, Hawthorne went one step further and committed the fatal
error of treating it with great seriousness. After various members of the party had visited him in Concord to provide him
with the details of Pierce's personal history and to remind him
of the party platform, Hawthorne sat down at his table and
reviewed his material. Perhaps after all, he reflected, Pierce had
been right in asking a "romancer" to write his life. This hopeful
view was, however, immediately invalidated by his determination to write the truth and nothing but the truth. The book
was therefore certain to be boring. But worse, he determined
to tackle the slavery question in all honesty—a determination
which could have only one effect, that of alienating the friendship and respect of those who were in daily contact with him.
Of this highly complicated constitutional problem he knew
nothing—and understood less.

"What luck Frank has!" Hawthorne kept repeating. One
man's luck was to be another man's misfortune, but Hawthorne
was of course quite unaware of this at the time and seems to
have remained quite unaware of it until the day of his death.
His wife no doubt kept from him the adverse criticism ex-

pressed on all sides because of his acceptance of Pierce's commission. Only a few years had passed since even Whigs had been made furious by the action of a local Whig committee which had turned Hawthorne out of his job in the Salem Custom House because of his supposed affiliation with the Democratic Party. His friends had witnessed his magnificent wrath. They had listened to his scathing remarks about his fellow place-holders in the custom house. They had noticed his attack, in a book published the year before, on Mr. Upham. Yet within eighteen months of the publication of that book Hawthorne was to publish a political pamphlet expressly written for a presidential campaign. It was disappointing, to say the least, to those who had vouched for his disinterestedness in political matters. And it was cold comfort to those who read the Life to discover that Hawthorne had very little idea of what was happening in America.

1853 is the year of the great anti-climax before the Civil War. For the past twelve years anti-slavery leagues, composed of those who wished for some gradual elimination of slavery in the South, and abolitionist societies, which on religious and philanthropic grounds demanded immediate liberation of all slaves, had slowly but surely gained members in the East. The outcome was never in any doubt in Southerners' minds: the East would one day become anti-slavery to a man, and there would be a solid anti-slavery block in both houses of Congress. The Northern States of the Middle West would follow suit. The rights of the slave-holders (and they did consider them genuine rights protected by the written Constitution) could only be protected in one way. Since representation in the House was established on the basis of population, the attack on slavery could better be withstood in the Senate (where each new state meant two more senators) by increasing the number of states in which the holding of slaves was permitted.

As long as the new states were equally proportioned between slave-owning and non-slave-owning territory, the balance of power in the Senate would remain much the same. The reason the East was disgusted by the Mexican War was, partly at least, that Abolitionists and those opposed to the extension of slavery saw it as a deliberate attempt, engineered by Southern Democrats, to carve out new states below the parallel 36° 30″, which by the Missouri Compromise of 1820 was to mark the division between free and slave territory. States so created would be slave states, and they would soon be sending senators to Washington.

With the Mexican War successfully concluded and the cession of California completed in 1848, the South claimed that the line of 36° 30″ must be extended from Atlantic to Pacific—though no one in 1820 had thought of a United States which stretched from ocean to ocean. The extension of this line would run through California; and the people of California and the people of the East were determined that no slavery should be allowed in ex-Mexican territory. Something had to be done, for the South now threatened secession, a dreaded word in the American political vocabulary. So we come to the disastrous Clay Compromise of 1850. It was a compromise which can only be described as amoral, unless one considers it as an effort of the party in power, the Whigs, to defer civil war. For the South came to an agreement with the North that if California, in spite of the Missouri Compromise of 1820, were to be admitted as a non-slave state the North and the East must accept and put into unqualified operation the Fugitive Slave Acts. The Clay Compromise of 1850 should be examined by all those who are destined to influence, however temporarily, the political fortunes of democratic countries.

For what those Democratic giants Clay and Webster had thought "good enough" under the circumstances, had within two years completely shattered the Whig Party. When Clay and Webster died, just before the presidential election of 1853, they left behind them a leaderless party, discredited in the eyes of most of its supporters. Franklin Pierce was elected by a land-slide, but one must admit that he himself had little to do with his success. And one cannot believe that poor Hawthorne's Life gained a single vote.

Granted that Pierce's experiences and Pierce's character were deadly dull material for a biography, however short, it cannot even be admitted that Hawthorne did the job well. By his praiseworthy determination to face up to the slavery question he succeeded only in offending his friends and relations. Any schoolboy of today can make out a case for the slaveholders, but in order to eliminate the twists and turns in the road, Haw-thorne chose a dangerous short cut. Pierce, he said, as far back in his career as the time when he was a Representative in Con-gress, had "fully recognized, by his votes and by his voice, the rights pledged to the South by the Constitution. This, at the period when he so declared himself, was comparatively an easy thing to do. But when it became more difficult, when the first imperceptible movement of agitation had grown to be almost a convulsion, his course was still the same. Nor did he ever shun the obloquy that sometimes threatened to pursue the northern man who dared to love that great and sacred reality—

his whole, united, native country—*better than the mistiness of a philanthropic theory*." Such an expression was guaranteed to arouse the ire of his immediate circle and of his own relations. The only materials in the Life which he could make readable were Pierce's experiences, brief and gallant, in the Mexican War; but unfortunately the Mexican War, too, was taboo in Hawthorne's circle. His young friend Lowell had given succinct expression to Boston and Concord opinion in the Biglow Papers:

> Thet the war is a damned war, an' them thet enlist in it
> Should hev a cravat with a dreffle tight twist in it;
> Thet the war is a war fer the spreadin' o' slavery;
> Thet our army desarves our best thanks for their bravery;
> Thet we're the original friends o' the nation,
> All the rest air a paltry an' base fabrication.

Having described Pierce's unwillingness to enter the lists as a nominee—which might or might not have value in America as propaganda—and having told, with some truth, how he preferred his simple and honorable existence as a lawyer to any other, Hawthorne was ready for his peroration. "He comes before the people of the United States at a remarkable era in the history of this country and of the world." Very true, but what follows is certainly unexpected. "The two great parties of the nation appear—at least to an observer somewhat removed from both—to have nearly emerged into one another; for they preserve the attitude of political antagonism rather through the effect of their old organizations than because any great and radical principles are at present in dispute between them." Could a complete misunderstanding of the political situation be more clearly expressed? "The measures advocated by the one party, and resisted by the other, through a long series of years, have now ceased to be pivots on which the election turns. . . . And thus men stand together, in unwonted quiet and harmony, awaiting the new movement in advance which all these tokens indicate." It is not bad English, in fact rather good; as prophecy it is wildly improbable; and as a considered judgment on the political situation it shows only ignorance— the ignorance which is understandable and forgivable, the ignorance of contemporary affairs which was to bring him so much unhappiness.

This small but so uncongenial task put a great strain on him. It was undertaken because of his loyalty to his Bowdoin friend. But one hardly knows whether to pity Hawthorne or his wife the more. To be at once the sister of Elizabeth Peabody, the Abolitionist, and the wife of Nathaniel Hawthorne, the author of the *Life of Franklin Pierce*, was certainly to be placed in an uncomfortable position. The volumes of letters which she wrote to her mother are proof of her loyalty and devotion to her family. Sophia's natural political inclinations ranged her with the Conscience-Whigs. She admired Sumner greatly, and vigorously defended Webster. For she failed to understand the damage Clay and Webster had done in splitting the party of which they were the chief adornments, damage which resulted ultimately in the formation of the Republican Party. On Webster's death—which occurred during the months when Hawthorne was writing the Life—she would hear nothing against him and even tried to reconcile the differences between the parties by accepting Pierce as an heir to Webster's views! Meanwhile, the Peabodys were asking Sophia what on earth her husband had to do with the despised Pierce and why?

"It hurts me, dear mother, to have you speak of General Pierce as if he were too far below Mr. Hawthorne to have Mr. Hawthorne indebted to him. You judge General Pierce from the newspapers, and the slanders spread abroad by the Whigs to prevent his election. . . . If you knew the man as we know him, you would be the first to respect him. . . . He is a man great from the very moral force which Webster lacked. . . . He is a man wholly beyond bribery on any score whatsoever. As regards the stories of his intemperance, if he ever did indulge unduly in wine, he is now an uncommonly abstemious man. And it is a singular fact that this particular weakness does not debase a noble mind as other vices do.[1] When it rises above it, it rises without the stains left by other vices. My own experience, in my young girlhood, with the morphine that was given me to stop my headaches, has given me infinite sympathy and charity for persons liable to such a habit. But the greater a man's fault has been, the greater is his triumph if it can be said of him, as it can of General Pierce,—*now* he is never guilty of it.

"As regards the Compromise and the Fugitive Slave Law, it is his opinion that these things must now be allowed—for the sake of the slaves. One of his most strenuous supporters said that 'viewed in itself, the Fugitive Slave Law was the most abominable of wrongs;' but that it was the inevitable fruit of the passionate action of the Abolitionists, and, like slavery itself, must for the present be tolerated. And so with the Compromise,—that it is the least of the evils presented. It has been said, as if there were no gainsaying it, that no man but Webster could ever be such a fool as really to believe the Union was in

[1] Sophia was known to have a horror of alcoholism.

danger. But General Pierce has lately, with solemn emphasis, expressed the same dread. . . ." The whole of this paragraph consists of Hawthorne's own views, ultra-conservative views based in some measure upon his own boyhood impressions of the threat to the Union at the time of the Hartford Convention during the War of 1812.

His own sisters whom he seldom saw and with whom he seldom communicated seem to have taken a very sensible view: they did not worry much about his political opinions (with which Elizabeth had always been in disagreement) but feared that his friendship with Pierce might divert his attentions from his proper and important work—which was literature. Louisa felt it her duty to write to him. She had met a friend of Hawthorne in the streets of Boston who detained her to "recount the glorious career which was before you in the diplomatic line, if General Pierce should be elected; and he stopped me in the street next day to repeat the list of offices. I remember being Minister to Russia was one of them. I, not by any means thinking office the most direct path to glory for you, very coolly told him I hoped you would have nothing to do with it. I believe he thought I was very ridiculous." Her brother could then have replied that he had no intention of accepting anything from Pierce. He was to change his mind. Louisa's letter is something like a warning. Her brother was at the height of his powers. He must, she thought, and rightly too, be kept at his writing table.

The same letter had begun with other information: "Mrs. Manning is very ill and I must put off coming to you till next week." The letter is dated July 1st, 1852. Mrs. Manning having recovered, Louisa still could not go to the Hawthornes at Concord since she had to take another relation to Saratoga Springs. She would come at the end of the month.

On the morning of July 30, a tremulous and excited Mr. Pike arrived at the Wayside. It was an unexpected visit; but poor Pike was always welcome. Mr. Pike behaved queerly. Then he came out with the words: "Your sister Louisa is dead. On the Hudson, in the *Henry Clay*."

The mention of the *Henry Clay* was sufficient to convey to the minds of the Hawthornes the idea of a ghastly death; for the papers had been full of the tragedy. The descriptions of the scenes on board the *Henry Clay*, a passenger steamer on the Hudson River, when she burst into flames just before her arrival at New York, had horrified Eastern America. No one knew or had reported that Louisa was a passenger. When the tragedy occurred she seems to have preferred being drowned to being burnt alive, but whether she had been burnt or drowned Mr. Pike did not know. It was early morning when Pike arrived. The whole family sat down to breakfast; but Hawthorne, unable to control his distress, left the table, went to his study, closed the door and remained there alone for the rest of the day. Mr. Pike hurried away. Mrs. Hawthorne had some "lovely" thoughts about Louisa and her mother in Heaven, which she sat down to record in a letter to her own mother who was still on earth.

His life's path had been shown to him in retrospect most clearly by his work for Pierce. And now Louisa, that sister who had been his best ally when they were children, that sister of whom he had seen so little since he married Sophia, Louisa who had seemed to be leading a happier and more normal life since the death of Madame Hathorne, had been either burnt to death or drowned. So events combined to fix his attention on the happy period when he and Pierce were boys at Bowdoin and then on the records of their two lives, the paths by which they had come to what they were now—the one the Democratic candidate for the Presidency of the United States, the other a writer of fiction who after years of obscurity had become known to the English-speaking world. After writing three works of lasting importance, Hawthorne's creative imagination was slack. The relaxation of the creative imagination leads to day-dreaming; and day-dreaming on the themes of Louisa's death and Pierce's success may have led Hawthorne to morbid reflection upon his own dreary and lonely course through life. It is understandable that Pierce's life should have seemed to him a successful one. At an early age he was able to cover up failure at the local Bar by becoming one of New Hampshire's delegates in the House of Representatives; and he became a senator almost as soon as he reached the Constitutional age. He returned to his state, as thousands have returned from Washington, with all the prestige of the ex-senator and a good deal of experience in impressing men of smaller experience. He returned to the Bar of New Hampshire with little law perhaps, but full of the self-confidence which results from office-holding; and by a series of highly improbable events in a Democratic convention he was raised from aspirant to candidate. Lord Bryce classified him as one of the three most colorless candidates ever to have won a Presidential election. Yet his party swept the country.

"What luck Frank has!" Nothing could be truer, provided one was content to be a Dark Horse, brought out of the stable when all the favorites had broken their knees. Yes, Pierce had

had amazing luck. But that was no real reason for Hawthorne to be depressed with his own. His popularity as an author had risen remarkably, and he had gained a place in European literature. He was making money, and Fields in England was arranging that he should make more. Louisa's death, which affected him profoundly, came just at the wrong moment. For it reminded him of their unhappy childhood, and set him to remembering the gloom of things past.

Would the wagoner who had so obstinately refused to hitch his wagon to a Concord star hitch it up to the "lucky" star of Franklin Pierce? The very suggestion annoyed him. He had undertaken to write the campaign life only if it was plainly understood that he did so because of a friendship of thirty years' standing and not because he could be bribed by promise of office or any other kind of reward which the President would be able to make to a novelist.

On Monday, August 30th, 1852, Hawthorne left Concord for a holiday. He was alone. The relaxing climate of Concord, the tragic death of Louisa, and the knowledge that he was doing something which was offensive to the ideological principles of Sophia's friends, by whom he was surrounded at the Wayside, made a change of scene and a change of air very necessary.

"Left Concord at ¼ 9. A. M. Rainy all day. Staid in Boston ½ past 2; took cars for Portland, where being delayed several hours at Kennebunk, arrived at about eleven P. M. Next day, at about one, left for Brunswick. In the evening, went to Bath to get a bed. September 1st, to Brunswick again; left for Portland

at ½ past six; spent the evening with Pierce . . . ; next morning, left for Portsmouth, arrived there about eleven, rode over
with Pierce to dine at Rye-beach, and returned in the afternoon.
Spent the night at Portsmouth, and (Friday, September 3rd)
set sail, at about ½ past ten, to the Isles of Shoals.[2] This is not
an enlivening passage but it is an enlightening one. He went to
Brunswick to attend the semi-centennial celebration of Bowdoin; and though neither Bridge nor Pierce nor Longfellow
were there, though he describes the visit as a gloomy affair
(partly because when he looked at his class-mates, he realized
how "damned old" he had grown), he nevertheless was reminded of his affection for that small group of friends. Longfellow had ceased for some years to be an influence in his life.
Bridge was not a man who could influence anyone. The same
might have been said of Pierce before the Baltimore Convention, but now he could and did influence Hawthorne.

The more he saw of Pierce the more convinced he became
that here was a man of honor—no one doubted that—and a man
with great reserves of power as administrator and as leader of
a great political party. On such a subject the opinions of a
novelist who knew nothing of administration or political leadership had really no validity. Poor Hawthorne took his stand in
politics and then found both feet slowly sinking in a bog of
incomprehension.

Pierce liked him, admired him and was flattered by his willingness to work for his election. It must be noted here for future
reference that Pierce was beginning to watch out for him. Busy
man though he was, he went over to the Isle of Shoals to see

[2] *American Notebook*, 1850–53.

that Hawthorne was all right. He fussed over him, possibly because he saw that Hawthorne was tired; he sent him cigars; he sent him fruit, and was continually asking about him.

On the Isle of Shoals Hawthorne vegetated happily—if indeed one could vegetate on those barren shores. He crawled about the rocks like a crab, fished in a desultory crab-like way, and filled page after page with the most boring details of his island experiences. Pierce's name appears frequently in his notes, but there is no comment on Pierce as a man.

It must surely have been here that Hawthorne finally decided to brave the obloquy of his critics and the disappointment of his true friends and to accept, if Pierce should be elected, what he had sworn to refuse, an official position. It was still mere daydreaming, for we know that he thought Pierce's chances of winning the election small. Searching the ground of that rocky island for bait, he perhaps found it amusing to build legations in the air, to envisage himself as American Minister to the Court of the Czar or as the representative of the United States in Portugal.

He returned to the mainland, to Concord and to his family. Then the book came out.

There was only one thing for his Concord friends to do, and they did it; they ignored the very existence of the book. There were no awkward moments or embarrassing incidents. His sister, Elizabeth, so as not to offend him (she was a hard-bitten Whig of the old-fashioned kind) nobly asked him for some copies of the book to distribute to the country bumpkins among whom she was living.

Was Hawthorne really going to like living at Concord? It

must always have been a matter of serious doubt with him. And now that he had written the *Life of Pierce* would he want to? These questions cannot be answered satisfactorily. By October 18, 1852, that is to say before the result of the election was known, he was writing to Horatio Bridge that he thought he had done the job pretty well. He had not sent Bridge a copy, because it was not, of course, literature—a curious explanation; for though Bridge cannot be called an amateur of letters, he was one of Pierce's most intimate friends. Of the life, Hawthorne writes: "I was terribly reluctant to undertake this work. . . . Before undertaking it, I made an inward resolution that I would accept no office from him; but to say the truth, I doubt whether it would not be rather folly than heroism to adhere to this purpose in case he should offer me anything particularly good. We shall see. A foreign mission I could not afford to take. The consulship at Liverpool I might. . . . I have several invitations from English celebrities to come over there, and this office would make all straight!"

It is clear, therefore, that by October, 1852 he had made inquiries about the emoluments of various offices in the gift of the President. Should Pierce win the Presidential election, this letter in Bridge's hands would be in existence to show which office he would like. He had always wished to see England; he had always felt rather "out of it" when his friends talked of their European experiences; the expenses of the Wayside were troublesome; and his dear wife would no doubt be happy to leave even Concord if she could accompany him to the country where he could get even with the "scribbling sons of John Bull" and she could be an official hostess. The Liverpool consulate was an office the holder of which would almost certainly be able to save money. There was every reason, it seemed to him, why he should go.

But to uproot so native a plant and send it across the Atlantic was a dangerous experiment. "In a day or two I intend to commence a new romance, which if possible, I intend to make more genial than the last." That fourth American novel was never to be written.

As soon as Pierce became President-elect, he offered the Liverpool consulate to Hawthorne, and Hawthorne accepted. As such matters are arranged in the United States, the official confirmation of the appointment could not of course be made until the following March. The winter was his, and he spent it in writing *Tanglewood Tales*, for which tens of thousands of children have since been grateful to him. He added a classic to the bookshelves of children's libraries, and the writing of the book gave him enjoyment. He knew that he had done good work and for once was entirely satisfied with the manuscript even as he wrote the last line. He openly expressed his certainty of its success—in his life a unique avowal.

James Fields, returning from Europe, found him packing up for his four years in England and quite properly wondered whether Hawthorne would find happiness there. His partner Ticknor had advised Hawthorne to go. It was strange advice, particularly from a bookseller-publisher to an author whose work was selling in increasing thousands. There can be no doubt that from a business point of view Ticknor made a gross error of judgment. And one can scarcely doubt that had Fields been in America, he would never have allowed his author to be uprooted. A visit to Europe, which with his sales he would soon have been able to afford, was one thing; to become the American consul in England's busiest port was another. Hawthorne had detested his life in the custom house. Was it not certain that he would detest his life in the consulate?

The novelist must become a hard-working and practical man of business. The erstwhile recluse of Herbert Street must stand up and face the public of Liverpool as the representative of his country. He must attend banquets, eat city dinners, and make public speeches. The venture was, to say the least, something of a gamble.

14

England

THE great day came at last. The boxes were packed and ready. The good-byes had been said. The troublesome details concerned with leaving a small property recently acquired had been settled. Cash and letters of credit were in the pocket. And so the great adventure began. For to the Hawthornes this journey to England was a great adventure.

On a very hot morning in the first week in July, 1853, they took the train from Concord to Boston. That same afternoon they went aboard their ship, the *S.S. Niagara*, a paddle-steamer and the pride of the Cunard fleet. One member of the Hawthorne family was even more excited than the other, and, though Hawthorne tried not to be silly about it, it was impossible for him to conceal his good spirits. Fortunately for them, an old friend and much-traveled man, George Ticknor, was sailing on the same ship. There was no end to the questions which one and all of them wanted to ask and which the kindly George Ticknor could answer.

After calling in at Halifax for mail and passengers the *S.S. Niagara* headed due east across a calm and sultry ocean.

To appreciate all that Hawthorne was to write of England, to understand his opinions of the English and to sympathize with him in his pleasures and in his trials during the period of the Liverpool consulship, one must always remember what sort of a man it was that Franklin Pierce had sent abroad. As Henry James put it, Hawthorne "was exquisitely and consistently provincial." Perhaps a better word than "provincial" would have been "regional," which today as well as then describes much American thought. It is true that his life had been passed in what would correctly be called small provincial towns, but his culture and his association with his famous contemporaries and his mind could not be accurately described as provincial. Much of the charm and much of the interest of the fiction he had written resulted rather from the "regional" qualities of the material and the mind which turned that material into romances. The light which Hawthorne's intelligence could throw upon a problem was often very bright, but it always shone from one direction. The topography and history of his region colored his opinions always. He was often wrong. However observant he might be, there was always the chance that because of this concentration of light on one side of an object he would be led to rash deductions concerning the nature of the parts which were in shadow. Even national problems he could not see in the round, since he considered every problem from the position of the Northeastern States. In his written opinions of England, the curious angle of his vision and the slight distortion in it combined to make his criticism peculiarly interesting. He was often unjust, often childishly incorrect; none the less in passages of splendid prose he did reveal with his spotlight cracks and flaws in British opinion and behavior which the English themselves and their more cosmopolitan critics had apparently missed.

Hawthorne, however, was on his way to England not to make a visit of inquiry but to take up an official position in

Liverpool, the center of the *entrepôt* trade between the Old World and the New. For four years he would have to talk, work, live, and deal with Englishmen, the vast majority of whom would turn out to be far more provincial in their outlook than he.

As he walked the deck of the *Niagara* he must have thought much about his job. There is every reason to believe that his thoughts were wildly inaccurate. Of ships and sailors in port he knew much, after his custom-house experience. But of the other work in an important consulate in the 'fifties, of the atmosphere of a large commercial town, he knew nothing. In Liverpool he would associate occasionally with aristocrats, but more usually with mayors, merchants, and members of the chambers of commerce—many of them *nouveaux riches*—among whom a superfluity of food on the table and gross overeating (but not overdrinking) were the hallmarks of success. Yet Hawthorne had never attended a public banquet or an official dinner in his life. He had never made a speech or "dressed for dinner." And he had never known a rich man. His life and the lives of those around him at Concord and Lenox (not all of whom had struggled as he did to make both ends meet) had been simple; their houses and more especially their food had been good, frugal, regional. A feast to him meant the seasonal enjoyment of fruit, a delicious meal of vegetables, or at most the excitement of roasting a whole loin and leg of lamb. He drank wine, smoked an occasional cigar, and in general enjoyed the kind of comfort which one associates with a well-run English vicarage. Hawthorne's clothes were of the simplest and most serviceable material without any concession whatever to modern fashion. About Society and its ways he knew nothing and showed little curiosity. He had no proficiency in polite small talk, and his experience of "parties" was limited to the enjoyment of big picnics. His behavior and manners were traditional and re-gional; they were correct, they were formal, and with his good looks and magnificent voice, they were impressive. Behind this façade of regional American deportment there was a mind hypersensitive, hypercritical. It was improbable that Haw-thorne would be happy in Liverpool society.

More important still he had allowed his mind to play with an idea—an idea which to him was fascinating: He imagined that the old English tree had sent out its roots beneath the ocean bed of the Atlantic and had sprung up and flourished in New England. The old trunk had perhaps decayed; in England he would find signs of a new growth from other roots. And while he would be able to claim collateral relationship with all that had grown within the last two hundred years, everything older was as much his as any Englishman's. This was indeed the dream of a romancer. In the eyes of Englishmen, the English tree, how-ever old, never decays or dies; it flourishes forever, and the New England growth is not the extension of its roots but the mere product of seeds sent over with the tiresome Pilgrim Fathers.

While the *Niagara* paddled frothily across a calm Atlantic, Hawthorne dreamed his dreams and played with the children. One thing he had discovered: he loved the sea more than ever now that it was something beneath the keel of a liner instead of something in which to paddle, bathe or fish.

They arrived at Liverpool and went for a day or two to a hotel where the children were miserably homesick, and then, after Hawthorne had taken over from Mr. Crittenden, the retiring Consul, they moved to Mrs. Blogett's, a famous boarding-house in those days and a rendezvous for Americans arriving or leaving by the steam packets. Here they were made comfortable and happy until they moved to a villa of their own at Rock Ferry up the river. Mrs. Blogett forever afterwards retained a place in their hearts. Hawthorne and his son were to spend a lonely winter there while Sophia and her daughters were in Portugal.

It was now midsummer in Liverpool, but the shivering Hawthorne came to the conclusion that there was no heat at all in England. And it rained almost every day. When he went to his office, he found a squalid sort of place, filled all day long with miserable and brutish sailors and stranded Americans—if indeed they were Americans; for there were no passports, and with the great influx of immigrants it was impossible to tell by their speech or their knowledge of topography what they were.

"A narrow and ill-lighted staircase gave access to an equally narrow and ill-lighted passage-way on the first floor, at the extremity of which, surmounting a door-frame, appeared an exceedingly stiff pictorial representation of the Goose and the Gridiron, according to the English idea of those ever-to-be-honoured symbols. The staircase and passage-way were often thronged, of a morning, with a set of beggarly and piratical-looking scoundrels, (I do no wrong to our countrymen in styling them so, for not one in twenty was a genuine American,) purporting to belong to our mercantile marine and chiefly composed of Liverpool Blackballers and the scum of every maritime nation on earth; such being the seamen by whose assistance we then disputed the navigation of the world with England. These specimens of a most unfortunate class of people were shipwrecked crews in quest of bed, board and clothing, invalids asking permits for the hospital, bruised and bloody wretches complaining of ill-treatment by their officers, drunkards, desperadoes, vagabonds, and cheats, perplexingly intermingled with an uncertain proportion of reasonably honest men. All of them (save here and there a poor devil of a kidnapped landsman in his shore-going rags) wore red flannel shirts, in which they had sweltered or shivered throughout the voyage, and all required consular assistance in one form or another."

Of his room in the consulate he writes: "It was an apartment of very moderate size, painted in imitation oak, and duskily lighted by two windows looking across a by-street at the rough brickside of an immense cotton warehouse." Julian, his son, could watch for hours the bales of cotton being lifted by pulleys to the upper floors of the warehouse. "One truly English object was a barometer hanging on the wall, generally indicating one or another degree of disagreeable weather, and so seldom pointing to 'fair,' that I began to consider that portion of its circle as made superfluously. The deep chimney, with its grate of bituminous coal, was English too, as was also the chill temperature that sometimes called for a fire at midsummer, and the foggy or smoky atmosphere which often, between November and March, compelled me to set the gas aflame at noonday."

Seldom in the history of the world has there been a harder life than that of a sailor in the smaller ships which passed between England and America in the 'fifties. Captains and mates, realizing full well the class of men they had taken on as crew, realizing too, that once they were outside the three-mile limit the laws of neither the United States nor Great Britain could be in practice sustained, kept discipline in their ships by brutality. The results of this savagery were a dozen times more noticeable in the Mersey than in any port of the United States, since the North Atlantic trade converged upon Liverpool. And it was these cases especially with which the consul had to cope, since the English staff attended to the routine business. Here was life in the raw. A typical story is that told by Julian Hawthorne of a man who claimed the right to see the U.S.A. consul. Hawthorne received him. The man asked him to have a good look at the hat he was wearing and particularly at the hole on it. Hawthorne looked and said briefly, "Noted." Then the man took off his hat and asked him to have a look at another hole, a revolting gash in his scalp. Hawthorne said once again, "Noted," but turned his eyes away because of the horror of the thing he had seen. At other times he visited the lunatic asylums; for lunatics are clever enough to demand an interview with the consul. Or he would have to follow alone the bier of some unknown American who must find burial in Liverpool. The work of Florence Nightingale was soon to humanize hospital treatment, but at the time of his arrival in England, visits to hospitals were experiences not easily forgotten. Nor was it easy to forget the prisons. Hawthorne performed his duties with exemplary conscientiousness. With grim determination he steeled himself against the impacts of painful experience.

One cannot defend today the social conditions prevailing in the large industrial and commercial towns of the period during which Hawthorne was in England. The reformers were at work; but to the eye of a foreigner their work must have seemed to have no effect whatsoever, however significant their achieve-

ments might appear in reports and statistics. Lord Shaftesbury
had not really roused the nation. He and many others had set
an example which was to be followed, but that the lowest-paid
workers in a town such as Liverpool were kept at a subsistence
level, removed only by a few pence per head from starvation,
is unfortunately true. Or even untrue, for there was much
starvation. They lived the lives of brutes, behaved like brutes
and were treated as such. Hawthorne was amazed and horrified
by what he saw. The half-naked children playing in the filth of
the streets on one of Liverpool's dirty, drizzling days disgusted
him. Yet they and their parents, illiterate and ill-clothed, were
often gay. That was the astonishing fact. Still more astonishing
was it that when a belted earl drove into Liverpool in his grand
carriage with four horses and postilions, the *canaille* did not
seem to resent it but seemed to get pleasure out of the sight.
Stranger still to him—for after all a chariot and four horses is
an object of pageantry to please the eye—was the unbelievable
disparity between the standard of life of the poor (if they could
be said to have any standard at all) and that of the shopkeeper
class; and the still greater disparity between their standard and
that of the upper middle-class business man. Opulence walked
the streets with and employed Destitution. There must, he
argued, be only one result: an end of the existing régime, a
revolution and—what he considered most important of all—an
end of British pride and power. He had never as an American
had any love of English institutions. Judging England by what
he saw in Liverpool during the first few weeks of his residence,
he became convinced that those famous institutions were now
at last cracking and crumbling.

He had not been in England long before the country to which

he was accredited became involved in a European war, "a contest entered into without necessity, conducted without foresight, and deserving to be reckoned from its archaic arrangements and tragic mismanagement rather among medieval than modern campaigns." [1] Troops about to leave for the Crimea poured into Liverpool. The ship in which he had come to England was made into a transport. If the patriotic fervor of the English did not rise to the pitch it has attained in subsequent wars, still the spirit engendered by the idea that Britain cannot be beaten—a spirit obviously very oppressive to foreigners—made the behavior of crowds and the conversation of individuals peculiarly unattractive to Nathaniel Hawthorne. What he saw and heard only convinced him the more of the vast superiority of his own people over the people of the Old Country. There was nothing at all to be said for the state of England, though there was a great deal to say about it. Fortunately for him, there was one living in Liverpool at that time with whom he could discuss all these things.

The year before Hawthorne left America a young Englishman had arrived in Concord on a visit to Emerson and he and Hawthorne had got to know each other. This was Henry Arthur Bright. Only twenty-two years of age, he had just come down from Cambridge where he had been unable to take his degree since, being a Unitarian, he did not wish to make the subscription required as a condition of graduation. Bright was to be described by Hawthorne's daughter. "He was thin, and so tall that he waved like a reed, and so shining-eyed that his eyes seemed like icebergs; they were very prominent. His nose was one of your English masterpieces,—a mountainous range

[1] *A History of Europe.* H. A. L. Fisher.

of aristocratic formation; and his far-sweeping eyebrows of delicate brown, his red, red lips and white doglike teeth, and his deeply cleft British chin were a source of fathomless study. . . . He and my father would sit on opposite sides of the fire; Mr. Bright with a staring, frosty gaze directed unmeltingly at the sunny glow of the coals as he talked, his slender long fingers propping up his charming head as he leaned on the arm of his easy chair." Such is the impression which became fixed in the memory of Hawthorne's young daughter, Rose.

Henry Bright was a young man of parts. He was rich and he was intelligent. His father was one of the best known ship-owners in Liverpool at that time; he was one of the plutocracy of the place, but came of an old family well established in the country in Worcestershire. Henry Bright was a passionate ama-teur of literature, and through literature had formed friendships with many of the famous men of the day, not because of snob-bery but because of a real enthusiasm for good writing, fortu-nate associations at Cambridge and an inquiring mind. He took also an active interest in the family business. If he wrote little that is of permanent value, with the exception of a book on gardening, his genuineness as a *littérateur* need not be ques-tioned. As soon as Hawthorne arrived in Liverpool, a man aged fifty, this young man of twenty-four quietly but firmly took him in hand. That rare thing in Hawthorne's life, an easily maintained friendship, was established. And the value of those visits of young Bright to the consulate or to Rock Ferry cannot be overestimated. Without Bright's friendship Hawthorne would have been hard put to it to bear the boredom of his official position. It was to Bright that he unburdened his soul of heretical opinions concerning the state of Old England, and

Bright was not the least bit offended. That says a good deal for
Bright. It is unfortunately true that the average Englishman in
the fifties had no hesitation whatsoever in making the most impertinent criticism of America to Americans, while at the same
time he was mortally offended if any American offered a
sentence of adverse comment on the Old Country.

Attendance at public dinners, mayor's parties and high
sheriff's luncheons and the making of speeches were unavoid-
able duties. Dislike them he might, but he could not get out of
them. Though the first attempts at making an after-dinner
speech were alarming, he soon gained confidence in himself
by listening to the failures of others. "It is inconceivable, indeed, what ragged and shapeless utterances most Englishmen
are satisfied to give vent to, without attempting anything like
artistic shape, but clapping on a patch here and another there,
and ultimately getting out what they want to say, and generally
with a result of sufficiently poor sense, but in some such dis-
organised mass as if they had thrown it up rather than spoken
it. . . . An Englishman, ambitious of public favour, should
not be smooth. If an orator is glib, his countrymen distrust him.
They dislike smartness. The stronger and heavier his thoughts
the better, providing there be an element of commonplace running through them. . . ." When it came to his turn to make a
speech, what surprised him most "was the sound of my own
voice, which I had never before heard at a declamatory pitch,
and which impressed me as belonging to some other person,
who, and not myself, would be responsible for the speech. . . .
I went on without the slightest embarrassment, and sat down
amid great applause wholly undeserved by anything that I had
spoken. Once, though I felt it to be a kind of imposture, I got

a speech by heart, and doubtless it might have been a very pretty one, only I forgot every syllable at the moment of need, and had to improvise another as well as I could." That, it may be noted, was more than Thackeray could do. Thackeray could learn by heart speeches which he claimed would be among the best delivered in his day. Forgetting every word of the speech as soon as he rose to his feet, he would bow, smile and sit down, usually amidst thunderous applause, and then turn to his neighbor and exclaim: "Just think what the audience has missed!"

In civic banquets Hawthorne was to show an almost pernicious interest. After his sojourn in England, though his powers as a writer of fiction dwindled and were soon snuffed out, he developed a new power in the writing of essays on English life. The "scribbling sons of John Bull," as he had called them in his Bowdoin days, now turned out to be Englishmen who so loved eating that "nothing is ever decided upon, in matters of peace or war, until they have chewed upon it in the shape of roast-beef, and talked it fully over their cups. Nor are these festivities merely occasional, but of stated recurrence in all considerable municipalities and associated bodies." "It has often perplexed me to imagine how an Englishman will be able to reconcile himself to any future state of existence from which the earthly institution of dinner shall be excluded."

Though Bright was always welcome either in the consulate or in their villa at Rock Ferry, it took some time for him to get Hawthorne to visit his father at Sandheys or his aunt, Mrs. Heywood, at Norris Green. Mrs. Hawthorne would have gone anywhere at any time. Just as she had been flattered by Emerson (originally because of his sympathy for her as the poor sick

sister of the "intellectual" Elizabeth Peabody) and had become
a Transcendentalist, so now in England she was heart and soul
for the aristocracy, and as there was no Burke's or Debrett's
handy, she recorded with evident pride what she believed to
be the aristocratic connections of those she met. One must feel
sorry for her at this time, for since her mother was dead and
her father understood nothing that was going on in the world
beyond what occurred a few streets from where he lived,
Sophia had no entirely satisfactory recipient of her long and
chatty letters. Though they were usually prose productions of
a mediocre order, her letters did undoubtedly throw the pattern
of regional American experience into high relief against the
background of English life. She was much flustered because
her husband at first refused to wear the "white cravat and tie,"
and insisted upon retaining his own sartorial conventions: he
"*will* hold on to black satin, let the etiquette be what it may.
He does not choose to do as the Romans do while in Rome. At
least, he is not yet broken in." An obvious threat. No detail of
domestic service or social behavior misses her inquiring eye;
and in her own inimitable style she describes them all. For Mrs.
Hawthorne was entirely bereft of a sense of humor. She wrote
a description of a cricket match which is enchanting in its in-
genuousness. Her description of a dinner party at the Hollands',
however, indicates more clearly the great divide which separated their old mode of life from the one they were now seeing
for the first time.

"The drawing room was beautiful. It was of very great size,
and at one end was a window in semicircular form, larger than
any but a church window. Depending from the lofty ceiling
were several chains, in different parts of the room, holding

vases filled with richly colored flowers with long vines streaming. Mr. Hawthorne as chief guest—there were twelve—took
Mrs. Holland, and sat at her right hand. The table was very
handsome; two enormous silver dish-covers, with the gleam of
Damascus blades, putting out all the rest of the light. After the
soup, these covers were removed, revealing a boiled turbot
under one, and fried fish under the other. The fish was replaced by two other enormous dishes with shining covers; and
then the whole table was immediately covered with silver
dishes; and in the centre was a tall silver stand holding a silver
bowl of celery. It would be useless to try to tell you all the
various dishes. A boiled turkey was before Mrs. Holland, and
a roasted goose before Mr. Holland; and in the intermediate
spaces, cutlets, fricassees, ragoûts, tongue, chicken-pies, and
many things whose names I do not know, and on a side-table a
boiled round of beef as large as the dome of St. Peter's. The
pastry of the chicken-pie was of very elaborate sculpture. It
was laid in a silver plate, an oakvine being precisely cut all
round, and flowers and fruits moulded on the top. It really was
a shame to spoil it. All these were then swept off in a very noise-
less manner. Grouse and pheasants are always served with the
sweets in England, and they appeared at either end of the table.
There were napkins under the finger bowls, upon each of which
a castle or palace was traced in indelible ink, and its name written beneath. The wines were port, sherry, madeira, claret, hock
and champagne. I refused the five first, but the champagne was
poured into my glass without a question."

The New Englander from the small towns pondered deeply
on what he saw. It was all very strange, and much of it was
offensive to him. In the ostentation and in the superfluity of

food he should have seen only a passing fashion, however deplorable. Not unnaturally he saw in it more than that. He looked at the women in the mob which always rushed to the pierhead or to the wharves whenever a transport was leaving with troops for the Crimea, troops equipped not for winter campaigns in Russia but for a military display on an English parade ground. He had never seen such women: so coarse, so undernourished and so primitive in their reactions. He looked at the women of the upper middle-class plutocracy, a class he was meeting at dinner parties in Liverpool; and he has given us his impression of one fifty year old specimen: "She has an awful ponderosity of frame, not pulpy, like the looser development of our few fat women, but massive with solid beef and streaky tallow; so that (though struggling manfully against the idea) you inevitably think of her as made up of steaks and sirloins. When she walks, her advance is elephantine. When she sits down, it is on a great round space of her Maker's footstool, where she looks as if nothing could ever move her. She imposes awe and respect by the muchness of her personality, to such a degree that you probably credit her with far greater moral and intellectual force than she can fairly claim. . . . Morally, she is strong, I suspect, only in society, and in the common routine of social affairs, and would be found powerless and timid in any exceptional strait that might call for energy outside of the conventionalities amid which she has grown up."

It is perhaps as ugly a picture of English womanhood as has ever appeared in print. Fat women were the fashion, and fashions, even in the female form, change with astonishing rapidity. Hawthorne was hardly reasonable in supposing that because the women he met in polite society had figures which were repellent to him, they would be found wanting in backbone or stamina in "any exceptional strait." Women, fat or lean, do not fail their countries in an emergency.

In his diagnosis, a visual diagnosis of the social disease which would soon prove fatal to the body politic of England, he was proved incorrect. He was wrong, not in supposing that that body was much diseased, but in his opinion that the disease was incurable. If one supposes that the British had lost the Crimean War—which because of the inefficiency of their organization they perhaps deserved to lose—then a very serious situation might have arisen in England. Then, as Hawthorne imagined, the *canaille* of Liverpool, whose appearance and behavior had so disgusted him when they rushed in a mob to cheer the departing troops, might well have rushed to wreak their vengeance on the plutocracy of Liverpool's suburbia. But it so happened that there was not to be a national day of mourning for defeat but an order for public rejoicing in celebration of a victory. And though the conditions in Liverpool were no doubt as bad as he painted them, he was mistaken in assuming that because of them the political situation was desperate. That a new plutocracy was arising in the United States, that conditions in Liverpool would soon be paralleled by conditions in New York, where the ostentation of Fifth Avenue and the poverty-stricken slums of the East Side lie side by side, Hawthorne did not of course realize.

Conflicting emotions sometimes produce effects of exaggerated strength. And that Hawthorne's mind was divided and therefore in conflict concerning England is no doubt true. At the time when he was writing his most abusive sentences and thinking his blackest thoughts about England, he was so deeply moved by the English scene that but for the climate, he had thoughts of living in England—thoughts but never a resolution. The English countryside enchanted him. What a place England must have been before the best of her blood had flowed out from her in the bodies of the men and women who had colonized America! Now all that could be admired was the place from which his ancestors came—the churches, the cloisters and college lawns; churchyards with their ancient tombs and their far more ancient yewtrees; above all, the parks belonging to country gentlemen and the common hedgerows in midsummer. "The English should send us photographs of portions of the trunks of trees, the tangled and various products of a hedge, and a square foot of an old wall. They can hardly send anything else so characteristic. Should there be nothing else along the road to look at, an English hedge might well suffice to occupy the eyes, and, to a depth beyond what he could suppose, the heart of an American." Among these hedgerow plants, growing wild, "are many of the kindred blossoms of the very flowers which our pilgrim fathers brought from England, for the sake of their simple beauty and home-like associations, and which we have ever since cultivated in gardens. There is not a softer trait to be found in the character of those stern men that they should have been sensible to these flower-roots clinging among the fibres of their rugged hearts, and have felt the necessity of bringing them over sea and making them hereditary in the new land, instead of trusting to what rarer beauty the wilderness might have in store for them." The town of Chester, so close at hand, was a never-failing delight to him and to Chester he took his American friends who passed through Liverpool. Poor Herman Melville was taken there, Melville who was already written out though still so young, and many others. And whenever Hawthorne visited Chester he discovered from the shop windows that even here his works were selling—in pirated editions. To Scotland, to Wales, and back and forth across England he went, now with his wife, now with Henry Arthur Bright, and now with Francis Bennoch. He covered much ground and many pages of his journal. Wherever he went and whatever he wrote, his wish to love England and the English is manifest. "We now emerged from the cathedral, and walked round its exterior, admiring it to our utmost capacity, and all the more because we had not heard of it beforehand, and expected to see nothing so huge, majestic, grand and gray. And of all the lovely closes that I ever beheld, that of Peterborough Cathedral is to me the most delightful; so quiet it is, so solemnly and nobly cheerful, so verdant, so sweetly shadowed, and so presided over by the stately minster, and surrounded by ancient and comely habitations of Christian men. The most enchanting place, the most enviable as a residence in all this world, seemed to me that of the Bishop's secretary, standing in the rear of the cathedral, and bordering on the churchyard; so that you pass through hallowed precincts in order to come at it, and find it a Paradise, the holier and sweeter for the dead men who sleep so near. We looked through the gateway into the lawn, which really seemed hardly to belong to this world, so bright and soft the sunshine was, so fresh the grass, so lovely the trees, so trained and refined and mellowed down was the whole nature of the spot, and so shut in and guarded from all intrusion.

It is in vain to write about it; nowhere but in England can there be such a spot, nor anywhere but in the close of Peterborough Cathedral."

Though there were many of these journeys of discovery, the greater part of every year had to be spent in or near Liverpool. So greatly did he dislike the town of Liverpool and his duties that but for the emoluments of his office he would have resigned and was in fact constantly thinking of doing so. One thing alone prevented him from asking the Secretary of State in Washington to relieve him of his consulship, and that was his belief that his position in Liverpool would, if he were very careful in his expenditure, enable him to save up a sum of money which would give him not security against want perhaps but at least a padding against the buffetings of misfortune. He would have after four years something to draw upon in case of necessity and a sum set aside for the Italian tour. But for the roseate dreams of a year's residence in Italy, the "brown soupy rain" and the soot-laden fogs of Liverpool would have been quite intolerable. It is understandable therefore that finance should have become something of an obsession. He was inclined to get into a fluster when he reviewed the prospects of his domestic budget, and he was inclined consequently to take gloomily inaccurate views of revenue.

That he should have been assessed for income tax by an over-zealous official of the Inland Revenue Department was of course an unfortunate mistake. He wrote the mildest of letters to Buchanan, the United States Minister in London, in which he questioned the right of England to levy taxes on American income, and Buchanan handed the letter over to Lord Clarendon who set the matter right with a note to the Financial Secretary of the Treasury. For President Pierce, whose vigorous foreign policy contrasted so strongly with his inept domestic policy, might easily have caused a good deal of unpleasantness over any British injustice to his friend Nat Hawthorne. Yet it was from Washington that Hawthorne received his greatest blow. No sooner had he made his forecasts of revenues and expenditure than a bill was introduced in the House of Representatives to reform the schedule of emoluments received by the representatives of the United States in foreign countries. The bill covered the scale of payments made to accredited ministers and to consuls, whose income was derived from fees out of which the consular staffs had to be paid their salaries. It was obvious to all those who had to recommend appointments in Washington that something had to be done about the inadequate salaries of ministers who represented the United States of America. But to make the bill so comprehensive as to cover both the consular and diplomatic services was perhaps a mistake, for in placing consulships throughout the world on a salaried basis instead of the basis of fees-minus-expenses, the government could avoid injustice only if it collected a great mass of statistical information which did not then exist. And it was unfortunate, to say the least, that the emoluments of the diplomatic corps should remain the same until the expiration of the Presidential term, while the changes in the remuneration of consuls should be made immediately.

Sound in principle, the bill was hastily drawn up and seemed to Hawthorne to have been viciously conceived by his worst enemy. Changes were made in it, though whether any of them were the result of the letters Hawthorne wrote to Horatio Bridge, who had the ear of the President, seems doubtful. As reported to him from Washington, the future emoluments of the U.S. consul in Liverpool were in his opinion inadequate. Such a scaling down would make the job unattractive or even impossible to hold. And while the Crimean War was increasing the north Atlantic traffic and consequently the receipts of the consulate, he would be deprived of all the benefits. He was hurt to the quick. At a later date he took a calmer and possibly more reasonable view of the income to be derived from his office, but for a man wishing to save money it was not very considerable.

The next shock to his equanimity was the opinion of a doctor that another winter in England might be the death of Mrs. Hawthorne—news which made him detest Liverpool the more. President Pierce, always solicitous for the welfare of the Hawthornes, hearing of this verdict through Horatio Bridge, suggested through Bridge again, that if Hawthorne's friend O'Sullivan should have to be removed, even temporarily, from his position as Minister in Lisbon to take up that of Minister in Vienna, the Hawthornes might like to go to Portugal with Nathaniel as *chargé d'affaires*. Hawthorne did more sums, afterwards proved inaccurate, and made the confession, afterwards proved correct, that though he read French he doubted whether he could speak it. He had no intention of trying to learn Portuguese, and on the whole he doubted—and he had reason—whether he were made for the diplomatic service. After several letters had passed between Washington and Liverpool, O'Sullivan himself suggested the compromise. Hawthorne and Julian should go to live in a lodging house; Mrs. Hawthorne and the girls should stay in Lisbon, gratis, with him. So Mrs. Hawthorne became a scout. She could make reports on the condition of Portugal—reports which turned out to be largely gossip about kings and dukes and courtiers—and if O'Sullivan had to go to Vienna, he would deposit Mrs. Hawthorne in Italy somewhere on the way.

Sophia must have known that her husband was ill-conditioned to be left alone with his son for three-quarters of a year in Mrs. Blogett's lodging house, and it is difficult to determine to what extent her chatty letters to the miserable Hawthorne were written in a style calculated to hide her unhappiness over their separation. Certainly Hawthorne went back to Liverpool, after parting with them at Southampton, with a heavy heart. On arrival he recorded how greatly he detested the very sight of the Mersey. Christmas at Mrs. Blogett's was made as gay as possible, but by January 16, 1856, he is recording in his diary, "I have suffered wofully from low spirits for some time past; and this has not often been the case since I grew to be a man, even in the least auspicious periods of my life. My desolate bachelor condition, I suppose, is the cause. Really I have no pleasure in anything, and I feel my tread to be heavier and my physical movement more sluggish, than in happier times. . . . My heart sinks always as I ascend the stairs to my office, from a dim augury of ill news from Lisbon that I may perhaps hear,—of black-sealed letters, or some such horrors. I have learned what the bitterness of exile is, in these days; and I never shold have known it but for the absence of Sophia. 'Remote, unfriended, melancholy, slow,'—I can perfectly appreciate that line of Goldsmith; for it well expresses my own torpid, un-enterprising, joyless state of mind and heart."

Sophia did not return until midsummer had passed and this entry was made in January.

In the spring of that year when Sophia was away in Portugal and Madeira Hawthorne made friends with Bennoch. It seemed to some, notably to Henry Bright and probably to Monckton Milnes, a strange and somewhat unfortunate friendship. Bennoch, a rich London silk merchant, was unquestionably a parvenu. He knew a number of the wrong people; he was overanxious and oversolicitous; and with money to spend, he gave the impression that he was trying to buy his way into London's literary society, which was then as closely guarded as a railed-in London square garden. Samuel Rogers had been head gardener for years. And Monckton Milnes, about to be made Lord Houghton, had every intention of succeeding to the post.

Bennoch claimed to be not only a patron of the arts but a poet. London society refused both claims: he was a silk merchant. This was harsh, but possibly good common-sense; rough justice, but sound.

Bennoch's career was a strange one. The son of a Dumfriesshire farmer, he had shown at an early age a facility for writing ballads and verses which had attracted the attention of Allan Cunningham. He came south to London and published in 1837 a slim volume of poems which was sent to Wordsworth for his opinion. Wordsworth reported favorably but begged the young and penniless Bennoch not to take up literature as a career from which to expect a living wage. This advice Bennoch took. He became clerk in the City, climbed rung after rung of the ladder of success and became senior partner in the firm of Bennoch, Twentyman & Rigg, wholesale merchants specializing in silk. He soon became a director of many companies. He had made good, this farmer's son, but not as a poet.

Hawthorne was not blind to his social shortcomings. Of the

vulgarity of some of Bennoch's friends he had embarrassing proof, and he was not impressed by his anecdotes of Wordsworth, Samuel Rogers, Walter Savage Landor. There was no reason why Hawthorne should be impressed. Of social cliques and of literary pretentiousness Hawthorne knew nothing, since he was unacquainted with London society, and he had never looked upon Bennoch as anything but a kindly silk merchant with an interest in literature. He had met too many would-be poets to be troubled by their failure to receive public notice. Bennoch was one of those unfortunate men who received satisfaction only in their obituary notices for what they have done and have strived to do, and by that time it is too late to appreciate the favorable judgments of one's contemporaries. What had seemed to some the vulgar dispensation of money made in the silk trade was at the time of his death called humble patronage. And by the time his obituary notices were written he had lost the greater part of his fortune.

Hawthorne became genuinely fond of Bennoch. What other men might think of him was no matter; he liked and was grateful to him. "If this man has not a heart, then no man ever had, I like him inexpressibly for his heart and for his intellect and for his flesh and blood; and if he has faults, I do not know them, nor care to know them, nor value him the less if I did know them."

This defiance of criticism is of the essence of Hawthorne, and the above quotation is reminiscent of many passages in the journals and letters concerning the much criticized Franklin Pierce. Much as he loved Henry Arthur Bright and appreciated the distinguished qualities of Monckton Milnes, both resembled too closely the men of letters, of learning and distinction he had left behind him in New England. Wherever he went and throughout his life Hawthorne, shy though he was, needed to meet men of simple and honest action; and the insignificance of the action was of no account. After his first great success with *The Scarlet Letter* it was presumed that, since he was an author, literary conversation was the dish to place before him at a party. Wherever Hawthorne went "literature" was discussed *ad nauseam*. As a novelist, he found it far more entertaining to hear men talk their own "shop" than to hear them, in flattery, try to talk his. Bennoch to him was a self-made man and a merchant, and as a Scot, he knew more about London and took more interest in London than any man he met. The extraordinary passages Hawthorne wrote in his English Notebook concerning the futility of the Blackwall Tunnel are inexplicable unless one remembers that Bennoch wrote propaganda for more bridges over the Thames. Bennoch was proud of his topographical knowledge of London, and being a City merchant, he could introduce Hawthorne to many institutions of which he would have seen nothing had he relied exclusively upon the guidance of grander friends. But his friendship with Bennoch certainly led him to some strange and unpleasant passes. The night when Bennoch gave a dinner in his honor at the Milton Club was a night not easily forgotten. Fifty guests made fifty speeches, and he was "toasted until he got roasted"— until, we gather, he was so mellowed by wine that he even accepted an invitation to a supper party.

Who but Bennoch could have suggested to Hawthorne that it would be enjoyable for them to stay as guests of the Mess of the Cork Rifles at Aldershot and drive out each day to see the maneuvers? Yet the occasion, oddly enough, turned out to be a success. Not even Hawthorne could stomach Martin Tupper; but a visit to Tupper at Albury was a success too, for he had never seen such a man or heard such conversation. And the idea that Bennoch and Tupper were poets never entered his head. Bennoch could produce moments of acute embarrassment too. There was the occasion on which they both arrived before the castellated entrance to Battle Abbey only to discover that it was not a visiting day. Hawthorne was prepared to turn around and go away. Not so Bennoch. He was all for presenting Hawthorne's visiting card, which would surely open the doors to them. And when Hawthorne flatly refused, Bennoch talked to a tradesman in the village who knew the domestic staff of Lady Webster's establishment. After a slight delay they were permitted to enter.

What neither Bennoch nor Hawthorne ever knew was that they were shown round the Abbey not by the French housekeeper but by Lady Webster's most intimate friend. On leaving, Bennoch pressed half-a-crown into her hand. Without a smile on her face the *grande dame* accepted it.

A greater variety of experiences came through his friendship with Bennoch than with any other man in England. It was from Bennoch's house on Blackheath that Hawthorne set out to tramp the streets of the city and the passages and alleys of the London slums of which later he was to write his Hogarthian description. It was Bennoch who introduced him to the commercial classes, of whose reforming zeal he formed such a contemptible opinion. One should remember that Hawthorne was seriously considering the writing of an English romance, and that Bennoch as a guide to English life had original if plebeian ideas. As a stranger from Dumfriesshire he, too, had once been excited by the sights and sounds of London, and he understood Hawthorne's desire for immediate and trustworthy information, his inquisitive appetite for all kinds and descriptions of London life. These things he was ready and, within limits, competent to supply.

With Monckton Milnes Hawthorne was never—to his loss—to get on intimate terms. They had met at the Heywoods' in Liverpool shortly after Hawthorne's arrival, for the Heywoods, the Brights and the Milnes were related. Milnes, finding his overtures ignored, not unnaturally supposed that Hawthorne found him unsympathetic. It happened that nothing was further from the truth. One must remember, in fairness to Hawthorne, that though as a New Englander he considered himself the equal of any man on earth, he had been rather overpowered by his first experience of Liverpool society; and that since Monckton Milnes had married the daughter and heiress of Lord Crewe and was himself a man of some personal authority (Hawthorne's Liverpool friends were always talking of his importance), a visit to Crew Hall was an experience for which he and Sophia were as yet unprepared. The hand of friendship was extended, and Hawthorne withdrew his. His reluctance was from his point of view, as he was later to discover, a great mistake.

It was only at a much later date that he accepted an invitation to the house of Monckton Milnes, and that was for a breakfast in Upper Brook Street.

The breakfast as a social function, even a breakfast at so late an hour as 10:30, would in our times be as unattractive to a host as to his guests. Even in the 'fifties of the last century the breakfast, or *dejeuner*, a foreign habit, was a form of entertainment given only by a selected few in London Society. It was a device to circumvent formality, a device for breaking a rule. Though London Society was already beginning to open its doors to the new industrial plutocracy, age and intellectual distinction rarely if ever were considered an excuse at formal parties for breaking the order of precedence. The most distinguished of Englishmen, who had the misfortune to have no title, would therefore find himself at a dinner party between two debutantes and, after the ladies had left the dining room, between two ensigns of the Brigade of Guards. A less formal occasion (most occasions were very formal) had to be found at which those who were blessed with brains and titles could entertain and be entertained by those who were blessed with better brains but no titles. And the breakfast was the answer. The most famous of these breakfast hosts had been Samuel Rogers. He was rich, the son of a banker; he was a poet; and he loved not only society but the company of clever men. His breakfasts became famous and an invitation to one of them was considered a compliment. In emulation of Rogers, Monckton Milnes, the rich bachelor, the young patron of the arts, also gave breakfasts in his room; and since he was himself a man of some brilliance, he could attract to his table very much the same kind of man who had accepted with such pleasure the invitations of Samuel Rogers. When Monckton Milnes married the daughter and heiress of Lord Crewe and moved to the house in Upper Brook Street, the breakfasts were continued.

At the time he received Milnes' invitation, Hawthorne was staying with Bennoch in the house on Blackheath. When the day came, he fortified himself with some cold beef and coffee and walked to Greenwich to catch the nine o'clock train for

Charing Cross. His original idea had been a sound one: he would walk from Charing Cross to Trafalgar Square and take a cab from there to Upper Brook Street. Seeing by the clock that he would arrive at Upper Brook Street before the hour for which he had been invited, he decided to walk. And he walked briskly in the wrong direction. He found himself presently in the most unexpected of places, the Guildhall, of which he made his usual thorough inspection. Having satisfied his curiosity, he set out once more, but again in the wrong direction. Realizing that he was by now due at his breakfast party Hawthorne hailed a cab. It was a long way, the cab-driver explained, at least half-an-hour's drive.

He was annoyed at being late, not because he had inconvenienced his hosts but because he had missed the opportunity to meet all his fellow guests. "Lord Lansdowne, an elderly gentleman, in a blue coat and gray pantaloons—with a long, rather thin, homely visage, exceedingly shaggy eyebrows, though no great weight of brow, and thin gray hair," made himself very pleasant with his simple manners and kind compliments. An old acquaintance from New England was there too, the great Ticknor of Boston and Cambridge, the historian of Spanish literature. Mrs. Milnes, his hostess, was always a success with Hawthorne, for he appreciated her unaffected ways, her simplicity of behavior and the naturalness of her manners, which reminded him of the best that could be found in New England. Only among the aristocracy, be it noted, did he find the simple dignity which he admired so much in his own people. They sat at a table so large that it was "worthy to have been King Arthur's." On one side of him he had the mother of Florence Nightingale; on the other Elizabeth Barrett Browning.

With Mrs. Browning his relations became almost immediately the happiest. They had friends in common, among them poor Margaret Fuller who had dined with the Brownings the night before she left on her ill-fated journey. After breakfast was over Browning introduced himself. "He is very simple and agreeable in manner, gently impulsive, talking as if his heart were uppermost. He spoke of his pleasure in meeting me, and his appreciation of my books; and—which has not often happened to me—mentioned that the *Blithedale Romance* was the one he admired most. I wondered why." Hawthorne and the Brownings were to see much of each other in Italy within the next few years. To one man there, whose appearance interested him very much, he was not introduced, but it was his own fault for being late. "He was a man of large presence,—a portly personage, gray-haired, but scarcely as yet aged; and his face had a remarkable intelligence, not vivid nor sparkling, but conjoined with great quietude—as if it gleamed or brightened at one time more than another, it was like the sheen over a broad surface of sea. There was a somewhat careless self-possession, large and broad enough to be called dignity; and the more I looked at him the more I knew that he was a distinguished person, and wondered who. He might have been a minister of state; only there is not one of them who has any right to such a face and presence." It was Lord Macaulay.

Here were the English men and women with whom Hawthorne would have found happiness; and if he had got to know them better, he would have formed a better opinion of the English people. That experience was denied him, partly by his consular duties in Liverpool, partly by an overzealous protective attitude towards his democratic principles. Too late he discovered how much he liked the aristocracy. "I liked greatly the manners of almost all,—yes, as far as I observed,—all the people at this breakfast, and it was doubtless owing to their being all people either of rank or remarkable intellect or both. An Englishman can hardly be a gentleman, unless he enjoy one or other of these advantages; and perhaps the surest way to give him good manners is to make a lord of him, or rather of his grandfather or great grandfather. In the third generation, scarcely sooner, he will be polished into simplicity and elegance, and his deportment will be all the better for the homely material out of which it is wrought and refined." Alas! the discovery came too late. He had already formed his opinion of England and the English.

He had received much kindness from all classes in England. He had been liked, and he had been admired as a man and as an author. He did not for one moment believe that the flattery he received was insincere. The sales of his books, though he was only profiting by the sales of one of them, and the intimate knowledge of his work shown by almost everyone he met were proof that the admiration was sincere. The visual pleasures of the English countryside he appreciated as much as any American who has ever come to live among the English; and he described them superbly. Why then did he have that fixed dislike and distrust of the English?

The distrust can be written off as traditional. He had been brought up to distrust the English. For though the United States was a Gargantuan child, growing in size and weight at a surprising pace, she was not as yet strong enough to take on Great Britain single-handed. Still quite certain of their material superiority, the British Government not infrequently treated the Government of the United States with scant respect; and the inevitable consequence was that the Federal Government became peculiarly offensive whenever the English seemed to have their hands full elsewhere.

This traditional distrust of England was no doubt partly responsible for Hawthorne's wishful prognostication of an immediate collapse of English institutions and a consequent destruction of the power of Great Britain. The wish was father to the thought, and the thought appeared to be confirmed by the conditions of life and the mentality of those who swarmed out of the slums of Liverpool, a city with a notoriously rough population of mixed races. "Ever since I set my foot on your shores—forgive me, but you set me the example of free speech—I have had a feeling of coming change among all that you look upon as so permanent, so everlasting; and though your thoughts dwell fondly on things as they are and have been, there is a deep destruction somewhere in this country. . . ." [2] Of London and the Thames below London Bridge he writes, "It seems, indeed, as if the heart of London has been cleft open for the mere purpose of showing how rotten and drearily mean it had become. The shore is lined with the shabbiest, blackest, and ugliest buildings that can be imagined, decayed warehouses with blind windows, and wharves that look ruinous: in so much that, had I known nothing more of the world's metropolis, I might have fancied that it had already experienced the Downfall which I have heard commercial and financial prophets predict for it, within the century." [3]

[2] *Doctor Grimshawe's Secret,* p. 199.
[3] *Our Old Home,* vol. 2, p. 132.

As a truly democratic American and an idealist, he was shocked by the institutions of England. "I do aver that I love my country, that I am proud of its institutions, that I have a feeling unknown, probably, to any but a republican, but which is the proudest thing in me, that there is no man above me,—for my ruler is only myself, in the person of another, whose office I impose upon him,—nor any below me. If you would understand me, I would tell you of the shame I felt when first, on setting foot in this country, I heard a man speaking of his birth as giving him privileges; saw him looking down on laboring men, as of an inferior race. And what I can never understand, is the pride which you positively seem to feel in having men and classes of men above you, born to privileges which you can never hope to share. It may be a thing to be endured, but surely not one to be absolutely proud of. And yet an Englishman is so." [4]

It was understandable perhaps that the poor and ignorant should dearly love a lord and should cherish a glimpse of his carriage postilions and horses. So far removed were the lives of Liverpool slum dwellers from the lives of the occupants of the great carriage that for the very poor the noble was a character in an entertaining fairy story. But that such men as Bright and Heywood, men of intelligence, birth and wealth, should accept without protest the existence of a privileged class of nobles above them, who, not because of their own worth but by hereditary right, could exercise powers of interference in the government of the country and in certain instances could claim the right to be tried not by judges of the court but by their own privileged equals—that to Hawthorne was inexpli-

[4] *Dr. Grimshawe's Secret*, p. 200.

cable. For he was not only one of those rare men who believed in equality; he believed also that in the great country from which he came equality of opportunity had been established in practice and would be maintained.

But did he in fact believe that all men are born equal, except in the very limited sense that every child will be given a chance —a chance to become President of the United States or a captain of industry? If he did then why was he so passionately interested in heredity? For thirty years he had thought continually of his own family history; he had spent much time in historical research concerning that family; and in the light of those researches he had formed in his own mind certain ideas concerning human existence. In scrutinizing the problems of heredity and of his heritage, Hawthorne must certainly have discovered that his passionate interest in his forebears could not be reconciled at all points with his detestation of hereditary privilege. And no doubt the English, who for the most part disliked criticisms of their institutions by an American (though nothing pleased them more than to criticise American institutions), pointed out to him that his republican and equalitarian theories went but poorly in double harness with his anxiety to get acquainted with the English stock from which the Hawthornes came. He had expected to find that the English would be just as much interested in what had become of their New England cousins as New Englanders were unquestionably in the life of their English forebears before the colonization of North America. The English were not and never had been the least interested in the fortunes of the descendants of Englishmen who went to America. They became Americans; that was the end of them. The effect of the Revolutionary War was to produce in the blood of Englishmen an anti-toxin against the poisons of failure. So that while every English schoolboy is taught the dates and places of the battles fought by Wellington —battles which added to the prestige of England—the lost battles of the Revolutionary War have been considered so unimportant that it has been thought unwise to tax children's minds with them. As for the War of 1812—the war which left so strong an impression upon the mind of the boy Hawthorne that he was able to argue in later life that the defeat of the English at the Battle of New Orleans portended the end of their power—there were those whose memories had to be jogged to remind them that such a war had ever been fought. The Battle of New Orleans was an unsuccessful "raid," to be mentioned perhaps in a footnote to the impressively long chronicles of English military endeavor. And there are few who read footnotes.

Hawthorne was to leave England with hurt feelings; how badly hurt is evidenced by the autobiographical passages in the tragically unsuccessful manuscript of the English Romance which he tried to write in Italy, *The Ancestral Footstep*. "The roots of his family tree could not reach under the ocean; he was at most but a seedling of the family tree." He had believed that "many English secrets might find their solution in America, if the two threads of a story could be brought together, disjoined as they have been by time and ocean"; but he found that if he was interested in his end of the thread, the English were not. The scant respect accorded to him by an official of the Records Office in London was one indication that England had no inclination to search for her end of the broken thread so as to join it to his. She welcomed him as an American author; but she did not see in him a long-lost cousin. "Whatever you may say about kindred, America is as much a foreign country as France itself. These two hundred years of a different climate and circumstances—of life on a broad continent instead of in an island, to say nothing of the endless intermixture of nationalities in every part of the United States, except New England—have created a new and decidedly original type of national character. It is as well for both parties that they should not aim at any very intimate connection. It will never do."

He felt he had no place in *Our Old Home* (the rather unfortunate title of his brilliant book on England) and this estrangement explains the passages in the published work which proved so offensive to those who had been kind to him during his consulship in Liverpool. He parted from the English with no regret.

15

Italy

PIERCE was not to get the Democratic nomination for a second term. It was a surprise to find that he wanted it, he who had been so reluctant to accept the position of Chief Magistrate. But he and his personal friends in Washington had been looking over the story of his career and were now pretty sure that Franklin Pierce had been born into the world to become President of the United States. If this were so, why not for two terms? Unfortunately, the delegates to the Democratic convention were not of the same opinion. They decided that if a member of the Democratic Party were to be elected President, his name would be James Buchanan.

This piece of news fussed Hawthorne considerably. If a Whig became President Hawthorne would surely be dismissed —and promptly. If Pierce became President for a second term he knew Hawthorne's plans and intentions well enough to remember to appoint a new consul in Liverpool with the least possible delay. But if James Buchanan were elected he might well think that the appointment of a consul in Liverpool was not very pressing. He was friendly with Hawthorne. He knew that the business interests of the United States in Liverpool and Manchester were safe in his hands. It was always rather satisfactory for a President to know that he had one good position which he could delay filling until it was convenient. There was always someone who wanted a job after all the jobs had apparently been filled. What Hawthorne feared was that he might be left in Liverpool for a whole year before he would be relieved. He wrote Horatio Bridge that he had decided that August 31, 1857, was the date on which he wished to hand over his office. Bridge must get the ex-President to help him press this matter with Buchanan.

It was an anxious wait; but they succeeded in doing for him what he had asked. He had only to stay on one month longer in Liverpool than he had intended.

Hawthorne was now as free as he had ever been in his life. He was even free from money worries, since he had always made up his mind to spend some if not all of the savings from his years at the consulate on the Italian tour. He would live beyond his income for at least a year, probably two years, but there would be some returns on the investment when he had shaped his Italian experiences into a novel or short romances. He was free now and he was in no hurry. After staying for a month in Leamington, he moved to London on November 10, meaning to cross over to France at the beginning of December. But while they were in lodgings at 24 Great Russell Street all the children came down with measles. It was not until the first week in January 1858 that they were able to pack their many pieces of baggage and say good-bye to England, a good-bye which Hawthorne could say with no regret.

And very early indeed they got up on their last morning in England to pack those bags. For though the train was due to leave London Bridge Station at 8.30 A. M., the cabs had been ordered to be at the door by 6.30 at which hour the Hawthorne party had been up and about for two or three hours.

The weather had become suddenly and intensely cold. The carriages had no form of heating except metal foot-warmers which warmed the toes perhaps but did not prevent frost from forming on the inside of the carriage windows. They were deposited at Folkestone beside a shingly beach, and then at 1 P. M., after spending two hours in the station waiting room, they went aboard. Two hours later—or so Hawthorne states—they were deposited on the shores of France. An hour's wait, and they were in another train bound for Amiens. "The frost hardened upon the carriage windows in such thickness that I could scarcely scratch a peep-hole through it. . . . My impression of France will always be that it is an arctic country.

"Weary, and frost-bitten,—morally, if not physically,—we reached Amiens in three or four hours, and here I underwent much annoyance from the French railway officials and attendants, who I believe did not mean to incommode me, but rather to forward my purposes as far as they could. If they would speak slowly and distinctly I might understand them well enough, being perfectly familiar with the written language, and knowing the principles of its pronunciation; but, in this customary rapid utterance, it sounds like a string of mere gabble. When left to myself, therefore I got into great difficulties."

So had Margaret Fuller when she first landed in France; and Margaret had taught French for years in Massachusetts. It is unfortunate that the French continue to speak without much regard for the Anglo-Saxons who are taught "French" in schools.

In Paris the cold was even more intense than in Amiens. After a week of sightseeing Hawthorne complains, "I am quite tired of Paris, and long for home more than ever." They left Paris on the twelfth and, still cold almost beyond endurance, took the train for Lyons where they put up at the Hôtel de Provence to be remembered for its passages of nightmarish length, quite dark, along which for one reason or another they spent dreary hours walking. A wretched breakfast was followed by the loss of a great carpet bag; they had a miserable day worrying about the luggage and another wretched breakfast in Marseilles. Hawthorne caught a cold, and when they went aboard the steamer *Calabrese*, he went to bed. The pitch and toss soon became too bad even for journalizing, and being in bed was "the best chance of keeping myself in an equable state." He got up to have a look at Genoa and was glad to get back on board and go to bed again. "And this is sunny Italy, and genial Rome!"

"*Palazzo Lazaroni, Via Porta Pinciana, February 30.*—

"We have been in Rome a fortnight to-day, or rather at eleven o'clock to-night; and I have seldom or never spent so wretched a time anywhere." He was uncomfortably housed, and indoors he was never warm. Out of doors he disliked the burning winter sunshine and feared the deadly chill of the shadows. He tramped the streets, seeing no beauty anywhere but much poverty and more squalor. He feared the Italian visit might be a fiasco.

A visit to William Story and his wife, who had an apartment in the Palazzo Berberini, was the first step towards a happier state of mind and an understanding of how Rome could be enjoyed. "William Story looks quite as vivid, in a graver way, as when I last saw him, a very young man. His perplexing variety of talents and accomplishments—he being a poet, a prose writer, a lawyer, a painter, a musician, and a sculptor—seems now to be concentrating itself into this latter vocation, and I cannot see why he should not achieve something very good." The Hawthornes paid another visit in the same street on C. G. Thompson, the painter, whom they had known in Boston. To visit the studio of one or another of the many American artists living in Rome soon became an almost daily habit. From them he learned the attitudes which were essential to the peace of mind of a foreigner living in Italy. The treasures of the country in which these voluntary exiles were residing must be considered as the common heritage of Western Civilization. Social conditions in Italy and the complicated politics of Italian states were *not* the concern of foreigners, and to enjoy Rome there was not the slightest need to know the Romans. The presence of French troops in Rome only confirmed the view that what "mattered" in Italy was not the people who could be described as Italians but the objects and the visual experiences which happened to be there. Similarly the Puritan mind must not be shocked or offended by the religious practices of Roman Catholicism, for even churches could be considered as museums occasionally disturbed by services. A life more remote from the reality of experience had never been conceived even in Hawthorne's imagination. The American exiles lived for Art and were under the erroneous impression that to live surrounded by masterpieces was to assume a position of advantage in the creation of contemporary work. Though the English poets of the nineteenth century found the Italian scenes and the Italian climate beneficial to their creative processes, the reverse is true of the painters and sculptors, both of America and of England. Long residence in Italy with its consequent relief from even the simplest duties of citizenship had its effect upon their work, whose idealism was not a sublimation of experience but a kind of mental exercise, part uncomprehending mimicry of the antique and part sentimentalized theory. The dangers as well as the delights of the life of the cultured exiles Hawthorne saw clearly. He was in no danger himself. There was no reason why, after so many years of intense activity as an author—and a regional and very American author—he should not wallow in romanticism. For him the Italian sojourn was a period of educational recreation which would do him no harm. But when his daughter Una "spoke with somewhat alarming fervour of her love for Rome, and regret at leaving it" he was worried that perhaps "we shall have done the child no good office, in bringing her here, if the rest of her life is to be a dream of this 'city of the soul,' and an unsatisfied yearning to come back to it. On the other hand, nothing elevating and refining can be really injurious, even if her life should be spent where there are no pictures, no statues, nothing but the dryness and meagreness of a New England village."

It is today difficult to conceive of a United States of America which had no pictures and no sculpture of the greatest periods. But Hawthorne was speaking no more than the stark truth. There were no pictures and no sculpture of any significance in his country when he left it—though there had been boatloads of reproductions. In our days the wealth of the United States in works of art of European origin is so great that it needs an effort of imagination to understand that a cultured man such as Nathaniel Hawthorne had never seen a great masterpiece in paint or marble or bronze before he left America to take up his consulship in Liverpool. At fifty-four years of age he began to train his eye and mind in the comprehension of the visual arts. He spent hours, days and weeks in the galleries and churches of Rome. With endearing honesty he describes the painful way of all those who late in life try to understand what is difficult enough even for those who begin their training as young men and women. It was exasperating for one who was so great an artist in words and had such a fine knowledge of the texture of language to find himself baffled by the problems of the visual arts. "It depresses the spirits to go from picture to picture, leaving a portion of your vital sympathy at every one, so that you come, with a kind of half-torpid desperation, to the end. It seems to me that old sculpture affects the spirits even more dolefully than old painting; it strikes colder to the heart, and lies heavier upon it, being marble, than if it were merely canvas." Day after day he laboriously records his impressions in his journal, and some of the passages produce an exceedingly strange effect.

Because Hawthorne wrote them, these careful descriptions of works of art are often originally and interestingly worded. But they are as incompetent in substance as they are competent in form. His sincerity and his craftsmanship beguile us into accepting the most childish and jejune statements without criticism. And though his knowledge became greatly improved after two years in Italy, he can never be said to have developed a sound opinion on either of the visual arts.

For two months he was happy enough and keenly interested in the artistic treasures of Rome. Then on the first day of April his conscience as the support of a family—growing in size and expense—awoke and he sat down at a writing table to begin the English romance. This was the manuscript we know as *The Ancestral Footstep*. Six years had passed since the publication of the *Blithedale Romance* and five since the publication of

Tanglewood Tales. Though he had done a vast amount of journalizing, he had not written a page of fiction, and as he sat down at that table he must have wondered how easy it would be for him to settle down once more to the lonely work of a professional author, blotting page after page to make the chapter and turning out chapter after chapter to make the book.

It is interesting to note that he had got so much into the habit of journalizing that he wrote as much as he ever finished of *The Ancestral Footstep* in the notebook, with dates given for each day's work. He wrote from April 1 until May 18.

It was very evident from those pages that it was not going to be at all easy for Nathaniel Hawthorne to take up his old craft again.

The time had come for the annual migration, for the exodus from Rome of the entire Anglo-Saxon colony. Soon the dreaded Roman fever brought to the city by the *mala aria* which rose from the Campagna after sundown on hot summer nights would make its appearance. And though Hawthorne had only been in the city for four months, he was as frightened of the pestilence as any of the American colony, who knew from long experience the toll of human life the "bad air" could take. He was going to run no risk with his young family. None whatsoever.

There were as many plans for the summer as there were voluntary advisers and of these there were as many as he had acquaintances. Fortunately for his peace and quiet both he and Sophia had long determined to move to Florence or to the neighboring countryside so that only two problems had to be settled by their friends: what house to take and how to get there. It fell to the lot of the egomaniac sculptor Powers to find them the villa or apartment and to his friend Thompson, the painter, to make arrangements for the journey. Hawthorne wished to hire a great carriage which would take the whole party; he wished to take the longer route, i. e. by Spoleto and Perugia; and he wished the contract which Thompson was to make with the *vetturino* to include every detail even down to breakfast foods and tips. The journey would take eight days, and during those eight days the Hawthornes would hand themselves over body and soul to the *vetturino*. There must be no haggling over tips on arrival. Did Thompson quite understand? Mr. Thompson did. But he also knew the lasting powers of the Roman *vetturino* in making a bargain. It would take many interviews and a long time, but it could and would be done entirely to Hawthorne's satisfaction.

Hawthorne became impatient. Then Thompson said he had found just the man and at a fair price: 100 *scudi* all-in. Hawthorne signed. Very early in the morning of May 24, they packed themselves into the great carriage and drove off. It was not a peaceful departure, however, for the two servants stood in the street shouting curses upon them and two porters followed the carriage demanding more money.

The experience of the foreigners from Salem and Concord was an enviable one. Those eight days of the Italian spring, spent traveling through Tuscany in a great carriage with every comfort arranged by a competent carrier-coachman—and all this before the invention of the automobile, gasoline pumps, macadamized roads and the hideous advertisements which clutter the modern villages—are indeed a pleasant prospect. The *vetturino* was a charmer. Though the travelers did not happen to like the wine, his catering was on a lavish scale and the hotels of his choice were modest but comfortable. If the start every morning was rather an early one—they had to be in the carriage by six A. M.—the slow pace was conducive to sleep. Long hours of sitting still could be varied by as much uphill exercise as anyone desired.

At the bottom of the steeper hills they would find a team of oxen—the contract had stipulated more horses but none ever showed up—waiting to be hitched on in front of the horses. It was then that Hawthorne and the children got out and walked.

So by long but slow stages the Hawthorne party traveled northward towards Florence. It was an expedition entirely after Hawthorne's heart, and they were all of them supremely happy. They could hardly have been otherwise.

The sculptor Mr. Powers was a gentleman with an artistic temperament. It was a disappointment (but would not have been a surprise had they known him) that when they reached Florence and drove up to the Casa del Bello, which they believed he had taken for them, they discovered that no definite arrangement had yet been made and that they must go to a hotel. The Casa del Bello was a three-storied *palazzo*. There had never been any question, as Powers explained, of their taking the whole place; only one of the two floors was for rent. Powers, who lived on the other side of the street, appeared in a dressing gown and slippers with his family of females in indoor attire, to accompany the Hawthorne family on an inspection of the great house. Hawthorne would have liked the top floor—which was not to let—but was content enough with the ground floor, which included a garden, terraces, and an arbor. "It has likewise an immense suite of rooms, round the four sides of a small court, spacious, lofty, with frescoed ceilings and rich hangings, and abundantly furnished with armchairs, sofas, marble tables, and great looking-glasses." The price was "only fifty dollars per month (entirely furnished even to silver and linen). Certainly this is something like the paradise of cheapness we were told of, and which we vainly sought in Rome." In these spacious surroundings he would talk a little, work a little but walk hardly at all. It was too hot for exercise and much too hot for picture galleries. The plan was an excellent one but with the loquacious Mr. Powers next door and the art-addict Sophia in the same house, it could not possibly work. And not just yet could he get down to his work.

Within the week Robert Browning called, rang the bell, dropped a card with an invitation written upon it in pencil for an evening party, and left. Half-an-hour later he rang the bell again; he had remembered that the card bore no address, and though everyone in Florence knew where the Brownings lived, the Hawthornes could not be expected to. This time he went in. Hawthorne was delighted with him, though he remained "surprised that Browning's conversation should be so clear, and so much to the purpose at the moment, since his poetry can seldom proceed far without running into the high grass of latent meanings and obscure allusions." That same night the Hawthornes went to the Casa Guidi. "We found a spacious staircase and ample accommodation of vestibule and hall, the latter opening on a balcony where we could hear the chanting of priests in a church close by." Browning "came into the ante-room to greet us as did his little boy, Robert, whom they call Pennini for fondness. . . . I never saw such a boy as this before; so slender, fragile and spirit like—not as if he were actually in ill health, but as if he had little or nothing to do with human flesh and blood. His face is very pretty and most intelligent, and exceedingly like his mother's. . . . I should not quite like to be the father of such a boy, and should fear to stake so much interest and affection on him as he cannot fail to inspire. I wonder what is to become of him,—whether he will ever grow to be a man—whether it is desirable that he should.

"Mrs. Browning met us at the door of the drawing-room, and greeted us most kindly,—a pale, small person, scarcely embodied at all; at any rate, only substantial enough to put forth her slender fingers to be grasped, and to speak with a shrill, yet sweet, tenuity of voice. Really, I do not see how Mr. Browning can suppose that he has an earthly wife any more than an earthly child; both are of the elfin race, and will flit away from him some day when he least thinks of it. . . .[1] It is wonderful to see how small she is, how pale her cheeks, how bright and dark her eyes. There is not such another figure in the world; and her black ringlets cluster down into her neck and make her face look the whiter by their sable profusion. . . . When I met her in London at Lord Houghton's breakfast table, she did not impress me so singularly; for the morning light is more prosaic than the dim illumination of their great tapestried drawing-room; and, besides, sitting next to her, she did not have occasion to raise her voice in speaking, and I was not sensible what a slender voice she has. It is marvellous to me how so extraordinary, so acute, so sensitive a creature can impress us, as she does, with the certainty of her benevolence. It seems to me there

---

[1] The fear expressed here is almost prophetic; for Mrs. Browning was to die after a few days' illness in the Casa Guidi some four years later to the bewilderment and dismay of Robert Browning.

were a million chances to one that she would have been a miracle of acidity and bitterness." This is indeed, in view of Hawthorne's reticence, a high and rather moving tribute to female beauty and charm.

For two months they remained at the Casa del Bello and led much the same life as they had led on their arrival in Rome; that is to say, they perambulated from one gallery to another, from church to monastery and from studio to *palazzo*. They were doing the sights once more, sights human and artistic. Both Hawthorne and his wife were happy at the Casa del Bello but two of the children, Una and Rose, were unhappy there and became pasty-faced and irritable. It was certainly very hot and as Hawthorne had begun to work again it seemed advisable to move. From the neighborhood of Mr. and Mrs. Powers they moved to the neighborhood of the famous Miss Blagden and took the Villa Montuato on the Bellosguardo hill.

Here Hawthorne found the most romantic, the largest, and the most sympathetic house he had ever stayed in. It was a house with a tower; and as we have seen, and as we will see, there was something in a tower which was emotionally satisfying to Hawthorne. Here was the "Monte Beni" of *The Marble Faun*. And here he found inspiration and wrote for two months in complete contentment. As his son Julian was afterwards to exclaim, "Would that he had been able to stay there for years; for had he continued in an atmosphere which so admirably suited him, there might have been not just one more romance to be published, but a whole series." But they had taken the house for just two months and so on October first they left their ancient tower, "threw a parting glance—and rather a sad one—over the misty Val d'Arno," and took the road to Rome.

After staying in Siena for ten days, not with the Storys (who had a summer residence there) but looked after by them, they proceeded by easy stages in a *vetturo*, with an even more charming *vetturino* than the one Thompson had found for them, and so returned to Rome, happy and full of plans for the winter.

"So we came to 68 Piazza Poli, and found ourselves at once at home, in such a comfortable, cozy little house, as I did not think existed in Rome." "Rome certainly does draw into itself my heart, as I think even London, or even little Concord itself, or old sleepy Salem, never did and never will." But within a week the sirocco had taken all the life out of him and blown away his love for Rome completely. "I have no spirit to do anything; indeed, all my pleasure in getting back—all my home-feeling—has already evaporated, and what now impresses me, as before, is the languor of Rome,—its weary pavements, its little life, pressed down by a great weight of death."

Another week passed; and then on November second he wrote in his journal the words, "Una has taken what seems to be the Roman fever." He closed the journal and was to write no more in it for four months. His eldest child, his Una, was dangerously ill.

At first the girl's condition was described as a slight touch of fever. Hawthorne was worried but not seriously disturbed. Since they had no cook in the house, their meals were supplied in tin boxes piping hot from a neighboring restaurant; and after the meal was over he was as ready as ever to play whist or euchre or old maid. Soon his anxiety spoilt the fun even of euchre. It was all very perplexing; for the Roman fever could not be caught, so he was told, in the last week of October. It was true that one of his sanitary regulations had been broken: he had stipulated that the family must be within doors by six o'clock every evening, and Miss Shepherd had one evening come home with Una an hour late. Miss Shepherd had wanted to finish one of her sketches of Roman ruins and the unexcused delay of this woman who was, incidentally, devoid of any talent for sketching, was no doubt responsible for Una's breathing the pestilent air.

The course which the disease was running was anything but satisfactory. It was of the intermittent type and with every recurrence of the fever the patient's temperature went higher and her resistance became weaker. There came a day when he was told that unless Una's fever abated before morning, she would die. Mrs. Hawthorne behaved with admirable fortitude. Hawthorne had long since given up hope. He cursed himself for ever having brought the family to Italy and then with much vehemence he cursed Rome. But Una did not die, though for three months her life was in the balance—three long months during which her father aged perceptibly with anxiety. Nor for many a long day, even when Una was strong and well, was Hawthorne to forget that vigil. "Una's illness" was to be a black and indelible scene in his memory for the rest of his life.

Mrs. Hawthorne's memory for horrors was as short as her husband's was long. Her social sense soon came back to her. Having nursed her daughter through the crisis of her illness she could sit down and write chatty letters about those days of the agony.

"Carriages were constantly driving to the door with inquiries. People were always coming. Even dear Mrs. Browning, who almost never goes upstairs, came the moment she heard. She was like an angel. I saw her but a moment, but the clasp of her hand was electric, and her voice penetrated my heart. Mrs. Ward, also usually unable to go upstairs, came every day for five days. One day there seemed a cloud of good spirits in the drawing-room, Mrs. Ward, Mrs. Browning, Mrs. Story, and so on, all standing and waiting. Magnificent flowers were always coming, baskets and bouquets, which were presented with tearful eyes. The American minister constantly called. Mr. Aubrey de Vere came. Everyone who had seen Una in society or anywhere came to ask. Mrs. Story came three times in one day to talk about a consultation. The doctor wished all the food prepared exactly after his prescription, and would accept no one's dishes. 'Whose broth is this?' 'This is Mrs. Browning's.' 'Then tell Mrs. Browning to write her poesies, and not to meddle with my broths for my patient!' 'Whose jelly is this?' 'Mrs. Story's.' 'I wish Mrs. Story would help her husband to model his statues, and not try to feed Miss Una!' General Pierce came three times a day. I think I owe to him, almost my husband's life. He was divinely tender, sweet, sympathizing and helpful." She added, "No one shared my nursing, because Una wanted my touch and voice; and she was not obliged to tell me what she wanted. . . . For thirty days and nights I did not go to bed; or sleep, except in the morning in a chair, while Miss Shepherd watched for an hour or so."

How very different the style of Hawthorne's entries in his journal!

The danger having passed, Hawthorne had thought he might be able to accompany Frank Pierce across to Ancona and then up the coast to Venice. But convalescence after so serious an illness was to prove a long drawn out business. "Una's terrible illness has made it necessary for us to continue here another month, and we are thankful that this seems now to be the extent of our misfortune. Never having had any trouble before that pierced into my vitals, I did not know what comfort there might be in the manly sympathy of a friend; but Pierce has undergone so great a sorrow of his own, and has so large and kindly a heart, and is so tender and so strong, that he really did me good, and I shall always love him the better for the recollection of his ministrations in these dark days. Thank God, the thing we dreaded did not come to pass. . . . I have found in him, here in Rome, the whole of my early friend, and even better than I used to know him; a heart as true and affectionate, a mind much widened and deepened by his experience of life. We hold just the same relation to each other as of yore, and we have passed all the turning-off places, *and may hope to go on together still the same dear friends as long as we live.* I do not love him one whit the less for having been President, nor for having done me the greatest good in his power; a fact that speaks eloquently in his favour, and perhaps says a little for myself."

With Una's convalescence and with the consequent knowledge that he would soon be able to leave Italy his spirits revived. He had bursts of unexpected hilarity. He even took part in the *Carnival*. To look on at a *Carnival* was to be soured by its futility and stupidity; but to be in the very midst of it was, just for a time, rather enjoyable. It must have been strange to see the dignified Nathaniel Hawthorne walking home with his hat festooned with streamers, his coat covered with flour and his hair spotted with confetti; stranger still to see that strong man engaged in a battle of serpentines with a lot of Italian boys and girls on the pavement.

Never, it was said, were so many New Englanders to be seen in Rome as during that winter season; never was the colony so gay. The gaiety was not for Hawthorne, but he met many old friends and made one new one. The new friend was John Lothrop Motley, who was still engaged on his monumental history of the Dutch Republic. Motley found him "the most bashful man I believe that ever lived, certainly the most bashful American, *mauvaise honte* not being one of our national traits, but he is a very sincere, unsophisticated kind-hearted person, and looks the man of genius he undoubtedly is." Charles Sumner was in Rome. Since the days, twelve years before, when he had interceded with Mrs. Bancroft on Hawthorne's behalf, Sumner had undergone an objectionable and painful experience. He had been beaten and severely injured by an infuriated political opponent on the floor of the senate. Hawthorne had not been the only New Englander to be profoundly shocked by the news of this incident. But he showed greater intelligence in wondering what might be the permanent effect of such an attack upon a psyche as sensitive as Sumner's. Others were to ask that question many years after Hawthorne was dead and a few years after the death of Abraham Lincoln. It is not impossible that many of the sufferings of the South may be traced to the *bouleversement* which that regrettable incident effected in Sumner's mind.

There were many famous New Englanders in Rome. And there were memories of others. Rome reminded one, for example, of Margaret Fuller.

By this time Hawthorne was taking rather a strong line with regard to Margaret. He had made his inquiries and had come to some rather unflattering conclusions. Mozier, the sculptor, to whom Margaret had sent her husband in the belief or in the hope that the stupid Ossoli might be discovered to have some artistic talent, had told Hawthorne some fascinating stories. "After four month's labor, Ossoli produced a thing intended to be a copy of the human foot, but the great toe was on the wrong side. He could not possibly have had the least appreciation of Margaret; and the wonder is, what attraction she found in this boor, this man without the intellectual spark,—she that had always shown such a cruel and bitter scorn of intellectual deficiency . . . as from him towards her I can understand as little, for she had not the charm of womanhood. But she was a person anxious to try all things, and fill up her experience in all directions; she had a strong and coarse nature, which she had done her utmost to refine, with infinite pains; but of course it could only be superficially changed. . . . She was a great humbug,—of course, with much talent and much moral reality, or else she could never have been so great a humbug."

Never had Hawthorne been more startled than when Mozier told him that Ossoli's elder brother was at that time "a working bricklayer," and that the sisters were "walking the streets without bonnets—that is . . . in the station of peasant girls."

Ossoli had been acting, to the best of Mozier's belief, in the capacity of a concierge or some kind of servant, but though he had been destitute of manners and even ignorant of his own language, he was the handsomest man he had ever seen.

It was not unnatural, in view of all this, that Hawthorne

should deny any resemblance between Margaret Fuller and the character of Zenobia.

Though his spirits and consequently his health had improved vastly by the time of their departure on May 26, he did not leave the Eternal City without delivering his curse upon her—a curse not entirely deserved, for though the Roman air had nearly killed his daughter, she had in reality escaped. She was, in fact, stronger at the time of their departure from Rome than her parents believed her to be, and consequently the journey to England via Geneva and Montreux took less time than they had anticipated. Hawthorne traveled with the first draft of *The Marble Faun* in one of his many canvas bags, and he planned to complete the manuscript when they got home to Concord. But this was not to be. For though Hawthorne had booked passages from Liverpool to Boston he was to cancel them. He was to write his last finished romance in England, and the family were not to reach their home for yet another year.

16

America Regained

ON his arrival in England in the early summer of 1859, Hawthorne had an interview with his publishers, the first object of which was to sell for cash the rights of the novel which he had been writing and which he intended to finish at the Wayside. Smith and Elder were anxious to obtain these rights and were willing to pay a high price for them. They very naturally wanted protection against the risk that they might pay and publish only to find that pirated editions appeared in English bookshops a few weeks later at a slightly cheaper price. They therefore explained that if he wanted a cheque in sterling he must finish the manuscript in England and remain in England until after its publication, so as to comply with such copyright regulations as then existed. If this proposal seemed as much to the advantage of Smith and Elder as it would be to the disadvantage of Ticknor and Fields, it was definitely the opinion of all that the risk of pirated editions of Hawthorne's work was less in America than in England. When Fields agreed to his proposition, Hawthorne canceled his reservations on the boat, accepted the terms with good grace, and apparently made up his mind at once to remain in England until July 1860, when he would have been away from his native land for seven years. He resolved also to rewrite *The Marble Faun* from cover to cover.

Lodgings or a house must be found where the work could be

done. They chose Whitby; disliked Whitby and removed to Redcar. And there "with the gray German Ocean tumbling in on me, and the northern blast howling in my ears" Hawthorne wrote of Rome and Florence, of sunshine and romance. Soon the severe climate proved too much for Mrs. Hawthorne. They moved to Leamington, where she was ill with bronchitis most of the winter but where Hawthorne finished his manuscript; and then moved on to Bath. He had got accustomed to frequent changes of residence and may even be said to have acquired a liking for pitching his tent wherever he pleased. Once the manuscript was in the publishers' hands he spent much of his time in London, renewing his friendships with Bennoch, Bright and Monckton Milnes. He was in excellent health and excellent spirits. For there is comfort even in fatigue when it follows the completion of months of incessant work.

The book was published. It appeared, much to Hawthorne's annoyance, not as *The Romance of Monte Beni* or as *The Marble Faun*, but as *Transformation*, a title invented by his London publishers and given to the book against the author's expressed wish. The press notices were by no means all good. That Hawthorne had published another book was most acceptable news to the reading public, and they eagerly bought it. But of unfavorable criticism, especially in intelligently written periodicals, there was a good deal. On both sides of the Atlantic the charge was made that after suggesting a plot which interested his readers, he had discarded it—not for a new plot, but for no plot at all. The reader was left bewildered by the number of questions posed but unanswered and by the number of threads which remained loose ends when the last page had been finished. The whole thing was far too improbable.

To these adverse notices Hawthorne at first paid little attention. The *Times* had been kind to him, and he for once had been pleased with his own work. "To confess the truth, I admire it exceedingly at intervals, but am liable to cold fits, during which I think it is the most infernal nonsense." Greatly encouraging were many of the notices the book received in America. Lowell gave it a good one in the *Atlantic Monthly*, Hillard an excellent one in the *Courier* and Whipple wrote "a really keen and profound article in which he goes over all my works." Hawthorne was satisfied. Not so Smith and Elder, who had given him a cheque for six hundred pounds. Though he had not paid much attention to adverse criticism, they had. They considered that if Hawthorne wrote an extra chapter—a chapter which would explain and pick up the threads—they could add it to the second edition, and everyone without exception would praise his new work. Hawthorne shrugged his shoulders. If an extra chapter was needed to please those foolish readers who refused to use their imagination, or who had none, he would write it. And write it he did. Needless to say, it was much too late to effect the required repairs—to have done that would have necessitated rewriting the entire book—and Hawthorne did little more than complicate the matter. At the same time he told the reader that if he or she wanted a modern novel, a "slice of life," his was not the fiction to read. The chapter was published, and Hawthorne was soon ashamed of it. He begged his friends, therefore, to close *The Marble Faun* when they had finished the penultimate chapter.

This was precisely the kind of controversy which would hurl Hawthorne back into the deepest shadow of his gloom. Never was an author more grateful to a friend than was Hawthorne to John Lothrop Motley, a man he greatly admired, for writing the perfectly sympathetic letter which was to restore his confidence. No adverse criticism after the receipt of this mattered a jot, for Motley understood him and appreciated his work.

"I admire the book exceedingly," he wrote from Walton-on-Thames. (The letter is published in full in Rose Lathrop's Memories of her father and is only quoted in part here.) "I don't suppose that it is a matter of much consequence to you whether I do or not, but I feel as much disposition to say so as if it were quite an original and peculiar idea of my own, and as if the whole world were not just now saying the same thing. . . . I am only writing in a vague, maundering uncritical way, to express sincere sympathy and gratitude, not to exhibit any dissenting powers, if I have any. If I were composing an article for a review, of course I should feel obliged to show cause for my admiration, but I am now only obeying impulse. Permit me to say, however, that your style seems, if possible, more perfect than ever. Where, oh where, is the godmother who gave you to talk pearls and diamonds? How easy it seems till anybody else tries! Believe me, I don't say to you half what I say behind your back; and I have said it a dozen times that nobody can write English but you. With regard to the story, which has been slightly criticised, I can only say that to me it is quite satisfactory. I like those shadowy, weird, fantastic, Hawthornesque shapes flitting through the golden gloom which is the atmosphere of the book. I like the misty way in which the story is indicated rather than revealed. The outlines are quite definite enough, from the beginning to the end, to those who have imagination enough to follow you in your airy flights; and to those who complain, I suppose nothing less than an illus-

trated edition with a large gallows on the last page, with Dona-
tello in the most pensive of attitudes, his ears revealed at last
through a white nightcap,[1] would be satisfactory. . . . I beg
your pardon for such profanation, but it really moves my spleen
that people should wish to bring down the volatile figures of
your romance to the level of an every-day novel. It is exactly
the romantic atmosphere of the book in which I revel."

Hawthorne was delighted.

Most of the month of May he spent in London. He accepted
an astonishing number of invitations and surprised himself by
his own sociability. Only six years had passed since, in refusing
an invitation, he had written, ". . . I am an absurdly shy sort
of person, and have missed a vast deal of enjoyment, in the
course of my life, by an inveterate habit (or more than a habit,
for I believe it was born with me) of keeping out of people's
way. It is too late to think of amendment. I never go anywhere
(as a guest, I mean) except sometimes to a dinner where there
is no possibility of avoiding it." So wrote the United States
Consul in Liverpool. Any such statement from the Hawthorne
who had just returned from Italy would have been untrue. He
had learned that social intercourse, in small doses, could be
very pleasant, provided, of course, that he mingled with people
whom he found sympathetic. In Rome and in Florence he had
found groups of English and Americans who were most sympathetic; not one of them had any intention or wish to convert
him to Transcendentalism, Abolitionism or Republicanism.
Men of the very first rank in European letters accepted him as

---

[1] The most futile of discussions had taken place concerning the question
of the "furiness" of a man's ear—were such ears possible or not?

one of themselves. On his return to England he found an equally sympathetic group of friends, who were pleased to hear of his return and anxious—but not overanxious—to enjoy his company. There were Bright, Mr. and Mrs. Monckton Milnes, the Motleys (who were at this time living in Hertford Street, Mayfair), Tom Hughes, Bennoch and many others.

He returned to London a man who knew his way about—not that he wanted to go about very much. In the secret places of his journal and in the still more secret places of the manuscript of *The Ancestral Footstep* he had expressed his disgust with the social conditions in England in the 'fifties. He had poignantly described his disappointment in discovering how little interested the English were in their distant cousins in the United States of America and his surprise at finding himself considered a foreigner in the Old Home. Since then he had lived for two years in Italy. And there, since he spoke no Italian, he really had been a foreigner.

No sooner had he got back to England than Bright and Monckton Milnes asked his advice on a subject in which, during his consulship, he had been known to be interested. They wanted a memorandum from him which would help Milnes to make a statement in the House of Commons concerning cruelty to seamen in the ships of the North Atlantic Trade. This opinion Hawthorne gave [2] and his name thus passed into Parliamentary Reports. His friend Tom Hughes, who belonged to a brilliant group of social reformers, showed him the practical efforts which were being made to improve the lot of the poor. He was beginning to know England from the inside, to feel instead of to observe. Murray's guidebook was set aside. And

[2] See APPENDIX.

what he had missed perhaps more than anything else in England —the sympathetic companionship of fellow countrymen—he now found with the Motleys and with James Fields, who was staying in London. Together they had some royal times. Without the presence of James Fields it is doubtful whether Hawthorne would have enjoyed as much as he did that memorable farewell party given by Barry Cornwall. The sight of old Barry Cornwall helping old Leigh Hunt (who was helping Barry Cornwall) up the stairs to "join the ladies" in the drawing-room, after the decanters had passed round the table more often than was good for sobriety, lingered pleasantly in his memory.

In June the Hawthornes, accompanied by James Fields and Harriet Beecher Stowe, set sail from Liverpool for Boston. "Hawthorne's love of the sea," wrote Fields, "amounted to passionate worship; and while I (the worst sailor probably in this planet) was longing, in spite of the good company on board, to reach land as soon as possible, Hawthorne was constantly saying in his quiet, earnest way, 'I should like to sail on and on for ever and never touch land again.' "

That Hawthorne had discovered late in life that he passionately loved to be on the ocean, that his appetite became voracious and that his spirits were never higher than on board a liner is perfectly true. It is possible, however, to attach another significance to his exclamation of eternal wanderlust. For he was not at all sure how much he would enjoy his native land after seven years' absence. Thankful though he was to be bringing back his family to America, all of them in good health (he who had at one time believed that his Sophia would be left in a cemetery outside Lisbon and that his Una would lie in a

Nathaniel Hawthorne. From a Photograph by Mayall, London, 1860

Roman grave), he not only had shown no haste to return but had repeatedly expressed a reluctance to take up residence in Concord once more. So soon as he put his foot upon American territory he would be expected to express an opinion on the political and social questions of the day. That his country was in a most unhappy state he knew very well; but after seven years' absence he was most inaccurately informed. He had been studying Italian art and writing a long novel. During those years in Europe he had discovered how regional his mind was, and he knew that the Commonwealth of Massachusetts was about as big a territory as his sympathy could cover. The United States of America had increased in size rapidly and enormously during his lifetime, but his understanding of American life had not, as he confessed, increased in proportion. He was going back to an America wherein almost everyone held a strong opinion on the two great topics of the day—Abolitionism and Secession. But many people hold strong opinions without a sufficient knowledge of affairs to justify the holding of even one. Though all Americans just then held strong opinions, very few citizens of the United States had any idea of the complexity of the forces which controlled their destiny. And certainly Hawthorne was not equipped to cope with those forces.

He was going back to Concord which was now a camp of fanatical Abolitionists. He was not an Abolitionist, but his sister-in-law, Elizabeth Peabody, was. Even during the consulate days she had pestered him with her pamphlets, which he had sent back unread. She had returned them by the next ship. He had written her curtly; then rudely; and finally had told her in plain unvarnished English what he thought of her. He had been brought up to believe in the inviolability of the

Union and any threat to the Union caused him immediate and painful anxiety. But the intelligentsia of Boston and Concord did not care a rap for the Union. All they cared for was Abolition. Hawthorne disagreed with them profoundly at many points. There was, for one thing, the furor over the John Brown incident. John Brown of Kansas, a fanatical Abolitionist but a man dignified in appearance and impressive in his zeal, had conceived the utterly fantastic idea that with eighteen followers, of whom five were Negroes, he could make private war against the slave-owners of the South. He seized a building which belonged to the Federal arsenal at Harpers Ferry, Virginia, and prepared to defend himself against the United States Marines who were sent to arrest him. Soon overpowered, he was tried and hanged. "Perhaps," writes James Truslow Adams, "no man in American history less deserves the pedestal of heroism on which he has been raised, but the North at once enshrined him as a saint, and more than ever convinced the South that there could be no peaceful solution of the conflict between the two civilizations unless it might be found in unopposed secession." [3]

A more unpatriotic and criminal act than John Brown's Hawthorne could not conceive. And the attitude of his Concord neighbors—of Emerson, Thoreau, Alcott, and Sanborn—shocked him profoundly. Sanborn, for example, made the proud boast that it was from his house in Concord that this fanatic had gone south upon his mad adventure. Emerson and Thoreau used their pens and their tongues to persuade their countrymen that John Brown was a national hero. Emerson declared that

[3] *The Epic of America*, p. 260.

the hanging of this martyr to the cause of Abolitionism had made "the Gallows as venerable as the Cross." That men of education, who took pride in the perfected discipline of their minds, should be among the first to help place John Brown on a pedestal for the mob to admire was to Hawthorne incomprehensible. "No man," he said, "was ever more justly hanged."

However strongly Hawthorne may have felt about the behavior and attitude of his Concord friends, there is no doubt that he was very pleased to see them as they were genuinely pleased to see him. He was, in fact, very fond of them all—even of Alcott. For Alcott's goodness was unquestionable. True, whenever he saw Alcott coming up the path he slipped out of the back door and climbed the hill at the back of the house; but then Alcott would read aloud his own poems, which was insufferable.

The heat, after the cooling breezes of the Atlantic, struck the Hawthornes as very oppressive. But the Wayside, which had been occupied by Sophia's brother during their absence in Europe, was in good order and the larch trees they had sent over from England seemed to be thriving. The only disappointment was to see how small their buff-colored house really was.

Soon carpenters were called in and estimates made. The house must be enlarged by three rooms so constructed that one would be raised above the existing roof. Hawthorne would have an upper room again, a treetop bower; he would have a workroom which was something like the towers which had always fascinated him. The workmen arrived and the Wayside garden was strewn with rafters and planks. The air was filled with the sweet smell of sawdust.

Abraham Lincoln was on his way to Washington. An unknown man to the Eastern States, he brought from Kentucky his rough manners, uncouth appearance and a strange pronunciation. He was not a fanatical Abolitionist. Far from it. He had only said that the area in which slavery was now permitted was on no account to be increased. He had stated in dignified words that the Union in his opinion could not survive half-slave, half-free. Federal Government could only operate successfully if the free states believed that the slave states would initiate a policy which would lead to the ultimate extinction of slavery in the United States. He did not pretend to advise the Southern States how this must be done. But he did go to Washington with confidence and an unalterable opinion on one subject. The majority of the people of the United States demanded the preservation of the Union at all costs.

Not Abolitionism but Nationalism had won the election. Nationalism precluded the right of the Southern States, though they formed a geographical, economic and social unit, to shape their own destinies. And this right the Southern States were determined to uphold. South Carolina seceded on December 20, 1860, and Alabama, Florida, Mississippi and Louisiana soon went with her. Just before Lincoln's inauguration in Washington, Jefferson Davis was elected President of the Confederate States, and other states soon followed their sisters out of the union: Virginia, Arkansas, and Tennessee in April; North Carolina in May. In April the fatal shot was fired at Fort Sumter, and the Stars and Stripes were hauled down. More than six hundred thousand Americans were about to die in the service of their country, though in the darkness of the next four years no one knew what that country was to be.

For a time, after the outbreak of hostilities, Hawthorne's spirits had been refreshed by the strong wine of nationalistic enthusiasm and by the invigorating atmosphere of youth's preparation for sacrifice. Six months passed, and though he took a tone somewhat more grim, he had lost little of his fervent belief in the cause of the North. The long and interesting letter (printed here for the first time) which he wrote to Henry Bright, his friend in Liverpool, sets forth his opinions on the war and shows clearly his state of mind in November, 1861. The belligerence of its tone is explained by the fact that Hawthorne and Bright were accustomed to bare-fisted bouts of controversy, which they both enjoyed and which hurt no one. Without this explanation Hawthorne appears unnecessarily rude.

The Wayside
Nov. 14th '61

Dear Henry Bright,

I duly received your note, and am rejoiced to hear of your happiness.[4] I hardly expect ever to witness it with my bodily eyes; for it will be the part of wisdom, in me, to stay at home and try to find my enjoyments and occupations in my own country. As a matter of taste, I am only too much inclined to live abroad; but as regards affection, I am happy to say that I feel a good deal for my native land, since our troubles began. By the by, you talk (in common with all other Englishmen) most wretched rubbish about this war. You are so wrong, that you and I have no common ground together, on which I can attempt to set you right. Can you see nothing in this view of the case?—for instance; if we had not fought, the North would unquestionably have lost its Capital, and its identity as a nation, and would have had to make an entirely new position for itself, and probably three or four separate

---

[4] Bright had recently been married.

positions. If we stop fighting at this juncture, we give up Maryland, Virginia, Kentucky, Missouri, all of which are fully capable of being made free soil, and will be so in a few years, if we possess them, but not in a hundred years if we lose them. We give up our Capital too, and retire under a load of disgrace, which, to my mind, would make national extinction the lesser evil of the two. Cannot an Englishman's common sense help you to see that this is so? Cannot your English pride of country win any sympathy from you for a people who have all their moral inheritance at stake? Who cares what the war costs in blood or treasure? People must die, whether a bullet kills them or no; and money must be spent, if not for gunpowder, then for worse luxuries. My countrymen choose to spend themselves and their property in war; and they find, at this very moment, an enjoyment in it worth all their sacrifices. I never imagined what a happy state of mind a civil war produces, and how it invigorates every man's whole being. You will live to see the Americans another people than they have hitherto been; and I truly regret that my youth was not cast in these days, instead of in a quiet time.

When we have established our boundary lines to our satisfaction, and demonstrated that we are strong enough to subjugate the whole South, I trust we shall cast off the extreme Southern States, and, giving them a parting kick, let them go to perdition in their own way. I want no more of their territory than we can digest into free soil; but now that we have actually come to swords' points, it would be a sin and shame to take less.

To drop this subject, (in which, of course, I do not expect you to agree with me, for I know Englishmen too well, and know that every man of you wishes to see us both maimed and disgraced, and looks upon this whole trouble as a God-send—if only there were cotton enough at Liverpool and Manchester), to drop the subject, however, I have spent personally a very quiet summer, seldom leaving home, except for a visit to the seashore, or an occasional dinner in Boston. The war at first drew my thoughts wholly to itself, but latterly, I am meditating a Romance, and hope to have it finished by the time the public shall be ready for any other literature than the daily bulletins, or treatises on warlike strategy. Sometimes I attend the monthly dinner of the Saturday Club, of which I am a member; and then I meet all the best people we have, and some of your friends among them. The dinner-table has lost much of its charm since poor Longfellow has ceased to be there, for though he was not brilliant, and never said anything that seemed particularly worth hearing, he was so genial that every guest felt his heart the lighter and the warmer for him. I have not met him since his misfortune [5] and tremble at the thought of doing so. He will never recover from the effect of this blow, though I think the effect will rather be perceptible intellectually, than on his spirits, which, I am told, are becoming tolerably good. But it has been like a stroke of palsy, and he has grown old, even to outward appearance, and white-bearded at once.

Lowell had a nephew (whom he dearly loved) killed, and another wounded, in one battle; and a son of Holmes received two wounds in the same. The shots strike all round us, but even the mothers bear it with wonderful fortitude.

Emerson is breathing slaughter, like the rest of us; and it is really wonderful how all sorts of theoretical nonsense, to which we New Englanders are addicted in peaceful times, vanish in the strong atmosphere which we now inhale. The grim endurance of the merchants, and even of the shopkeepers, surprises me. The whole world, on this side of the Atlantic, appears to have grown more natural and sensible, and walks more erect, and cares less about childish things. If the war only lasts long enough (and not too long) it will have done us infinite good.

[5] A reference to the tragic death of Longfellow's wife in July, 1861. Mrs. Longfellow had been sealing up a little package of her daughter's curls when a lighted match set fire to her voluminous dress. In spite of her husband's efforts to put out the flames—efforts in which he himself was badly burned—she was so terribly injured that she died the next day. Hawthorne's prognostication that his mind would never recover from the shock was correct. Though Longfellow lived for another twenty years, hale and, apparently after some years, hearty, his life had in many respects ended on July 6, 1861.

All the family are particularly well, including myself, whose health had hitherto not been so good as in England. We often speak of you, and wish we could see you by your own fireside. Do not take any offence at my belaboring your sentiments about our war. You have those sentiments because you are an Englishman, and can no more help yourself than a cockney can help dropping his H; and therefore I should not like you half so well if you agreed with me.

With kindest regards to Mrs. H. Bright,

> Sincerely your friend
>
> (Signed) Nath Hawthorne

Brother was fighting brother, and history was inscribing on the American record a tale more gruesome than any Hawthorne had ever told, a tale whose horrors were eventually to overwhelm him. But in this letter he is stating his own case for the war. Though everyone in New England saw the need for such a statement, not many would have agreed with Hawthorne's. He had always believed that it was ethically wrong for the white man to hold the black man in slavery, but he believed it far worse for the white man to kill his brother in order to set the Negro free. All his life he had been passionately devoted to the Union, and now that the Southern States had destroyed the Union, he realized his *casus belli*. But the ultimate solution was difficult to discover. When he said that once the North had beaten the South there was no reason the South should be happy in the Union, he raised one of those painfully searching questions which are inadmissible in the midst of internecine warfare. And he could only reach the strange conclusion that in the event of Northern victory, the Northern slave states should be forced into a new union, while the rest should be expelled forever into outer darkness. As a wartime slogan this would hardly do. Not even Frank Pierce had a word to say for it.

When he wrote that "it is really wonderful how all sorts of theoretic nonsense, to which we New Englanders are addicted in peaceful times, vanish in the strong atmosphere which we now inhale," he was expressing what so many of his contemporaries confessed, namely, that everyone seemed suddenly to have acquired a new strength and a new maturity. Motley wrote to his wife, "One thing, however, is certain. There is no difference of opinion here.[6] There is no such thing as party. Nobody asks or cares whether his neighbor was a republican, or democrat or abolitionist. There is no very great excitement now—simply because it is considered a settled thing which it has entered no man's head to doubt, that this great rebellion is to be put down, whatever may be the cost of life and treasure it may entail." Motley goes on to tell how he had been out to Brook Farm, now Camp Andrew, and how he had wished that Hawthorne would revisit the place and write another romance of Blithedale during the Civil War.

All this explains, too, how it was possible for Hawthorne, who was unsound on Abolition and the friend of Frank Pierce, to be happy at the meetings of the Saturday Club. When Holmes was asked to write out the names of the members—and nothing ever gave him so much pleasure as the Club of which he was unofficial secretary—he gave them in the following order: Emerson, Hawthorne, Longfellow, Lowell, Motley, Whipple and Whittier; Professors Agassiz and Peirce; John S. Dwight, Governor Andrew, Richard H. Dana, Jr. and Charles

[6] Boston, June '61.

Sumner. There was an immensely long list of others "also invited" to gather around the table at Parker's Hotel in Boston on the last Saturday in every month. How good the conversation was at those dinners it is impossible now to say; but it was then and for many years considered brilliant. Certainly Lowell and Holmes were a pair of wits well matched and in a class of their own. If Emerson, whose talk was reported to be so much better than his writing, became too Transcendental, there was always that much beloved Swiss, Agassiz, whose knowledge was so great that Holmes nicknamed him "Liebig's Extract."

Agassiz was as plain-spoken about the scientific knowledge of his American associates as a man could well be; but because he combined great personal charm with honesty of purpose and determination, he could say nothing offensive. He was among the most popular of the inner group of the Saturday Club. Longfellow's conversation may not have been brilliant, but it retained that peculiar quality which made him so excellent in the capacity of host and, when he put it to more serious purposes, so effective in teaching the undergraduates of Harvard the proper approach to European literature and European languages.

Hawthorne must have attended the meetings of the Club infrequently, and dinner table talk was not his forte. He was, however, an excellent listener, and of listeners there were few enough among the members of the Saturday Club.

Outsiders tended to identify the interests of the Saturday Club too closely with those of the *Atlantic Monthly*, and when they dubbed it the "Atlantic Club," Holmes used to get very angry. He had no objection to those who called it the "Mutual Admiration Society," for "if there was not a certain amount of mutual admiration amongst some of those I have mentioned [the list quoted above], it was a great pity, and implied a defect in the nature of men who were otherwise largely endowed." A typical quip from the Autocrat. But though the members may never have called it the "Atlantic," others had perhaps good reason to make the connection, for all those of the inner circle had contributed something to the magazine. Lowell had been its first editor; Holmes, though he was a professor of anatomy, had made his reputation as the "Autocrat" in its pages. And though he would not have believed it in 1861, all of the work which Hawthorne was henceforth to publish would appear first in the *Atlantic*.

During the winter of 1861–62 Hawthorne sat at his writing desk and found himself "blotting successive sheets of paper as of yore." He was making a second attempt at his Anglo-American romance. Fields believed that he was writing *The Dolliver Romance*, but he was in fact writing *Dr. Grimshawe's Secret*, though he himself never gave a name to the manuscript. There were moments of inspiration in that upper room, which was so infernally hot or so damnably cold, but they were rare enough. It was hard work. For what did the art and craft of fiction amount to at such times and in such a place? Brother was fighting brother. Women were volunteering for the hospitals, and little Louisa Alcott was off to the front. The ladies of Concord held sewing bees. His own son was drilling in case the war continued for years and years. Every now and again, overcome by the apparent futility of the novelist's task, he would cease work altogether and take up the newspapers and the bulletins. He sat and thought about the war—and then turned back to his manuscripts. His industry was responsible, after all, for the feeding of a wife and three children.

In the spring Horatio Bridge, now Paymaster General of the Navy and a very busy man, invited Hawthorne to stay with him in Washington. There were several objections to accepting the invitation. "For instance, I am not very well, being mentally and physically languid." This was known and was one of the principal reasons for sending the invitation. "Also I am pretending to write a book . . . each week finds me a little more advanced, and am now at a point where I do not like to leave it entirely." And that was a very sound reason for not going, for indeed the long book was destined never to be finished. Then too since the book trade—especially that portion devoted to fiction—was expected to do a poor business during the War, he must save every cent. When he discovered, however, that James Fields, his own publisher, encouraged him to go, that a long paper on his experiences in Washington during war time would be acceptable to the editor of the *Atlantic*, and that Ticknor would accompany him, he accepted Bridge's invitation.

As they traveled southward, snow and frozen ponds were exchanged for slush. They met the thaw and then the spring. Hawthorne's health and spirits reacted favorably, and he was soon in the best of humors.

The farther south they went, the nearer the war they got; but like many another tourist who visits a battle front, they anticipated by more than a hundred miles the sounds and signs of warfare. Hawthorne seems to have expected a great change even in the appearance of New York City. There was a change discoverable, one which his democratic and pacifist mind found vastly amusing. The shops which had formerly exhibited gents' suitings in their windows now were exhibiting magnificent displays of swords, gilded and decorated scabbards, and other articles of officers' accoutrement. "A great cannon at the edge of the pavement" made him think that "Mars had dropped one of his pocket pistols there, while hurrying to the field." There was, in fact, nothing in New York to suggest the terrible tragedy which had befallen his beloved country; there were only the signs that his fellow countrymen had entirely lost their sense of the ludicrous. Farther south he noted that the people looked more peaceful than usual, no doubt because the restless element of the population would have been among the first to join the colors.

How much would James Fields approve of these observations for publication in his pompously patriotic *Atlantic?*

In the train taking them towards Washington, he conversed with every stranger he met and observed that in a democratic army, which was proud of military rank but which for a time spurned the outward and distinctive marks of rank, there was every opportunity for the boastful sergeant to describe himself as a captain and for the captain to talk of himself as a colonel. Hawthorne looked ahead to a time when the war was over. "Every country neighborhood would have its general or two, its three or four colonels, half a dozen majors, and captains without end—besides non-commissioned officers and privates, more than the recruiting office ever knew." How boring the conversation would be!

As they approached Washington, they became aware that the "air was full of a vague disturbance." General McClellan was about to act at last: he was about to lead the Federal troops into the ghastly fiasco of Bull Run. But Hawthorne arrived too late to see the troops streaming out of Washington; he walked for hours without hearing a shot and found the whole affair a great anti-climax.

What struck him most about Washington was the "singular dearth of imperatively noticeable people there. I question whether there are half a dozen individuals, in all kinds of eminence, at whom a stranger, wearied with the contact of a hundred moderate celebrities, would turn round to snatch a second glance." There was one man in Washington he was determined to see, Abraham Lincoln, "(temporarily, at least, and by force of circumstances) . . . the man of men." How to see him was something of a problem, until someone suggested that he should attach himself "to a deputation that was about to wait upon the President, from a Massachusetts whip-factory, with the present of a splendid whip." Here then was Hawthorne, one of America's most distinguished men, shuffling into the presence of the President at the tail-end of a sordid little delegation of manufacturers. The whole occasion seemed so ludicrous to him that his reverence for the Chief Magistrate vanished.

Hawthorne's account of that interview is historically interesting because it is amusing, familiar and totally lacking in reverence. If one reads the whole article of fifteen thousand words as a contemporary piece of reporting one sees how well he did his job, but one sees also what a problem the manuscript must have been to the editor who had commissioned it. Irreverence towards the President might amuse the New Englander but would infuriate the rest of the North. Those who were fighting for the Union would feel a certain amount of satisfaction that

Hawthorne, a New Englander, by his visit to Harper's Ferry, had found an opportunity for a sly dig at all fanatical Abolitionists and had made fun of Emerson and Whipple when it came to the martyrdom of John Brown. With a judicious use of the scissors, *Chiefly About War Matters* might well have been turned into a lampoon. But could James Fields use his scissors to cut out what was offensive to his readers and still preserve everything that represented sensitive reaction, sound common sense and interesting observation? Fields was an honest man, and, as we know, he approached this difficult task with misgivings. Out must come the intimate sketch of Uncle Abe. That certainly his readers would not stand for. When he asked Hawthorne's permission to do this (for he might well have been told to publish the manuscript as it was written or return it by the next post), Hawthorne agreed. He thought Fields was unnecessarily nervous; and he claimed that his little portrait of Abraham Lincoln was of historic interest. In return for the censorship of Fields, Hawthorne apparently claimed the right to add footnotes to the article, footnotes to be written in the style of a shocked and patriotic Aunt. And in this form the article appeared in the *Atlantic*. From the subscribers' point of view, it was a bad joke; for letters poured in protesting that Hawthorne's article had been cut and objecting to the impertinent style in which the footnotes had been written. And some of those who discovered later that Hawthorne himself had written the notes thought that he had played them a very poor joke. Perhaps it was not a joke in the best possible taste; but it had solved an editorial controversy, one which was to plague the mind of honest Fields for years. Long after both Abraham Lincoln and Hawthorne were dead, when Fields was writing his memorial of Hawthorne, he felt it his uncomfortable duty to publish the passage which he himself had expurgated and so to place himself in a doubly invidious position. No one has ever questioned that he did the right thing by Hawthorne.

With *Chiefly About War Matters* Hawthorne became a regular and well-paid contributor to the *Atlantic*. Soon the rewritten or edited passages from his English notebook which we know as *Our Old Home* were enchanting the readers of the magazine. Hawthorne had excellent material and he had chosen the passages well. For his article on Stratford-on-Avon he had the almost perfect story of the dotty Miss Bacon; and if he used the poor lady as copy, he at least did not exploit his own great kindnesses towards her. He had no qualms whatsoever about using the story of the parson who besotted himself in the gin taverns of Liverpool; for, as he said, he had no respect for the feelings or the friends of such a man. The Swiftian article on fat women he published without a blush. Hawthorne did not shape these articles to suit the market. They happened to be published at a time when Northerners were, if not eager, at least well pleased to listen to any American writer who would put the English in their place. Hawthorne's readers did not know, of course, that he had written most of them before the Civil War, at a time when New England was favorably disposed toward the Old Country.

James Fields, ever ready to assist his friend and aware that the articles had been well received by the subscribers to the *Atlantic*, came forward with a suggestion that the material should be published in book form, in two volumes, and persuaded Smith, Elder & Co. to pay one hundred and eighty.

pounds for the English rights. This pleased Hawthorne greatly, as well it might.

The book must have a dedication, and Hawthorne not unnaturally wished to dedicate it to Franklin Pierce. Pierce was his dearest friend; he had sent him to England and made possible the experiences without which he could never have written *Our Old Home*. Fields, however, objected. He maintained that those who were expected to buy the book would take great offense if Hawthorne were to dedicate it to an ex-President whose term of office had better be forgotten during the Civil War. He claimed that he had reached this conclusion only after many of his friends had begged him to see to it that Hawthorne should do nothing "to jeopardize the currency of his new volume." A publisher, like all men, occasionally makes a grave error of judgment, and in this instance Fields was certainly in the wrong. "I find," Hawthorne wrote him, "it would be a piece of poltroonery in me to withdraw either the dedication or the dedicatory letter." And he added, "My long and intimate personal relations with Pierce render the dedication altogether proper, especially as regards this book, which would have had no existence without his kindness; and if he is so exceedingly unpopular that his name is enough to sink the volume, there is so much the more the need that an old friend should stand by him." He was prepared to alter certain phrases; but that was all, and Fields must accept his decision or refuse the manuscript. He accepted; and though in England the book received very severe notices and in America encountered some adverse criticisms, it sold well and was widely read. There were even those who were glad of Hawthorne's testimony that Frank Pierce had always been and still was wholeheartedly for the Union. His very dear friends in England did not even pretend to be pleased with what they considered a caricature of English life; but that was perhaps inevitable.

Hawthorne had had another success.

17

Envoi

WHEN Fields, in the summer of 1863, commissioned his friend to write *The Dolliver Romance* in serial form for the *Atlantic*, he did not know how Hawthorne had struggled during the past few years to write another novel or how many manuscripts he had discarded or how many thousands of words he had actually got down on paper. He knew that Hawthorne was reported to be in a poorer state of health than either his letters or a short talk with him showed. He knew that as time went on and sacrifice of human life was piled on sacrifice, the Civil War had cast a chill shadow over his spirit. He knew that Hawthorne was worried about money. And he believed that what Hawthorne needed most was encouragement. He could best give encouragement by placing his friend under a contract which necessitated timed production and immediate publication. As Hawthorne wrote, the work in progress would be printed in the *Atlantic*. What Fields did not know (and if he had been told he would have been greatly surprised) was that when he started upon the commissioned *Dolliver Romance* Hawthorne had, secreted in his tower, some twenty-eight thousand words of *The Ancestral Footstep*, at least eighty-five thousand words of *Dr. Grimshawe's Secret* and sixty thousand words of *Septimius Felton*. Though in need of cash, though ill and dispirited, his opinion of this work must have been poor indeed; for with Fields' commission in his pocket he started afresh and wrote sixteen thousand words of *The Dolliver Romance*.

There were at the time of his death four manuscripts in various stages of completion; but there were not four distinct stories or four plots. In all of them he used some of the same material, and in no one manuscript did he use all his ingredients; some one or two are missing from each rewriting. Nevertheless, the materials were there; they had been there, ready to use, for certainly six and probably nine years. And the tragedy of Hawthorne's end is probably to be found not in the quick decline of his physical powers but in his secret struggle to make of this heterogeneous material, which for some strange reason he seemed to treasure, an original and pleasing whole.

Mrs. Ainsworth, his hostess at Smithell's Hall, Bolton-le-Moors, Lancashire, who had asked Hawthorne to dine and spend the night, had showed him one of the most interesting features in the famous old house of which she was the *châtelaine*. This was the bloody footstep, the indelible stain on one of the flagstones, which, as legend had it, the foot of the martyred George Marsh had made as he was dragged out of the house. *The Bloody Footstep*, therefore, had about it an air of legend and historical interest. Mrs. Ainsworth asked Hawthorne to write a ghost story or "thriller" around Smithell's Hall, asked him to invent another explanation of the Bloody Footstep. And thereafter the brown imprint became an obsession with him.

In Italy he began to fashion a plot and to write out in his journal his ideas for a humorous novel. But he was working with a millstone round his neck. One would hardly expect the author of *The Scarlet Letter* to deal lightly with such an idea as the Bloody Footstep, and indeed in the next one hundred and eighty-six thousand words of his fiction there is not one amusing incident.

The English had shown only apathy toward his quest for ancestral information and they had paid scant attention to his idea that English roots had come to life again across the sea. Hawthorne was hurt, and his feelings not unnaturally colored the abortive novel. He decided that the disinherited heir should return to claim his right to a fair and ancient property like Smithell's Hall, and that he should prove it by his possession of the key to a secret cupboard or box. On such a foundation a grotesquely unrealistic and amusing romance might well have been constructed. But in the process of writing Hawthorne could not conceal the venom of his resentment, and the manuscript unhappily combined satiric passages with sections reminiscent of *Fanshawe*, the novel of his immature youth.

Returned to America after the publication of *The Marble Faun*, Hawthorne took up his pen again and remembering the manuscript of *The Ancestral Footstep* (a title which he did not invent) he began another, which we know as *Dr. Grimshawe's Secret*. It is not very good Hawthorne, but his son proved that it was at least a publishable and profitable novel. The "footstep" now appears on a gravestone in the old Salem cemetery, which was next to the house where he had courted Sophia; but as in *The Ancestral Footstep*, Hawthorne was determined to place his hero in the Old Country and he presently carries his readers to England. The key, the locked box, the disparaging attitude of the English toward the New Englander in search of his ancestors are included again. Admirably written descriptions of English life and a fuller treatment of the Leicester hospitalers make excellent reading, though spiders and spiderwebs —Hawthorne here recalls a disgusting plague of giant spiders at the Florentine villa—now assume a strange significance.

He then discarded *Dr. Grimshawe's Secret* and began on the manuscript of *Septimius Felton*, which he wrote secretly. Although he had up to this time talked freely of work in progress, no member of his family had any idea of the existence of *Septimius Felton* until after his death. Hawthorne started with some new material; the locus of the story is the Wayside and the period is that of the War of Independence; a happy choice it seemed to him, for the day of which he was writing and the day in which he was living were both periods of nationalism and heroism. And he based this work on a new idea, in fact, on the story which Henry Thoreau had told him, that the Wayside had once been occupied by a man who believed he would live forever. The improbability of such a central theme would make it necessary for Hawthorne uniformly to maintain the level of fantasy, and this he failed to do; for the times were too painful and too exciting for him to keep flashes of contemporary comment and observation out of the manuscript. Into this work he cast many of the old ingredients: the footprint, now quite redundant, the spiders, a key, the iron box (which had once been a masterpiece of marqueterie) and a flower which the head gardener at Eaton Hall had once shown him in the hothouses. The book breaks off with an author's note that he had visited Smithell's Hall while in England and considered that the Bloody Footstep was nothing but a "natural reddish stain in the stone."

Had Fields been allowed to read any of these manuscripts he

would never have commissioned *The Dolliver Romance*. He would have seen that the intuitional selection of material, a great and rare gift but one essential to the creation of great works of fiction, was no longer in Hawthorne's grasp. It had gone, and gone forever. The shadow of war, ill-health, a sense of the futility of what he was doing and—what is so strange in a writer who had always been all too intimate with his readers— a thinly veiled contempt for those who would read such stuff as he was producing for them—these were the signs that Hawthorne the romancer was "written out." Had Fields seen those manuscripts he would have understood at once that Hawthorne must now be kept to writing pungent and satirical articles for the *Atlantic* on contemporary affairs. He did not see them. And when Hawthorne, invigorated by a visit from Fields, talked of the work he was about to write, he talked so well that the publisher was enthusiastic and encouraging. Fields went back to Boston, and Hawthorne wearily climbed all those stairs to his tower workroom, the room with a view. He sat down at his writing table and began *The Dolliver Romance*. He imagined a new doctor living in the same house as that occupied by Dr. Grimshawe; a little girl whom we seem to have met before many, many years ago; an Elixir of Life; and a bloody footstep. And after that? Great craftsman though he was, he had to confess to himself that he was beaten. Nothing could be made of all this. For years and years he had tried to do something with this material, and now he knew that there would be no *Dolliver Romance*, nor any other.

Thoreau died. The Hawthornes went to his funeral and afterwards walked round by the Old Manse to look at their first residence in Concord. Hawthorne was in a reminiscent mood. Thoreau had first come into his life during those first happy months of his marriage—Thoreau with his music box, Thoreau with his beloved boat which became Hawthorne's *Pond Lily*. He would dedicate his new book to Thoreau and write a memorial of him. But the book was never completed, and the memorial was never begun.

Theirs was a curious friendship. "He despises the world, and all that it has to offer, and, like other humorists, is an intolerable bore," he wrote to Monckton Milnes. "I shall cause it to be known to him that you sat up till two o'clock reading his book [Hawthorne was a great admirer of Thoreau's prose and distributed his work when in England]; and he will pretend that it is of no consequence, but will never forget it . . . he is not an agreeable person, and in his presence one feels ashamed of having any money, or a house to live in, or so much as two coats to wear, or having written a book that the public will read— his own mode of life being so unsparing a criticism on all other modes, such as the world approves." Now his friend Thoreau was dead, and he had something more to say about him. What that more was we shall never know. For Hawthorne himself was about to die.

A few days after Thoreau's funeral Sophia wrote in her diary, "My husband looking very ill"; then again, "My husband quite ill. Everything seems sad when he is ill." Lassitude, hesitancy to begin anything and long periods when he stood and stared at nothing in particular were alarming signs. He detested the summer climate of Concord, with its steam and fog and oppressive heat. And after years in Europe he found that the cold winter, which had invigorated him when he was younger, was too severe for him at fifty-nine. He became thin and very pale.

Not until the late autumn of 1863 did his condition create real alarm among his intimates and relations. His brain was still perfectly clear for short efforts, and he was writing excellent letters. But in December he had to leave home, in bitter cold weather, to attend the funeral of Mrs. Franklin Pierce. Pierce, though overwhelmed with his own sorrow, watched over Hawthorne like a nurse and kept bundling him up against the cold. On the return journey he stayed in Boston with Fields, who reported that he appeared ill and nervous.

At home he was very "difficult;" he refused to see a doctor; he was adamant in his determination that he would go to see the doctor and that the doctor should not come to see him. Had he something to tell the doctor which he did not want Sophia to know? That the fainting fit up in the tower was perhaps a slight stroke? It seems probable that he himself thought that he was about to die, not perhaps immediately but at some not far distant date. He was prepared for the end; and he seems to have been determined that the end should not be a "bedside scene" surrounded by his devoted family.

By the new year he seemed a little better. "I am not quite up to writing yet, but shall make an effort as soon as I see any hope of success. . . . Seriously, my mind has, for the present, lost its temper and its fine edge, and I have an instinct that I had better keep quiet." Within five weeks he wrote to Fields again, asking him to inform the subscribers of the *Atlantic* that he was unable to continue *The Dolliver Romance*. The letter is a long one and admirably expressed. "It is not quite pleasant," he said, "for an author to announce himself, or to be announced, as finally broken down as to his literary faculty." He made several suggestions how this should be done, but left the choice to Fields, who if he liked could say, "Mr. Hawthorne's brain is addled at last." He goes on, "I am not low-spirited, nor fanciful, nor freakish, but look what seem to be realities in the face, and am ready to take whatever may come. If I could but go to England now, I think that the sea voyage and the 'Old Home' might set me all right. This letter is for your own eye, and I wish especially that no echo of it may come back in your notes to me." He spoke of his intention of going to Boston to discuss his "sanitary prospects." But he did not go until the end of March and then did not see a doctor.

Meanwhile Ticknor, remembering what a wonderful recuperative effect their journey to Washington had had on Hawthorne in 1862, proposed that they should repeat that journey. Hawthorne accepted. He stayed with Fields in Boston and Fields was terribly shocked by his appearance. His limbs were shrunken, his vigor quite gone, and he seemed very deaf. But off they went on the night of March twenty-eighth. In New York, where they put up at the Astor House, the weather was abominable, but Hawthorne had stood the journey well and a rest in the city would do him no harm. Ticknor, who was an excellent nurse, sent a daily bulletin to Mrs. Hawthorne. His patient was doing well. "He seems afraid that he shall eat too much, as he says his appetite is good. I assure you he is very prudent, and there is no fear of his eating too much." Though Hawthorne was gaining strength, they stayed in New York for a week and then moved on to Philadelphia. The northeasterly wind still blew. Ticknor was quite determined that his patient should not go to sea, which seemed now his one desire.

They had no plans but would probably go on to Baltimore.

On Saturday evening, while they were still at the Continental Hotel in Philadelphia, Hawthorne sat down and scribbled a note to Fields, telling him that their mutual friend had gone to bed ill. The next morning W. D. Ticknor died.

The wrong man had died—the nurse, not the patient. There had been some colossal mistake somewhere. Hawthorne became dazed and crazed. He hurried back to Boston and on to Concord. There was no cab at the station, so he walked to the Wayside and arrived wet with sweat. His physical and mental distress was very painful to witness; "so haggard, so white, so deeply scored with pain and fatigue was the face, so much more ill he looked than I ever saw him before," wrote Sophia.

Some five weeks of life remained to him. And during those five weeks the behavior of everyone, with the exception perhaps of Hawthorne himself, becomes entirely inexplicable. Never has a deathly sick man been surrounded by more devoted or more irrational human beings.

Within that same month of April Mrs. Hawthorne wrote to James Fields of her alarm at her husband's condition—weakness, weariness of spirit, uneasy somnolency by day and great restlessness by night, and an acutely painful neck. He was so fatigued by dressing that he had to lie down for some time afterwards to recover from the exertion. Within the week she wrote another letter saying that he was miserably ill but that she was pleased with Frank Pierce's plan to take him on a trip—a serene "jog-trot in a private carriage into country places, by trout streams and to old farmhouses, away from care and news. . . ." The next day she wrote again: her husband was much weaker; she would bring him to Boston where she could hand him over to Pierce. His steps were uncertain and his eyes very uncertain too. Could Fields arrange a meeting between Hawthorne and Dr. Oliver Wendell Holmes, as if it were a meeting between old friends, and would Fields or Holmes write to her? Her husband, she believed, would talk to Holmes about his health but would not submit to medical examination. No doubt Sophia did her best, but the choice of the Autocrat, the ex-Professor of Anatomy, as a diagnostician was a strange one, Holmes' career as a general practitioner had been short and most undistinguished. The arrangement, however, was carried through.

When Holmes caught sight of Hawthorne in the street, he immediately took a very serious view of his appearance and of his hesitating and feeble gait. They walked slowly along for half an hour, Hawthorne complaining of the trouble he was having with his digestion, for which Holmes provided a palliative. Later Fields saw him and recognized that his speech and movements indicated severe illness. Yet no one prevented his leaving on the trip and no one seems to have given a thought to Frank Pierce.

The next night Pierce and Hawthorne left by train for Concord, New Hampshire. The letter written by Pierce to Horatio Bridge on May 21, 1864, explains with dignity and simplicity how the end came:

I met H. at Boston, Wednesday (11th), came to this place by rail Thursday morning, and went to Concord, N.H. by evening train. The weather was unfavourable, and H. feeble; and we remained at C. until the following Monday. We then went slowly on our journey; stopping at Franklin, Laconia, and Centre Harbour, and reaching Plymouth Wednesday evening (18th). . . . The conviction was impressed upon me, the day we left Boston,

that the seat of the disease from which H. was suffering was in the
brain or spine or both. H. walked with difficulty, and the use of
his hands was impaired. In fact, on the 17th I saw that he was becoming quite helpless, although he was able to ride, and, I thought,
more comfortable in the carriage with gentle motion than anywhere else; for, whether in bed or up, he was very restless. I had
decided however, not to pursue our journey beyond Plymouth,
which is a beautiful place, and thought, during our ride Wednesday that I would the next day send for Mrs. Hawthorne and Una
to join us there. Alas! there was no next day for our friend. We
arrived at Plymouth about six o'clock. After taking a little tea
and toast in his room, and sleeping for nearly an hour upon the
sofa, he retired. A door opened from my room to his, and our
beds were no more than five or six feet apart. I remained up an
hour or two after he fell asleep. He was apparently less restless
than the night before. The light was left burning in my room—
the door open—and I could see him without moving from my
bed. I went however, between one and two o'clock to his bedside, and supposed him to be in a profound slumber. His eyes were
closed, his position and face perfectly natural. His face was towards my bed. I awoke again between three and four o'clock, and
was surprised—as he was generally restless—to notice that his position was unchanged—exactly the same that it was two hours before. I went to his bedside, placed my hand upon his forehead and
temple, and found that he was dead. . . .

I came from Plymouth yesterday and met Julian in Boston.
. . . The funeral is to take place at Concord, Monday, at one
o'clock.

On May 23, 1864, Longfellow wrote, "And Hawthorne too
is gone! I am waiting for the carriage which is to take Greene,
Agassiz, and myself to Concord this bright spring morning to
his funeral." And on May 25: "You have doubtless read some
description of Hawthorne's funeral. It was a lovely day; the

village all sunshine and blossoms and the song of birds. You cannot imagine anything at once more sad and beautiful. He is buried on a hill-top under the pines."

Longfellow, Lowell, Holmes, Agassiz, Hoar, Dwight, Whipple, Norton, Alcott, Hillard, Fields, Judge Thomas and Emerson acted as pall-bearers. Ex-President Pierce was in attendance upon the family.

The last words shall be Emerson's:—

"I thought there was a tragic element in the event, that might be more fully rendered,—in the painful solitude of the man, which, I suppose, could not longer be endured, and he died of it.

"I have found in his death a surprise and disappointment.

"I thought him a greater man than any of his works betray, that there was still a great deal of work in him, and that he might one day show a surer power. Moreover, I have felt sure of him in his neighborhood, and in his necessities of sympathy and intelligence,—that I could well wait for time,—his unwillingness and caprice,—and might one day conquer a friendship. It would have been a happiness, doubtless to both of us, to have come into habits of unreserved intercourse. It was easy to talk with him,—there were no barriers—only, he said so little, that I talked too much, and stopped only because, as he gave no indications, I feared to exceed. He showed no egotism or self assertion, rather a humility, and, at one time, a fear that he had written himself out. One day, when I found him on the top of his hill, in the woods, he paced back the path to his house, and said, 'This path is the only remembrance of me that will remain.' Now it appears I waited too long."

FINIS

Bibliography

I. Works Concerned Wholly or Mainly with the Life of Hawthorne

Arvin, Newton. *Hawthorne*. London: Noel Douglas, 1930.

Birrell, Augustine. *Nathaniel Hawthorne*, Life and Letters. London, 1928, vol. I.

Bridge, Horatio. *Personal Recollections of Nathaniel Hawthorne*. New York: Harpers, 1893.

Conway, M. D. *Life of Nathaniel Hawthorne*. London: W. Scott, 1890.

Dhaleine, L. *N. Hawthorne, sa Vie et son Oeuvre*. Paris: Hachette, 1905.

Fields, Annie. *Nathaniel Hawthorne*. Boston: Small Maynard, 1899.

Fields, James T. *Yesterdays with Authors*. Boston: Houghton Mifflin, 1900.

Hawthorne, Julian. *Hawthorne and His Circle*. New York: Harpers, 1903.

  Nathaniel Hawthorne and His Wife. Boston: J. R. Osgood, 1885.

Hawthorne, Nathaniel. *The American Notebooks* (ed. Randall Stewart). New Haven: Yale University Press, 1932.

  Letters to William D. Ticknor. Newark: Carteret Book Club, 1910.

  Two Letters in *Second Book of the Dofobs*. Chicago: Society of the Dofobs, 1909.

James, Henry. *Hawthorne*. New York: Harpers, 1880.

Lathrop, G. P. *A Study of Hawthorne*. Boston: J. R. Osgood, 1876.

Lathrop, R. H. *Memories of Hawthorne*. Boston: Houghton Mifflin, 1897.

Pickard, S. T. *Hawthorne's First Diary*. Boston: Houghton Mifflin, 1897.

—— *Proceedings of the One Hundredth Anniversary of the Birth of Nathaniel Hawthorne*. Historical Collections of the Essex Institute, vol. 41, 1905.

II. Other Historical and Biographical Works

Adams, James Truslow. *The Epic of America*. Boston: Little Brown, 1931.
 The Founding of New England. Boston: Atlantic Monthly Press, 1921.

Brooks, Van Wyck. *The Flowering of New England*. New York: Dutton, 1936.

Bryce, James. *The American Commonwealth*. London: Macmillan, 1893–1895.

Canby, H. S. *Thoreau*. Boston: Houghton Mifflin, 1939.

Emerson, Ralph Waldo, *Journals* (ed. Emerson and Forbes). Boston: Houghton Mifflin, 1909–1914.
 Works (2 vols.). London: George Bell, 1876.

Fisher, H. A. L. *A History of Europe*. London: Arnold, 1937.

Freeman, John. *Herman Melville*. New York: Macmillan, 1926.

Hale, Edward Everett. *James Russell Lowell and His Friends*. Boston: Houghton Mifflin, 1899.

Howe, M. A. De Wolfe. *The Life and Letters of George Bancroft*. New York: Scribners, 1908.

Laidler, Harry W. *A History of Socialist Thought*, Chapter XI. New York: Crowell, 1933.

Longfellow, Samuel. *The Life of Henry Wadsworth Longfellow* (2 vols.). Boston: Ticknor and Fields, 1886.

Lowell, James Russell. *Letters* (ed. Charles Eliot Norton). New York: Harpers, 1894.

New Letters (ed. M. A. De Wolfe Howe). New York: Harpers, 1932.

Morse, John Torrey. *The Life and Letters of Oliver Wendell Holmes*. Boston: Houghton Mifflin, 1896.

Ossoli, Margaret Fuller. *Memoirs* (2 vols.). Boston: Phillips Sampson, 1852.

Poe, Edgar Allan. *Complete Works*, vol. XI (ed. J. A. Harrison).

Sanborn, F. B. and Harris, W. T. *A. Bronson Alcott*. Boston: Roberts, 1893.

Sanborn, F. B. *Henry D. Thoreau*. Boston: Houghton Mifflin, 1899.

Shepard, Odell. *Pedlar's Progress: the Life of Bronson Alcott*. Boston: Little Brown, 1937.

Wade, Mason. *Margaret Fuller*. New York: Viking, 1940.

Weaver, R. M. *Herman Melville, Mariner and Mystic*. New York: Doran, 1921.

Wendell, Barrett. *Cotton Mather*. New York: Dodd Mead, 1891.

Williams, E. I. F. *Horace Mann*. New York: Macmillan, 1937.

Woodberry, George E. *The Life of Edgar Allan Poe*. Boston: Houghton Mifflin, 1909.

III. Encyclopaedias and Works of Reference

Bibliography of Collected Biography
Catholic Encyclopaedia
Dictionary of American Biography
Dictionary of National Biography
Modern English Biography (Frederic Boas)
New International Encyclopaedia

IV. First Editions of Hawthorne's Works

[Anonymous.] *Fanshawe, a Tale*. Boston, 1828.

Twice-Told Tales. Boston, 1837.

The Gentle Boy: A Thrice-Told Tale. With an Original Illustration. Boston, 1839.

The Sister Years: being the Carrier's Address to the Patrons of

The Salem Gazette, 1st January, 1839. Salem, 1839.

Grandfather's Chair: a History for Youth. Boston, 1841.

Famous Old People: being the Second Epoch of Grandfather's Chair. Boston, 1841.

Liberty Tree: with the Last Words of Grandfather's Chair. Boston, 1841.

Biographical Stories for Children. Boston, 1842.

Samuel Johnson. The Sunday School Society's Gift. Boston, 1842.

The Celestial Railroad. Boston, 1843.

[Anonymous.] *A Visit to the Celestial City.* Revised by the Committee of Publication of the American Sunday School Union. Philadelphia, 1843.

(Edited.) *Journal of an African Cruiser.* New York, 1845.

Mosses from an Old Manse. New York, 1846.

The Scarlet Letter; a Romance. Boston, 1850.

The House of the Seven Gables, a Romance. Boston, 1851.

True Stories from History and Biography. Boston, 1851.

The Snow-Image and other Tales. London, 1851.

The Blithedale Romance. Boston, 1852.

A Wonder-Book for Girls and Boys. Boston, 1852.

Life of Franklin Pierce. Boston, 1852.

Tanglewood Tales for Girls and Boys: being a Second Wonder-Book. Boston, 1853.

[Anonymous.] *A Rill from the Town Pump.* London, 1857.

The Philosophy of the Plays of Shakespere Unfolded. By Delia Bacon. With a Preface by Nathaniel Hawthorne. London, 1857.

The Weal-Reaf: a Record of the Essex Institute Fair. Containing letter and original contribution by Hawthorne. Salem, 1860.

The Marble Faun; or the Romance of Monte Beni. Boston, 1860.

Our Old Home: a Series of Sketches. Boston, 1863.

Passages from the American Note-Books. Boston, 1868.

Passages from the English Note-Books. Boston, 1870.

Passages from the French and Italian Note-Books. London, 1871.

Septimius Felton; or, the Elixir of Life. Boston, 1872.

The Dolliver Romance and other Pieces. Boston, 1876.

Legends of New England. Boston, 1877.

Legends of the Province House. Boston, 1877.

Tales of the White Hills. Boston, 1877.

A Virtuoso's Collection, and other Tales. Boston, 1877.

Doctor Grimshawe's Secret, a Romance. Edited, with Preface and Notes, by Julian Hawthorne. Boston, 1883.

Sketches and Studies. Boston, 1883.

Appendix

Redcar,
July 30th, '59

My dear Mr. Milnes,

Our friend Henry Bright has given me great pleasure by telling me that you mean to bring the subject of the cruelties on board ships in the English and American trade before Parliament. A better or more necessary thing could not be done—nor one in which the legislators of both countries ought more heartily to combine. It is impossible to imagine, unless compelled (as I often was, in my office of American Consul at Liverpool) to investigate the matter, what an immense mass of cruelty falls into the ocean between your laws and our own, and remains absolutely unpunishable. Finding myself almost utterly powerless either to protect the victims or punish the offenders, I frequently addressed my own Government on the subject; but there are such international difficulties in the way of a reform, that the voice of an individual can never have sufficient emphasis.

You will please to observe that I acknowledge these evils a little more readily, because I do not consider the character of my own seafaring countrymen as solely or principally involved in them. In a vast majority of the cases that came under my notice, the perpetrator of the cruelties was not an American; and very frequently it turned out that the single American among the officers of the ship (that is to say, the captain) was the only person against whom no cruelty could be proved. These men, as a class, were fully capable of appreciating and deploring the evils of the system under which they acted, and I feel confident that none would more rejoice at the possibility of a better state of things.

It seems to me entirely practicable that England and America should confer together on this matter, in a friendly and generous spirit.

Wishing that I could do anything to promote so excellent an object, I am

very sincerely yours
(Signed) NATH HAWTHORNE

R. Moncton Milnes, Esq., M.P.

Index